BEST
FOOD
WRITING
2005

BEST
FOOD
WRITING
2005

Edited by
HOLLY HUGHES

Marlowe & Company
New York

BEST FOOD WRITING 2005

Copyright © 2005 by Holly Hughes

Published by
Marlowe & Company
An Imprint of Avalon Publishing Group Incorporated
245 West 17th Street • 11th Floor
New York, NY 10011-5300

AVALON
publishing group incorporated

Library of Congress Cataloging-in-Publication Data is available.

ISBN 1-56924-345-X

9 8 7 6 5 4 3 2 1

Designed by Michael Walters and Susan Canavan
Printed in the United States of America

Contents

Cooks at Work

Baking Up a Storm

Drinking Again

Dining Out

Grabbing a Bite

Someone's In the Kitchen

Appetites

Introduction

by Holly Hughes

This summer my family tried a dangerous experiment: each of my three children was made responsible for cooking dinner one night a week.

As far as I was concerned, phoning for pizza was an available option any time—after all, it's an option I myself use frequently enough (especially at deadline time!), and we live in New York City where delivery pizzas can be excellent. But none of my kids ever took the delivery option. They *wanted* to try cooking.

Well, the experiment yielded brilliant results. My 10-year-old daughter discovered the alchemy of putting meat into an oven—meatloaf, brisket, a roasting chicken—and waiting for the savory aromas to emerge. My 12-year-old son found his inner grillmeister and was thrilled to sear anything over an open flame. And my oldest son, the teenager, soon became a wok wizard, improvising with ingredients and stir-frying up a storm. My family ate well all summer, and I had a much–needed kitchen break (because cooking every night for a family is tedious, no matter how you slice it). But more important was that these three young people began to discover how much fun it is to mess around in the kitchen.

I suppose it's partly the feminist in me that wants my sons as well as my daughter to become competent home cooks. But it's also because I want to inculcate in all three of them the love of food. That is a lifelong pleasure, and it's not always just about eating; it's about feeding other people too. For once, they had to pay attention to the raw ingredients, their freshness, their quality. They came to realize why technique matters—why all the stir-fry ingredients should be cut into similar sizes, why the meatloaf mixture should be worked by hand (my daughter happily squished eggy ground beef and breadcrumbs through her fingers for fifteen minutes—a whole lot more fun than Play-Doh). The eating end of things improved, too, which I hadn't expected: Our family made quite a to-do at the table every night, praising each other's cooking, savoring the tastes. We all had a renewed appreciation of the art of cooking. It wasn't just food being thrown in front of us anymore.

I know I won't be able to keep up this regimen once the school year begins, when homework and piano lessons and soccer games inevitably begin to crowd out the cookery. But for one leisurely summer, it was a great beginning.

When I tell people that I edit this annual anthology of food writing, they usually respond that it sounds like fun. Well, I won't deny it: It is a fun project to do, year after year. For one thing, the food writers that I have gotten to know around the country are some of the most delightful, open, generous people I've ever worked with, as eager to share praise of their colleagues as they are to promote their own work. For another thing, reading massive amounts of food writing makes me interested in eating and in cooking all over again, every year.

Here are the dishes I look forward to cooking, based on this year's collection: Margit Bisztray's Baby Greens with Roasted Beets and Potatoes (p. 283), John Thorne's Chinese fried rice (p. 289), Lisa Yockelson's layer cake (p. 142). My grill-happy son is employing all the Waldy Malouf pointers learned from David Leite's article (p. 286), and from Monica Bhide (p. 102) my teenager has learned to listen to his stir-fries to tell when the ingredients are perfectly melded.

I've thought about certain tastes in a whole new way, thanks to Dara Moskowitz ("Pucker Power," p. 105) and Suzanne Martinson

"To Win a Cook's Heart, Butter Her Up," p. 74). Gina Mallet has inspired me to enjoy apples and eggs again and stop worrying about food scares, Dan Barber (p. 14) has made me understand at last why it's best to buy organic food, and Dorie Greenspan (p. 128) has reassured me that it's okay to take kitchen shortcuts—after all, the most elegant hostesses in Paris do it all the time. And though the highlight of my dining-out year was probably a dinner at Thomas Keller's new Per Se restaurant in New York City, I'm also looking forward to eating at the West Hollywood burger stand Jonathan Gold describes on page 228.

This is my sixth year now editing the *Best Food Writing* series, and I must say no two years are the same. Food writing is hot now in a way it wasn't when I began this enterprise back in the year 2000–food writing courses have sprung up everywhere, from adult-education classes to the top culinary colleges in the country, and well-known novelists and nonfiction writers blithely try to muscle in on the territory of those dedicated food writers who've been doing this sort of things for decades. It's a bit like the realm of children's books (another of my professional areas)–the Big Names stroll in, take a cursory glance, and assume that this stuff is easy to do, that it's a great way to make a buck. And because they are Big Names, they get the gigs, if only because their writing is easier to promote.

But just because you know how to eat and you know how to write doesn't mean you are qualified to be a food writer. It also helps to know how to cook. Many of the writers represented in this collection have worked as chefs (Jason Sheehan, Patrick Kuh, Emily Kaiser, John Kessler come to mind) and others like Gabrielle Hamilton, Rick Bayless, and Dan Barber still run very successful restaurant kitchens, with writing only an occasional sideline. Others are dedicated foodists who have been covering this field for years, like John Thorne, with his encyclopedic knowledge of cookbooks, or Judith Jones, the near legendary cookbook editor who first brought Julia Child's classic French cookbook to the American public. These people *know food* and when they write, they share with us a special expertise. The fact that they also write wonderfully is just the icing on the cake.

This doesn't mean, though, that passionate amateurs shouldn't be invited to the table. At the end of this book, you'll find a sampling of excerpts from various food-oriented Weblogs (a.k.a. blogs) I've found on the Internet. After days and days of browsing though blogs, I can say that there's a lot of sloppy writing out there, but there's also some very good stuff, full of a refreshing curiosity and excitement about food. These people are writing about food—shopping for it, cooking it, eating it—because *they love food*. And that's what makes all the best food writers such a pleasure to read.

BEST
FOOD
WRITING
2005

The Food Biz

As Asian as Apple Crumble

by Gina Mallet
from *Last Chance to Eat*

Part culinary history, part memoir, part opinionated diatribe against scaremongering in the food industry, *Last Chance to Eat*—written by a Toronto-based theater and restaurant critic—is a passionately argued, delightful read.

All self-respecting English country houses had an orchard, and Mr. Haggie's property was no exception. The orchard at the end of the long driveway of chestnut trees bloomed scores of pink and white candles in the spring. From 1939 to 1946, the orchard went to seed, and the only apples we children found were small, green, and hard. When we bit into them, they tasted bitter, so we fed them to the ponies, or let our neighbor David use them as targets for his pop gun. He would climb over the fence, his gun pointed down while he recited: "Never let your gun / pointed be at anyone," then fire away.

The pictures of Adam biting into the apple suggest he had no trouble finding one. In fact, an apple is an exotic everywhere but Central Asia. Apples did not spring up spontaneously anywhere else. They were brought to the West along the Silk Road from Kazakhstan, where wild apples still grow copiously, mostly yellow and orange and tart to the taste. It took a good deal of work to acclimatize the apple, but its taste so entranced Europeans that they crossed and cosseted it to produce any number of varieties. Apples were bred to be eaten alone, or so they cooked well, and their tastes varied according to when and how they would be eaten.

We children knew the little green apples were not the real thing. For England, the greatest apple in the world was a Cox's Orange Pippin—every nation feels this way about their favorite apple. The Cox is a modest-sized, yellowish apple, with irregular pink markings and some russeting, or rough skin. It doesn't look like anything. Only when you bite into the Cox is its greatness revealed. Then, as with wine, or cheese, or strawberries, the flavor opens up. A Cox may be compared to a vast, ancient soprano, who seems totally unsuitable as Mimì until she opens her mouth and starts to sing. Then, of course, reality falls away and she is the most beautiful woman in the world. First comes the spark of acid; then the firm but not too crisp flesh and the subtle fragrance of orange blossom that you smell and taste simultaneously; and finally, a mellow aftertaste. These were the apples our aunt grew.

I never knew why my aunt decided to grow apples, and she didn't care to explain, at least to me, but she gave indications of boredom with the ceremonial role of diplomat's wife. She and my uncle lived on the Isle of Oxney in Kent, in a mellow brick Queen Anne rectory. The house had been transformed by the Edwardian architect Edwin Lutyens into something proconsular, an imposing edifice with a garden facade that had a line of French doors opening onto a stone terrace, flanked by rosebeds, a wide lawn, and a view extending over the marshes toward the sea. You could throw a formal garden party at the drop of a hat.

Beyond the garden was the orchard, a snowy cloud in spring, which stretched away in every direction in carefully tended rows, in and around old footpaths, the odd cherry tree, and barn. My aunt never did anything by halves, and she took her apple growing very seriously, picking her crop with care. Cox's, of course, were the top crop. She had no trouble getting rid of them locally. Apples grown this way in a small orchard were a calling rather than a profit crop. As a photograph of my aunt sorting apples along with village helpers shows, apple growing and harvesting were communal and organic pursuits, followed in similar orchards all over Britain. We got a box of Aunt Peggy's pre-industrial apples at Christmas, and they were fresh to the bite. In the space of a few decades, the great Cox would be on the endangered apple list.

My cousin Philip Mallet eventually inherited the house in Kent, keeping the orchard—which remained a calling, not a profit center—and the apples were still snapped up locally. Philip kept to such classics as the Egremont Russet, which was probably what the little green apples in our orchard had been originally. The Egremont Russet, bred as a dessert apple for the Victorians, was not too sweet, and tasted of hazelnuts, a perfect accompaniment to a glass of port. In those days, the high point of apple eating was after dinner. Queen Victoria was a lifelong lover of an American apple, the Newtown Pippin, a big yellow apple that tasted disarmingly of pineapple. At first bite, the Queen found the Newton Pippin so good that she directed the import duty on it lifted. Those were the days when a monarch still had real food power. If only science had been more advanced, the Newtown Pippin might be more than a hobby apple today. But it declined because nobody understood that the tree, which grew hugely, leached all the calcium from the soil, and without calcium it couldn't thrive.

In the past couple of decades, Philip has had more and more difficulty selling his apples. The local shops in nearby towns shut down one after another as the supermarkets took over. The supermarket grip on food distribution is even tighter in Britain than it is in North America, because Britain is smaller. Today, only a handful of chains sell most of the food, and they've closed down almost all competition. The supermarket buyers don't listen to customers, of course, but buy the apples that make the most profit. Nowadays, these are the apples approved by the European Union as the only "real" apples—they must be a minimum of two and a half inches in diameter and come from an approved list of varieties. Red and Golden Delicious, Fuji, Royal Gala, and the Jonagold which, although American, has become the national apple of Belgium. The Cox is a miserable failure: it doesn't look like a beauty queen and it sometimes doesn't conform to the EU's size standards. All over Europe, the old varieties are being discarded. Until the 1950s, the Finkenwerder Herbstprinz—a juicy red russet—was the most loved variety grown in the orchards around Hamburg, one of the big apple-growing regions in Germany. But thirty years later, the Prinz had almost disappeared from production because the supermarkets didn't want it. Thus, an apple unique to a region is no longer good enough, and local tastes are trampled on. The result is predictable: many varieties are dying.

Britain still grows more than seven hundred varieties, but for how long? Even the most enthusiastically patriotic supermarket stocked only ten varieties, all the usual suspects, in 2002.

Philip still grows Bramleys, the unique English cooking apple. Philip's wife, Mary, made an heirloom Bramley apple crumble for lunch. It was really good. The English, unlike North Americans, differentiate a cooking from an eating apple. The Bramley is named for a nineteenth-century butcher and it meets the EU template for a large apple, but that still hasn't got it onto the EU list. It is a big green apple with pink streaks, and it is creamy, grainy, and acid. As it is cooked, it melts down into a thick purée. The nearest thing to a cooking apple elsewhere is the Granny Smith, the slightly sour soda pop apple originally from Australia.

Philip tried to keep up with the trends. He planted Fujis and Royal Galas, a Cox cross that could be called Cox Lite, designed for the modern palate, which is addicted to sweets.

Sugar is the industrial narcotic, so bland is preferred over any taste that causes the mouth to pucker even a tiny bit. This is increasingly true of all the new fruit: some huge new Bing cherries called Lappins taste like a candy bar. Even the superior Rainier, a blush cherry that tastes of strawberries and cream, has only a tiny spike of acid.

RATING THE POP APPLES

In the fall in Toronto, I count the varieties of apple in the markets. I live in the heart of good apple-growing country; the little villages that still survive amid spreading exurbia have apple fairs and cider tastings, and some heirloom apple orchards still sell the resolutely untelegenic Cox. In a small Korean market, I saw fourteen kinds of fresh apples in baskets on the sidewalk. I selected seven modern hybrids, Golden Delicious, Royal Gala, Jonagold, and Fuji, as well as McIntosh, Red Delicious, and finally an Elstar—a Dutch apple I'd never heard about. They all looked rather alike, I thought, pink and green, so under the suspicious eye of the storeowner, I marked each one with a felt-tipped pen.

Then I went home, chopped the apples up, and ate slices in sequence.

I started off with the Golden Delicious, the apple grown most frequently through the world. Golden Delicious (not related to the

Red Delicious) was a seedling that grew in the Appalachians in West Virginia, and it is highly variable. Depending on where the apple is grown, it is either anemic or robust. Reportedly, the taste is exceptional in the Auvergne in France. My Golden Delicious was pale yellow. I thought it tasted watery, and its bite was far from crisp and inviting.

When I bit into the Royal Gala, there was a world of difference. Royal Gala is bred in New Zealand, and it is a cross between the Golden Delicious and the great Cox. The Royal Gala had just a hint of acid in its bite, and the flesh was firm; an immensely edible apple that melted in the mouth. However, it didn't have the Cox's orange aroma or the Cox's complexity.

At first I thought Jonagold filled every taste requirement. A spurt of acid on the first bite, the crunchy flesh, and then a pleasant melonlike flavor. After letting the aftertaste linger in my mouth, however, I decided I didn't like it as much as the Royal Gala.

Fuji, the most expensive, was a letdown. This Japanese apple, another Golden Delicious cross, had abrasive skin—I felt I had to fight to eat it. It was very sweet. When I read later about Fuji, I learned that the apple "improves" if kept for a month. It grows sweeter!

I compared two red apples, McIntosh and Red Delicious, directly. The McIntosh is brusque to the bite, then turns to mush. It makes a good cooker, and seemed better than the Red Delicious. The Red Delicious, like the Fuji, had a defensive skin, and only a faint, watery taste.

Then I tasted the Elstar. The champion, I decided. Nothing to look at, a disappointing bite, flesh on the soft side—but none of that matters. The Elstar's taste has legs. It begins crisp, even chippy, then mellows into a satisfyingly loamy flavor. Beside it, the Royal Gala tasted flat, and too sweet, as were all the other apples. I have never again found an Elstar.

When I told a grower how much I had liked the Elstar, he said, "Oh, you like an acid apple, so you'd love Pink Lady." I tried Pink Lady, a new breed that growers have great hopes for, but it was just as sweet as any of the soda pop apples.

THE OTHER SIDE OF PARADISE

Philip's troubles in England are magnified a thousand times in Washington State. Once proclaimed apple grower to the world, the home of the mighty Red Delicious, Washington has been brutally humbled by a combination of bad science, supermarket economics, and the rise of an apple empire in China.

North Americans never ate as many apples as Europeans, and now they're eating even fewer. Apples just can't compete with manufactured snack food or the ease of opening a plastic pack. You have to be proactive to eat an apple, and, of course, the modern apple bought from the supermarket doesn't taste very good. Not only do supermarkets have a very small selection but they are mostly the same innocuous varieties approved by the European Union. Further, the apples have mostly been picked unripe, which means they will never fulfill their potential. They are usually old. Ripe or not, the industrial apple is picked in the fall; most are then put into cold storage and brought out when necessary to restock the shelves throughout the rest of the year. When you buy an apple in July, you are buying a senior citizen. It will taste stale, its initial crispness lost. And it will invariably taste bitter because the apples are buffed with something like furniture polish, which cannot be washed off.

Lastly, the supermarket owners couldn't care less. They pay very little for apples now because they are in the catbird seat. They force farmers to grow the apples they want to buy and then make them compete to sell them.

The only apple supermarket owners really want is the Red Delicious. It is the brand-name apple that sells regardless of how it tastes, though it's hard today to find a single apple eater who doesn't complain about the taste.

The melancholy fall of the Red Delicious traces the life and death of the American industry itself. At first, apple growing was an all-American pastime, innocent and life-giving. More than a century ago, homesteaders started growing apples in the fertile Wenatchee Valley in Washington State. It turned out that the Wenatchee had one of the most perfect apple climates anywhere, comparable to the apple's original home in Central Asia. The soil is volcanic, rich in nutrients, the whole region irrigated by the inexhaustible Columbia River. The valleys themselves are protected from the Pacific damp by the Cascade Mountains, the dawn unfolding into sunny, dry days, and the dusk heralding the cool nights so essential to bringing a blush to the apple's cheeks. The air was clean and so was the water. The region was a paradise—before the Columbia River became so polluted that neither human nor salmon could swim in it safely, and even wet-suited Para-Sailors and sailboarders feared being dunked in it.

The first farms were small, some as small as twenty-five acres, and apple growing was as much a calling to the families who grew them as a profit center. They were immensely proud that their Red Delicious, an apple developed in the Middle West, found its true home in the Wenatchee. In those faroff days, the Red Delicious did not merely look tempting, a blood red molar, but actually tasted good as well. Apple historians speak of a snappy bite, a cider sparkle. The Red Delicious was never as good as the Golden Delicious, an entirely unrelated American apple, which has a more complicated taste, honey and lemon mixed, at least when it's picked ripe. But the Red Delicious was so beautiful, so popular, that it became first the state apple, then the national apple.

There was one problem about the Wenatchee. It was hours from any large population center; obviously the farmers couldn't eat all the apples themselves, and far too few visitors came to the region. So they had to send their apples miles away, to supermarkets across the mountains, across the country, and beyond. Even so, there were plenty of food outlets then, and many of them couldn't get enough of the Wenatchee apples. By the fifties, the farmers' standard of living was not only good but getting better all the time. The export market in particular looked rosy. America at this time was number one in apple production. And so, the first worm i' the bud.

Wenatchee's success drew Goliath growers—outsiders who saw a good thing in apple speculation. Big companies began to muscle into the market. There was no land left in the Wenatchee for them to buy, so they went south to the irrigated lands around Spokane, where the climate was not so good for apples—a small but significant step toward lowering the state's apple standard. The Red Delicious would start to lose its luster as it became more and more commercialized.

Most apple eaters have never known, and apparently still don't know (or perhaps don't want to know), just how difficult it is to grow an apple. Even a small orchard has to use a range of chemicals if its apples are to survive to maturity without being consumed by a multitude of pests or falling prey to any number of diseases.

Industrial growers, who need the highest possible percentage of perfect apples, drench the trees with chemicals. In the past, up to four hundred chemicals might readily be used to grow an apple tree. Even organic farms use poisonous natural pesticides, since organic soil, despite the claims of the founders of the organic movement, cannot repel either disease or pests. An apple tree cannot be left to grow by itself: it needs constant attention. Left to its own devices, it will simply produce masses of small apples, the more seeds the better, since its main intention is to reproduce itself, not satisfy consumers.

To produce an apple large enough to bite into with satisfaction, or to match the European Union apple template, the grower must take a firm hand and routinely thin the trees. If you're producing apples for sale on a large scale, you need a good deal of help, not only to thin the trees but also to pick the apples once they're ripe, before they've fallen and lie rotting on the ground. The answer is chemicals. Alar, a chemical hormone designed to stop apples falling prematurely from the tree, was used extensively.

Alar proved to be the industry's downfall. The Alar case was a perfect storm of ambiguous science, extreme environmentalists, government foot-shuffling, and ignorant consumers ignited by mass media sensationalism.

Every processed food we eat has chemicals in it, and chemicals often change as they are processed. When Alar-treated apples were cooked for applesauce and apple juice, a toxic byproduct formed. Scientific analysis of unsymmetrical dimethyldrazine (UDMH) revealed that it was mildly carcinogenic. Even so, the risk was considered slight by the National Cancer Institute. But in the eighties, the National Resources Defense Council (NDRC), an adversary group, pressured the Environmental Protection Agency to conduct more experiments on UDMH. The results were inconclusive. Fifty-two mice were fed UDMH in amounts analogous to a person drinking 19,000 quarts of juice made from treated apples daily and for life. Eleven mice developed cancerous and non-cancerous tumors, while eighty died prematurely, poisoned by the massive dose of UMDH—which it turned out was a key ingredient of rocket fuel.

The Alar scare was unsubstantiated by any peer review journal, yet the media swallowed it whole. In 1989, Phil Donahue—a crunchy granola in his own right—said on his daytime talk show in his folksy way, "Don't look now, but we're poisoning our kids. I wouldn't lie to ya." The claim was repeated on CBS's flagship show *60 Minutes*, and beamed to a prime-time audience. Immediately, Alar was fingered as a killer. That was all it took for the apple's innocence to be lost forever. Celebrities rushed to condemn it. Once, an endorsement by a movie star for anything but Chanel No. 5 or Obsession would have been dismissed out of hand. The public used to know a fantasy when they saw one. They liked their movie stars to be fantasies, the way John Wayne was a fantasy, and Marilyn Monroe. But as movies declined, the stars began to take themselves seriously as tribunes for the common person, using their fame as a platform from which to air political views.

Meryl Streep, a concerned mother herself, went before Congress pleading for all mothers whose children were being threatened by the carcinogenic apple. She was put up to it, according to the investigative journalist Robert James Bidinotto, writing in *Reader's Digest* (October 1990), by the National Resources Defense Council. Bidinotto writes that Streep "came up with the idea of setting up a group called 'Mothers and Others for Pesticide Limits,' which was an NRDC front operation from the word go." Before and after the *60 Minutes* segments, Streep also played a prominent role in speaking out against Alar in the media.

Panic ensued. Schools went on an apple-dumping spree. Naturally, the bottom fell out of the apple market, and the financial reverberations have never stopped since.

Did the crusading movie star wish to put an end to family farming? Because that is what happened. Despite the fact that a consensus of scientists cleared Alar, the chemical was withdrawn in America although, interestingly enough, it is still used in green Europe. The victims of the Alar scare were the family farms, built by the original homesteaders. When the market shrank in the mid-1990s after the furor, the small farmer was left at the mercy of supermarket buyers as the chains became fewer and exerted more power. The supermarkets, sensing weakness, wasted no time in putting pressure on the growers, playing Goliath against the Davids of the family farms, pushing down prices as low as they could. More and more, the small growers were squeezed out of a diminishing market because the big producers could survive the downturn better. Today, less than half of the growers in the valleys are small growers, and they grow the best apples.

As the small growers go broke, the supermarkets make money, even though apple sales are not what they were. The supermarkets can now buy apples so cheaply that they make more money from them than they do from selling Coca-Cola or potato chips. And they don't want to rock the boat. Recent consumer research for the Washington Apple Commission shows that consumers are not wedded to the Red Delicious or, for that matter, any red apple. They want crisp, juicy apples, regardless of color. But the supermarkets don't want to take chances. The computer printouts show that overall, red sells best. The grower can do nothing about it. The supermarket pays higher prices for red apples, so the growers, their backs to the wall, continue growing them. The growers can actually grow far better Red Delicious than are found in the supermarkets, but they aren't red enough.

One Wenatchee grower, Ron Skagen, has been quoted as saying, "You have this disconnect between financial returns and what the consumers want." This is the unacceptable face of industrialized food, the middleman deciding what consumers will eat based on his profit margins.

The last straw was the downturn in the export market. All industrial food is now produced to be exported; that's where the largest profits lie. But as more and more countries become players, the game has grown as daunting as chess, a series of moves and counter-moves often leading to deadlock. Every self-respecting country has an armory of trade barriers that it juggles to suit the political mood. The European Union's rule that a banana may only be called a banana if it's straight is one way to keep out curved bananas from the Caribbean, all part of the United States vs. Europe banana war, and, said an EU official, to prevent bananas from being mistaken for a "bicycle wheel."

The Americans had counted on the Japanese market, always tough to crack, opening up to their apples; but the Japanese were wily. They rejected the proposed exports for, among other things, not being sweet enough for Japanese taste. This seemed at first plausible as the Japanese are sugar junkies. They have their own sweet organic apples—Kinsei, Orin, and Shizuka—large, golden apples that sell for five dollars apiece. And the Japanese produce their own Fujis, whose sweetness they love. They eat their apples peeled, thus eliminating the tastiest part of the fruit. On the other hand, the rejected apples were hardly tart: the Red Delicious and the Golden Delicious are both sweet and bland. Stalemate.

The Washington growers turned this way and that in desperation. They tackled head-on the problem of chemicals. They followed an integrated pest management schedule that lessened chemical use, even coming up with sex traps to stop insects breeding, and they achieved some success. But one insect simply couldn't be got rid of, and it was the most lethal.

Of all the pests that attack apples, the most destructive is the codling moth, as devastating to apples as the European corn borer is to corn. The codling moth emigrated along with the apple; it flourished because it had no natural predators outside Central Asia. In Kazakhstan, native wasps feed on the moth. As a result, only a small number of apples there have the telltale mothholes in them. So, American scientists have mounted wasp-catching expeditions to Central Asia, returning with several species of predator. But the wasps are sensitive. They haven't been happy in Washington State— the food, the water, who knows? Anyway, they don't gobble up the codling moth the way it was hoped.

If ever a crop cried out for genetic modification, it is the apple. And in fact a recent discovery could change the apple's fortunes. The gene for the peptide protein that prevents tooth decay has been identified, and one suggested application is to splice it into apples. An apple a day keeps the dentist away! No sooner had this news got out than there was what seemed now the de rigueur protest from Europe. A transgenic apple would not be the right kind of apple; it would no longer be our old familiar apple (as if the Asian apple was ever really ours).

The future looks bleak for Western apples. In a few years, the Chinese apple will be as supreme as Chinese apple juice is now. The big question is, when the Chinese achieve a monopoly, just how many varieties they will think it necessary to grow. The Red Delicious, or the Fuji?

Before the apple returns to Central Asia, there are recipes that mustn't vanish. Who knows, the Kazakhstan apple might become a tourist attraction, Westerners journeying to Central Asia just to taste it, and bringing home a box or two of the precious fruit. Then, as the apple becomes more and more desirable, some bright fellow will say: "I believe we could grow apples here . . ." And the whole cycle will begin all over again.

Food Without Fear

By Dan Barber

from the *New York Times*

Chef and co-owner of Manhattan's Blue Hill restaurant and its farm-based Westchester sister, Blue Hill at Stone Barns, Barber cooks with a passion for quality ingredients that can inspire us all.

N ow that the bloom is finally off the Atkins diet rose, now that the instinct to, say, make a purée of potatoes feels slightly less suicidal, let us take a moment to realize that, when it comes to food, Americans have the tendency to lose all reason. With the same collective head-scratching that goes on when we look back at the big hair and shoulder pads of the 80's, we would do well to ask: What were we thinking?

This question, of course, applies not just to the Atkins diet but to pretty much every diet fad Americans have followed over the last 30 years. In addition to catchy names, these we eat comes from or how it was grown. Good nutrition has been conveniently, and profitably, reduced to an ingredient list. (Remember the grapefruit diet?) That's a shame—and there's no better time to explore the ways in which we've been led astray than during Thanksgiving week, a time when Americans are particularly focused on food. (And, coincidentally, a time when we are blessedly between diet fads.) With a little scrutiny, we can see that our reductionist diet logic dissolves like a lump of sugar. Just consider the traditional Thanksgiving spread: it may appear to represent the American pastoral, but looks can be deceiving.

Start with the turkey. If your image of a turkey's life is one of green grass and rolling hills, look more closely. Nearly 300 million turkeys are raised today on factory farms where they live in windowless buildings illuminated by bright lights 24 hours a day. (This keeps the turkeys awake and eating.) The birds stand wing to wing on wood shavings and eat an overly fortified diet that enables them to reach an ideal dressed weight of 15 pounds in 12 to 14 weeks. The most popular breed is the Broad Breasted White, aptly named because these turkeys develop disproportionately large breasts, which makes it difficult for the birds to walk (if they had room to do so) and procreate (assuming they'd want to) without artificial insemination.

So what kind of bird would fit more accurately with our agrarian fantasies? Well, how about one that spends most of its life outdoors? Such birds—called pastured birds—are able to move around freely. Instead of having to be injected with antibiotics to stay healthy, they doctor themselves, seeking out certain plants at certain times of the year for pharmacological reasons. Because they expend so much energy moving around, they also grow more slowly; it takes a month longer for them to reach slaughter weight than factory birds, which is one of the reasons pasturing is less attractive to industrial farmers. Scientific research comparing the health benefits of conventionally raised turkey to pastured turkey is scarce, but some work has been done on chickens. A study sponsored by the Department of Agriculture in 1999, for example, found that pastured chickens have 21 percent less fat, 30 percent less saturated fat, 50 percent more vitamin A and 400 percent more omega-3 fatty acids than factory-raised birds. They also have 34 percent less cholesterol.

The pasture principle isn't limited to fowl. Compared to most American beef, which is raised on a grain-intensive diet, pasture-fed beef offers 400 percent more vitamin A and E. It is also much richer in beta-carotene and conjugated linoleic acids, all of which inhibit cancer. It's also higher in omega-3 fatty acids, which are a major inhibitor of heart disease. These benefits don't exist at these levels in animal that are fed an unvaried and unnatural diet.

The pasture principle can be applied to vegetables as well. We don't live off the food we eat—we live off the energy in the food we eat. So while Mom asked us, "Did you eat your fruits and vegetables?" today we might well ask: "What are our vegetables eating?"

It seems axiomatic but it's worth remembering that in order to experience the health benefits of the roasted broccoli at the Thanksgiving table, that broccoli needs to have been healthy too. We can be forgiven for ignoring the obvious because most every diet I've seen treats a head of broccoli the way Gertrude Stein talked about a rose – but a broccoli is not a broccoli is not a broccoli, especially if you consider how and from where it's grown.

Sadly, the broccoli and the other brassicas on your holiday table (brussels sprouts, cabbage, turnips, kale, mustard greens) were most likely grown in a monoculture—a place where, with the help of large amounts of chemical fertilizers and pesticides, nothing but the crop is allowed to grow. Fertilizers are as pervasive in these large farms as tractors, especially synthetic nitrogen. And you can understand why: the chemicals bulk up vegetables beautifully and quickly, enabling them to withstand the rigors of long-distance travel so that they can arrive at your supermarket unbruised and brightly colored. But it's a little like dating someone on steroids: the look and feel may be an initially appealing, but in the end it's all kind of disconcerting.

And think what gets lost. A serving of broccoli is naturally rich in vitamins A and B, and has more vitamin C than citrus fruit. But raised in an industrial farm monoculture, shipped over a long distance and stored before and after being delivered to your supermarket, it loses up to 80 percent of its vitamin C and 95 percent of its calcium, iron and potassium. Fruits and vegetables grown organically, however, have higher levels of antioxidants. That's largely because a plant's natural defense system produces phenolic compounds, chemicals that act as a plant's defense against pests and bugs. These compounds are beneficial to our health, too. When plants are grown with herbicides and pesticides, they slow down their production of these compounds. (Even more important, from a cook's point of view, organically grown fruits and vegetables taste better—their flavors practically burst from the ground and demand to be expressed, and we chefs merely comply.)

The same rules apply to the root vegetables, whether potatoes, sunchokes, beets, parsnips, or carrots. Seek out ones grown in nutrient-rich soil for the greatest flavor and benefit. You can't buy good quality soil in a bag any more than you can buy good nutrition in a pill. Most organic farmers encourage complex relationships between crop roots, soil microbes and minerals – relationships that become wholly disrupted by chemical additives.

What about the milk and eggs that go into Thanksgiving pies and tarts? The industrialization of our food supply did not spare the dairy industry.

Not surprisingly, pastured dairy cattle and laying hens produce more nutritious milk and cheese—pastured eggs in particular, with their glowing yellow yolks, have up to three times the amount of cancer-fighting omega-3's of eggs that come from factory hens.

As a chef, I am often mystified as I hear diners, rooting around for a nutrition and dietary cure, ask for this steamed and that on the side, and in the process deny themselves pleasure. Choosing what dietary advice of the moment to follow by putting a wet finger up to the wind, our patrons decide, or succumb, en masse, to a pummeling of such wearisome regularity that it begins to resemble the "rosebud" of "Citizen Kane": the clue that solves everything but means nothing.

There is an ecology of eating. Like any good ecosystem, our diet should be diverse, dynamic and interrelated. In 1984 Americans were spending roughly 8 percent of their disposable income on health care and about 15 percent on food. Today, those numbers are essentially reversed.

An ever-more reductionist diet—protein this year, carbohydrates next year—ignores plant and animal systems loaded with genetic complexity, and the benefits that complexity passes down to us.

So as you're getting ready for Thanksgiving, think of yourself less as a consumer of the harvest bounty and more, in the words of Carlo Petrini of the Slow Foods movement, as a co-producer. Try to remember what you know intuitively: that we can't be healthy unless our farms our healthy; that the end of the food chain is connected to the beginning of the food chain; that we can't lose touch with the culture in agriculture (it dates back to before Dr. Atkins). To the extent possible, shop at farmers markets for your Thanksgiving foods. Try to choose diversity over the abundance that the big food chains offer. Your food will be tastier, fresher and more nutritious. You'll be able to have your cake (and your bacon and your bread and your potatoes) and eat it too.

Two Americas, Two Restaurants, One Town

by Rebecca Skloot

from the *New York Times Magazine*

In the restaurant business, success does not always follow fine cooking. Skloot compares two competing restaurants in one small West Virginia town, almost a microcosm of the great divide nowadays in American gastronomy.

To call Baristas a restaurant would be a serious understatement. It is a restaurant, but it's also a barbershop. And a coffeehouse. And, of course, a massage parlor. Naturally, it's run by the same guy who turned the funeral home around the corner into a gym, with cardio machines in the viewing room and free weights in the old embalming chamber.

Baristas occupies a huge turn-of-the-century white house in New Martinsville, W.Va., with steep fire-engine-red steps, a porch full of rainbow-colored tables and pillars painted to look like cloudy skies and candy canes. You walk inside to high ceilings, oak floors, purple walls and one of the owners, Jill Shade, making her famous mocha crushes or hopping around singing an old Cher song she has had stuck in her head for weeks. When I first walked in, Shade pointed to a huge wooden board behind her. "Menu's up there," she told me, "but if you're craving something you don't see, just holler and I'll try to make it."

Baristas' menu is not exactly an exercise in overwhelming choice—a couple of homemade soups, a salad, some appetizers, sandwiches and one dinner special on Friday nights. But ambience is another story. You can eat in the basement pub, with its low oak ceiling and stone walls. You can eat on the patio overlooking the Ohio River, in the garden next to the hibiscus plants or in the cafe surrounded by walls of local art. You can get a haircut or a bona fide Swedish massage while you wait, then sit at a table covered in quotes from Camus or Malcolm X. It's exactly the kind of place I love, and exactly the kind of place I would never expect to find in New Martinsville, where I live part of each year. It's a town of about 5,000 people and 36 churches, a town full of all-you-can-eat buffets, Confederate flags, "No Trespassing" signs and folks who still feel the need to point out the local lesbian couple. But then again, I never expected to find Jeff Shade in New Martinsville either.

Shade is a local boy, a 38-year-old former high-school football star who left West Virginia with dreams of becoming a minister. But he lost God somewhere in Texas and got kicked out of seminary, he says, for "asking too many questions." He studied philosophy and theology at Princeton, then went to massage school in Manhattan while serving as the pastor for a New Jersey church where he preached from The New York Times instead of the Bible. A few years later, he headed back to New Martinsville with his wife, Jill, their 2-year-old son, Soren Aabye Shade (as in Soren Aabye Kierkegaard), and degrees in Greek, theology, philosophy and massage. With all that education, he and Jill decided they wanted to expand the minds of the folks back home. The tool they chose was the burger.

The Barista burger is the creation of Tammy Wilson, a compact, ponytailed whirlwind with tie-dyed flip-flops and a T-shirt that says "Save the drama for your mama." Wilson is Baristas' main cook, and she works in a kitchen that looks more like a home than a restaurant. Teenage girls run in and out asking her questions about prom dates and haircuts, Jill appears from the garden with a bag of peppers for roasting and Jeff wanders around tasting soups and sauces while cracking jokes about politicians or saying things about Foucault that nobody understands. Wilson spends hours each week pressing fresh garlic and adding it to vats of ground beef for burgers; when she's done, she rolls up her sleeves and plunges her hands into the meat. "I learned to cook from my hillbilly grandma, and I'm proud of it," she told me. "And if there's one thing I know, it's that burgers only taste right when you mix the spices by hand."

Clearly, she's onto something. People drive 60 miles up and down the Ohio River for her burger: a juicy half-pound of ground beef with hints of ginger and garlic and soy, some spices, a touch of West Virginia honey and enough sweet smokiness from the grill to make you think she cooked it over fresh mesquite. Mix that with a salad fresh from the garden and hand-cut fries, and you've got a room full of people who simply can't believe anyone *wouldn't* want to eat at Baristas.

But in fact, a lot of locals can't imagine even walking into Baristas, let alone eating there. The truth is, most of them would rather go to Bob Evans.

The first time I drove up to the New Martinsville Bob Evans, Billy Joel's "Just the Way You Are" was echoing through the parking lot from the speakers above the doors. Everything about the place said "national chain." I walked past a red-white-and-blue banner into a world lined with plaid curtains and Old Fashioned things, like copper teakettles and washboards that looked so new they might as well have still had price tags on them. The eggnog- and pecan-pie-scented candles by the cash register overwhelmed any smells from the kitchen. A short woman in black polyester slacks and a white button-up shirt with a Bob Evans logo stitched on it smiled at me, menu in hand, and said: "Hi, welcome to Bob Evans. One for dinner?"

Baristas and Bob Evans are less than a mile apart, but they might as well be in different cities. Baristas sits on Main, a quiet tree-lined street with wide sidewalks and a historic courthouse. You're guaranteed to miss it if you don't know to turn toward the river at the BP station. But you can't miss Bob Evans. It has the tallest sign on this strip of Route 2, a highway lined with a Wal-Mart, a McDonald's, a Dairy Queen and a Pizza Hut that could be anywhere in the country.

There is only one Baristas, but there are 576 Bob Evanses, in 21 states; in 2004, the company rang up $1.2 billion in sales. Bob Evans is part of a giant and fast-growing retail category known as "full-service family-style dining" (you know the kind: Cracker Barrel, Denny's, Friendly's); it's a sit-down restaurant that leans more toward down home than fast food, with a serious emphasis on all-day breakfast. Like most Bob Evanses, the one in New Martinsville is in a red-and-white "farmhouse" with a sprawling parking lot and a few benches out front.

The goal at every Bob Evans restaurant is to be the same as every other Bob Evans restaurant. "We want to make sure the experience someone has in New Martinsville is the same as the one they'd have in Orlando, St. Louis or Baltimore," said Tammy Roberts Myers, the P.R. director at the Bob Evans headquarters in Columbus, Ohio. The company's guiding principle is simple: consistency, in everything from ambience to the distance between tables to the arrangement of food on your plate.

"Going out to eat is risky," said Steve Govey, the Bob Evans regional manager for the Ohio Valley. "You never know what you're going to get. But at Bob Evans, that's not true. Our strategy is being completely predictable, something people know they can count on."

Bob Evans was packed when I arrived. It was full of customers of all ages and sizes, with lots of khakis, denim shorts and camouflage hats with pictures of guns or slogans like "National Wild Turkey Federation." There were three women at three different tables wearing identical neon orange T-shirts. I'd just come from Baristas, where people danced at the counter to Ray Charles and talked across the room about how so-and-so woke up with a weird rash yesterday and what John Kerry said at the rally in Wheeling about helping millworkers. At Bob Evans, I sat alone at the counter. The people around me stared at their plates and ate in silence; behind me, people spoke so quietly I could barely hear their murmurs over the clanking silverware.

I ate a raspberry grilled-chicken salad with exactly four slices of strawberries, four chunks of pineapple and a tough sliced chicken breast with raspberry vinaigrette. I followed that with a classic turkey dinner. The stuffing was great, but the rest was just barely edible—a little dry, too salty, with oily biscuits and mashed potatoes that tasted like fake movie-popcorn butter. Honestly, I didn't get it.

But I went back to Bob Evans the next day, and I kept going back and kept trying things on the menu. I was determined to understand why so many people in town chose this place over Baristas. (The prices at the two restaurants, by the way, are about the same.) I ate a southwestern omelet smothered in jack cheese, and a pork chop dinner that took four people to make. None of the chefs spoke while they cooked; they just threw still-frozen vegetables and meat straight onto the griddle. (They let me watch.) They measured lettuce and arranged the food on my plate so it would look exactly like the instructional diagram hanging on the kitchen wall: pork chop over here, frozen vegetables over there, one sprig of parsley right there.

After a waitress put the whole package down in front of me, I took a bite and thought, They're right, it *is* just like grandma used to make. Thing is, my grandmothers couldn't cook. From my New York grandmother, I got burned matzo brei and gefilte fish from a jar. From my southern Illinois grandmother, I got food that tasted just like Bob Evans's: soggy vegetables, rubbery bread and meat so over-cooked it crumbled when you bit it.

I'd gone meat shopping a couple of days earlier with Tammy Wilson from Baristas, and I watched her hand-pick every pound of meat from the butcher's counter as he leaned through the window and told her it had just come in fresh. "He gets most of his meats local," she told me. I wanted to find out the same sort of thing about the Bob Evans pork chop, so I called the folks in Columbus. Tammy Roberts Myers said she would be happy to trace my dinner for me, all the way from the animal to the table. But a couple of weeks later, she called to say that someone at headquarters had a change of heart. "Sorry," she said. "We can't tell you that, because it's proprietary information. What I can tell you is, it was on a farm somewhere at some point."

I didn't start to understand the appeal of Bob Evans (for other people, anyway) until I met Daisy and Wally Kendall. They eat at Bob Evans nearly every day, sometimes more than once. They sit in a maroon vinyl booth giggling and finishing each other's sentences. When I asked why they eat at Bob Evans all the time, Daisy said: "It's clean, and there are no surprises. I know what I'm going to get."

Wally shrugged and said: "People say, 'Why do you only go to Myrtle Beach for vacation every year? Don't you want to see somewhere else?' We never know what to say—we tried it, we know we like it, why risk spoiling our vacation somewhere new we might not like?"

When I asked other people why they chose Bob Evans over Baristas, most folks just smiled and shook their heads. One young woman told me her father doesn't like her eating at Baristas because "it's like feeding your money to Satan." One regular said he didn't know why he ate at Bob Evans, but he thought it might have something to do with it being so consistent. "I'm not big on change," he told me. "That's why I'm voting for George W. It's just too dangerous to change stride now. It's best to leave well enough alone."

One woman lowered her voice and whispered: "Baristas' problem is, they try to make fancy food. We're simple people here. We don't like a lot of spices and stuff. A little salt and pepper is good enough for us. You have to develop a taste for that fancy stuff, and we don't really want to."

Another woman pointed to my pork chop dinner and said: "You've got to remember, this is what we were raised on. If people want to go into Baristas for a bean-sprout sandwich, that's fine, but around here, we don't do that sort of thing."

In fact, Baristas' menu is full of traditional New Martinsville food (hamburgers, grilled-cheese sandwiches, steaks, fried green tomatoes), and there isn't a bean-sprout sandwich in sight. But there are a few things on the menu that give some locals the creeps: hummus, pesto, eggplant, feta. The way they see it, Jeff's a local boy, and New Martinsville loves him, but that doesn't mean they're about to eat weird food in a restaurant that sounds as if it might as well be a brothel, what with all the drinking and massaging going on there.

Daisy and Wally have known Jeff Shade since he was a kid. When I asked them why they'd never gone to Baristas, they looked at each other as if it had never occurred to them. "We love Jeff," Daisy said. "The only reason we haven't gone there is really just negligence.

"We were going to go there once," Daisy went on, "but a deer ran into the car." Then she paused. "We really should go sometime," she told Wally.

How about now, I asked. I'll go with you.

"Oh, no," they said in unison, then giggled. "We're expecting a call from Wally's doctor later."

Daisy and Wally have always been Bob Evans people, but they didn't start going daily until they came down with severe health problems—lymphoma for Wally and serious respiratory problems for

Daisy—which they attribute to years of breathing in toxins while working at a local chemical plant. They got sick and weak, they couldn't cook and Bob Evans became their life. Daisy looked at me and whispered: "You know, the food here is wonderful. We've never had a bad meal. But really, we don't come for the food. We come for the people." She gestured around the restaurant. "This is our social life."

When I walked back into Baristas after a few days of nothing but Bob Evans, I literally felt as if I had come home. The walls were the exact shade of purple that I painted my bedroom when I was a teenager, and these days my kitchen is maroon, just like Baristas' back dining area. One of my favorite Jayhawks songs was playing, and I sat down at the bar next to Gary, a former airplane-engine specialist who lives in an octagonal penthouse he built on top of an old hog barn.

I told him what I'd been doing, and he looked at me as if I were crazy. "I can't imagine hanging out at Bob Evans every day," he said. "I just find that place so . . . so . . . the same." I knew what he meant. I loved talking to Daisy and Wally and a few other regulars at Bob Evans, but I couldn't handle going in there every day. I'm a Baristas person to the bone—just as Daisy and Wally are pure Bob Evans. The question is: Why? What makes them Bob Evans people and me a Baristas person?

Some of it is simple aesthetics: I think fresh food tastes a lot better than frozen, and I want herbs instead of salt. Local art on colorful walls makes me happy, and fake old-fashioned teakettles make me sad. Mostly I love Baristas because of the buzz, the energy I feel when I'm in the midst of people who thrive on resisting predictability, like the Catholics who come to Baristas to hear Buddhist monks speak about reincarnation, or the Republicans who came in to meet the Kerry people who stopped by one night to stump.

Maybe I had an idea that I could convert people—that I could persuade some Bob Evans folks that they should be open to change, that the food really was better at Baristas; and maybe persuade some Baristas people that the Bob Evans people are interesting and funny and friendly, too. But in all my time shuttling back and forth between the two restaurants, I didn't change a single person's mind. At some point, it hit me: it's not just New Martinsville. Bob Evans people and Baristas people live together all over the United States.

They often go to the same stores and send their kids to the same schools, but try as they might, they simply can't understand why anyone in his right mind wouldn't eat the way they do, think the way they do and vote the way they do. Unfortunately, I'm not sure a burger can change that, not even a really, really good one.

Barista Burgers

Adapted from Tammy Wilson, chef at Baristas.

1 ½ pounds ground round
1 ½ pounds ground chuck
¼ cup finely chopped onion
2 to 3 cloves garlic, minced
5 tablespoons soy sauce
5 tablespoons honey (preferably ThistleDew Farm
    West Virginia honey)
¼ teaspoon Emeril's Essence (or Bayou Blast! Essence for a
    spicier burger)
1 ½ teaspoons ground ginger.

1. Preheat a grill. In a large bowl, blend the ground round, ground chuck, onion, garlic, soy sauce, honey, Emeril's Essence and ginger.

2. Shape the mixture into six patties. Grill to taste. Serve on sourdough buns with lettuce, tomato and onion.

SERVES 6

Big Cheese

by Cynthia Zarin

from *The New Yorker*

This in-depth profile traces how one dynamic entrepreneur fell into running a famous Greenwich Village cheese shop, and what that has done to raise cheese's profile in the gourmet world.

Before I met Rob Kaufelt, the owner of Murray's Cheese Shop, in Greenwich Village, what I knew about cheese could be wrapped in a chestnut leaf. When people came to dinner, I bought Brie to have with drinks. At Christmas, my aunt, an Anglophile, supplied Stilton. I made grilled-cheese-and-apple sandwiches with supermarket cheddar, and wrapped the leftover cheese in plastic. (For cheese, this is roughly the equivalent of putting a plastic bag over your head. Use waxed paper.) Years ago, I'd had a glimpse of a different world, where cheese was treated with the easy reverence that might otherwise be reserved for a home-town starlet. It was in Sperlonga, a seaside town south of Rome. On our first two mornings, we bought buffalo mozzarella at a tiny *latteria*. The animals were milked at dawn; the cheese was made fresh every morning, in a formidably clean kitchen behind the shop. It was sublime nursery food, tasting of grass and clouds. We ate it on the spot. The third morning, we went for a swim. When we came for our cheese, the girl behind the counter shrugged. The cheese was no good now. It was done. Finished. When I mentioned this episode to Rob Kaufelt one morning, drinking coffee at the Grey Dog, on Carmine Street, he said, "Fanatics. There are people who think there's only ten minutes in the life of a Camembert when it's *à point*, when you should eat it. Anything else is junk." At fifty-six, Kaufelt is a wryly handsome, jumpy man. He grinned and added, "But they're right."

Murray's Cheese Shop is at the corner of Cornelia and Bleecker Streets. (There is also an outpost in the food market in Grand Central.) In the past few years, the cheese landscape in New York—what kind of cheese you can buy, who makes it, who's eating it, and where—has changed dramatically; it's like the moment when black-and-white TV turned into full-spectrum color, and in that world Kaufelt is key. Steve Jenkins, who is the cheese expert at Fairway, the food mecca on the Upper West Side, says, "Rob's a hipster. He's magnificent. The incredible thing is that he found some deep peasant virtue in what we do. Murray's is a vehicle for Rob, and it's driven by him. He was tapped on the shoulder by a fairy who told him cheese was magic."

Four years ago, Murray's had only ten or fifteen restaurant clients, and only a handful served a separate cheese course: Le Bernardin, Jean Georges, Lutèce. Murray's now supplies cheese to seventy-five restaurants in the city; the wholesale division accounts for half of Kaufelt's business. If you go out to supper and eat cheese at the likes of Gotham Bar and Grill, Town, or Daniel, it's probably from Murray's. Even so, the Grey Dog is Kaufelt's breakfast and lunch joint. It's also where he holds meetings with his staff. At Murray's, there's nowhere to sit down—it measures just nine hundred square feet. The crammed, narrow shop is redolent, heady, a miniature city of cheese. At any one time, three hundred cheeses—squat, tall, pyramid-shaped, cylindrical—pack a sixteen-foot display case on the left side of the shop. Five staff people, wielding knives, work behind it, bumping into one another. On the right wall, bakers' shelves hold bottles of olive oil and vinegar, jars of jams and chutneys, and boxes of artisanal pasta and crackers. Murray's sells, on average, between five and six thousand pounds of cheese a week, primarily cheeses imported from France, Spain, Italy, and the British Isles, as well as a growing number of American farmstead cheeses. At Christmas, the amounts triple. Kaufelt has found some of these cheeses himself, in Welsh villages, Alpine hamlets, and on farms in Vermont; many are unavailable anywhere else in New York. In two hours one spring afternoon, I counted eighty-five people—locals, tourists, cheese lovers—who came in to browse, take deep whiffs, and carry away shopping bags marked with the red-and-yellow legend "This Is Murray's Cheese." The store's basement office is reached by an almost perpendicular flight of steps: the most benign adjective that the twenty-five people Kaufelt now employs use to describe it is "submarinelike." But more space is forthcoming: in September, for the second time since Murray's opened, in 1940, the store is moving.

At the Grey Dog, Kaufelt was on the phone with the architect for the new store. In conversation, he repeats crucial thoughts three times; it's a verbal tic that he shares with his father, Stanley Kaufelt, the New Jersey supermarket mogul, who can say in one sentence—in this case, about his reaction when Rob bought Murray's Cheese, in 1991—"I was amazed, I was astonished, I was flabbergasted."

"Look," Kaufelt said into his cell phone. "We need to think about the walls. We need to think about the floor. We need to think about the storefront. Do you have any cool lights? No, not cool-looking. Cool temperature. Yeah, special bulbs. That make cheese look cheesier?"

The move is just across Bleecker Street, twenty-five steps if you bear a little to the south-southeast. The shop will go from very small to somewhat bigger: twenty-seven hundred square feet, including upstairs offices and a conference room. There will also be a climate-controlled storage space in the basement. Kaufelt is buying the retail part of the building, and he plans to rent out part of it to complementary food shops: a seafood store, maybe, or a bakery. But, in a city where the Whole Foods chain, banking on the current interest in natural and organic groceries, has recently opened a fifty-nine-thousand-square-foot store, twenty-seven hundred square feet is nothing. For Kaufelt, the point is that he's not moving far, and not getting too big. He sees himself as a steward of the Village, of neighborhood store owners. It's a quandary: how can he expand his business and stay local at the same time? It's especially fraught for Kaufelt, because he comes from an entrepreneurial family, where bigger is better.

Robert Ian Kaufelt ("My mother was in a Scottish phase") was born in 1947 into a family of grocers in Highland Park, New Jersey. His paternal grandfather, Irving Kaufelt, who emigrated in 1914 from Poland, owned a store called Kaufelt Bros. Fancy Groceries, in Perth Amboy. (Rob's maternal grandfather was a Talmudic scholar.) On Fridays, they made sausage and sold it for twenty-five cents a pound. From the time Rob's father, Stanley, could stand, he measured out flour and sugar into brown paper bags. Over breakfast at the St. Regis, Stanley Kaufelt recalled, "For my bar mitzvah, I got a bicycle. On Monday, my father put a basket on it and told me I was going to deliver the orders!" The year Rob was born—he's the middle child of three—Stanley persuaded his father to close the Perth Amboy store and buy a six-thousand-square-foot supermarket in nearby North Brunswick. Big supermarkets were new—there were only two in New Jersey. Two years later, the Kaufelts opened up another, and DuPont approached them with an offer: the store's butcher would precut the meat, wrap it in DuPont's plastic film, and the customers would serve themselves. Until then, customers waited to order their meat at the counter. "How can you do this?" Irving Kaufelt asked his son.

"It's horrible!"

"It was marvellous!" Stanley told me. "You just put it in the case." On the first day, a forty-eight-foot meat counter sold out in an hour. In 1952, Stanley bought five stores, and a few years later he bought fifteen more from Food Fair, a competing chain, for twenty-seven million dollars. In the early eighties, Stanley was negotiating to buy a supermarket chain that was later sold to A. & P., but at the East Brunswick store the landlord wouldn't hand over the lease: he didn't like A. & P., so he signed with the Kaufelts.

By then, Rob was president of the company. He'd graduated from Cornell University in 1969, dipped in and out of the counterculture, and briefly tried law and architecture. In 1971, he travelled around Europe with a girlfriend (she later became his first wife), and they returned hoping to open a bed-and-breakfast in Vermont. Instead, Rob went to work for Stanley. Pathmark had pioneered one-stop shopping—in addition to groceries, it ran a pharmacy and a photo shop, and sold beauty aids—and it was beginning to dominate the business. Between 1978 and 1979, the Kaufelts had tripled the size of their company, Mayfair Supermarkets, but were losing money, and it seemed to Rob that what they needed was their own identity.

Interesting things were happening in New York: at Dean & DeLuca, Zabar's, and Balducci's, the emphasis was on food, not price. He decided that Mayfair should follow their example, and focus on quality and service. He was also interested in prepared foods, which, according to Kaufelt, were becoming popular not just because more women were working ("Nah, I don't think grocers are that clever") but because it made sense for the retailer. "The grocers realized, 'I can cook the produce, I can cook the meat, I can cook the chicken I didn't sell the day before, and I can make twice as much money!' It's not a glamorous notion. But once quality is in the equation it becomes about the perception of value."

He prevailed on his father to let him try innovations in East Brunswick: a bakery; fish displayed European style, on ice; a salad bar, which was a good way to salvage vegetables that would otherwise go bad; a custom butcher shop in addition to prepackaged meat; fresh pasta made to order from hand-cut dies. Their average cost to fix up a new venue was two hundred thousand dollars. Several months into the project, they were a million dollars over budget. The Kaufelts liked to open new stores in September. October passed, then November. "I was completely beside myself," Rob recalls. "Stanley said, 'Stop screwing around and open it!'" Rob was so nervous that one morning, on the way to work, he drove under a jack-knifed truck. He woke up in the hospital. That weekend, his family opened the store without him.

The average profit margin in the supermarket business is about two per cent. Before the renovation, the East Brunswick store's gross weekly sales were a hundred and sixty thousand dollars; the first week in the new store, the Kaufelts took in a million dollars. (The gross levelled off to about six hundred thousand dollars weekly.) In 1980, Mayfair Supermarkets was a public company, trading under the name Foodtown, at two dollars a share. Within two years, it had revamped many of its existing stores. The stock price skyrocketed and the stock split twice. In 1982, Foodtown had one of the greatest increases in percentage return on equity on the stock exchange. In the following years, many more upscale supermarkets opened, and one result was that many local retailers (bakeries, fish markets, butchers) in New Jersey and elsewhere went out of business.

Rob Kaufelt left the company in 1985. "Dad and I were not getting along," he says. "I was thirty-eight. I was impetuous. I was sure I was right. I was inexperienced. The idea that one needs to be politic within one's own organization and staff—it didn't occur to me."

At the end of that year, he opened a specialty food store in Summit, New Jersey, and, two years later, one in Princeton, called Kaufelt's Fancy Groceries, in honor of his grandfather. (Kaufelt told me, "I have a romantic vision of my grandfather's shop. I think I have a romantic vision, period.") After the crash of 1987, the Princeton store went out of business. Kaufelt sold the remaining store and left New Jersey for Manhattan—he'd been living in Princeton—eventually moving to 17 Cornelia Street, just up the block from the original Murray's Cheese Shop. (He currently owns a house on Greenwich Avenue.) Murray Greenberg, who had fought in the Spanish Civil War—"New York has had a fair number of Marxist capitalists shrewd with a buck," Kaufelt says—opened the store in 1940, when the neighborhood was almost entirely Italian. (A number of local stores survive from that time: Faicco's pork store, O. Ottomanelli's & Sons meat market, and Rocco's Pastry Shop; A. Zito & Sons bakery closed in May.) Almost everyone had a big family, and everyone shopped at Murray's for pasta, olive oil, parmesan, and provolone. "In the cheese business, there has always been a gray market," Kaufelt said. "Back then, everyone paid cash. New York industrial cheddar came in forty-pound blocks, and it got moldy quick. They'd buy it for fifty cents a pound, scrape off the mold, and sell it for one-fifty. Later, they bought Brie that was starting to run, took the skin off, spooned it into containers, and called it Brie spread."

Who bought it? I asked.

"Everyone bought it. You bought it. The upscale of 1984."

One day in 1991, Kaufelt was standing in line at Murray's to buy cold cuts and heard that Louis Tudda, who had bought the store after Murray Greenberg retired, in the nineteen-sixties, had lost his lease. Tudda was working behind the counter, and Kaufelt suggested that he move across the street; Durando's, an old butcher shop, had recently closed. But Tudda wanted to retire; he wanted to move to Italy. "So I bought it," Kaufelt told me, grinning. "Louis said, 'There's nothing to buy—I've got no inventory, no equipment.'" Kaufelt paid fifty thousand dollars for the name and remaining stock, moved the store to Durando's, and hung a photograph of his grandfather's Perth Amboy store above the register. He shook his head. "Durando told me, 'I was a shepherd in Sicily. When a guy messed with my sheep, I hit him with a two-by-four.'" He paused and added, "When I told my father I had bought a cheese shop on Cornelia Street, he said, 'You're out of your fucking mind.'" Kaufelt knew next to nothing about cheese. And in those low-fat, low-cholesterol days few people were interested in it.

In 1995, Stanley Kaufelt sold Mayfair Supermarkets, which then owned and operated about thirty stores in New Jersey, with gross sales of more than six hundred million dollars annually, to Ahold, a Dutch conglomerate. He and Rob's mother, Florence, now live in Boca Raton. Florence jokes, "When our friends in Florida hear about Murray's, they think we rejected Rob and he had to go into business by himself."

When Rob Kaufelt showed up in the Village, other changes were occurring: Cornelia Street was becoming a restaurant row. Pó, Mario Batali's first venue, which he opened on a shoestring (Kaufelt lent him five thousand dollars), was at No. 31. At No. 20, David Page was cooking at Home, which featured American food. There was a communal, collegiate feeling, the sense of something exciting going on. One morning, I was standing on the corner of Bleecker and Cornelia, next to Murray's, with Kaufelt, who was wearing an old tweed jacket, jeans, and a black T-shirt. He leaned against the street sign. Every third person who passed said hello. Looking up the street, Kaufelt said to me, "We'd hang outside and talk. Mario was discovering his Italian roots, and David was discovering his Wisconsin roots. We were all proselytizing for new flavors. The cheeses I was beginning to find were new, but they were old. The chefs were supportive of the old shops. David bought sausages from Faicco; the bread at Pó was from Zito. There was a generation of guys my age who were looking to reinvent food. None of us were really sure we were going to be able to make a living!"

There was a lull in the traffic, and an old woman in a head scarf yelled from across the street, "Hey, Rob, get a job!" He waved back, then said, "Look, some people want to protect this, some people want to protect that. I have the constant sense of something important being lost. Shops like mine are dinosaurs. This one—Murray's—is being saved. I think what I was seeking for myself after I left the grocery business was redemption." He grinned at me. "Of course, it's innately ridiculous. Cheese? Why do we say, 'Say "cheese"'? It even sounds funny!" He sighed. "In my case, it's compounded by the name Murray."

Liz Thorpe, who is twenty-five years old and graduated from Yale with a degree in art history and American studies, runs Murray's wholesale department. She's the face that Murray's presents to restaurant clients. When Thorpe sells cheese to a new restaurant, she often does a mini-tutorial for the staff. Cheese, she tells them, began as a way to preserve milk. There are five major groups of cheeses: fresh cheeses, such as chèvres, which are greeted in Europe as harbingers of spring; bloomy-rind cheeses—Brie, Camembert—which are exposed to mold, form a crust, and ripen from the outside in; cheeses like Epoisses and Taleggio, which are washed with marc or brine; cheddar and Morbier (to which a layer of ash is added between milk from the morning and the afternoon milking), which are pressed; and blue cheese, into which mold is injected, producing veiny markings. When a traditional French cheese plate is served properly, she explains, the different cheeses are placed in order from the mildest to the strongest, starting at twelve o'clock on the plate, and there should be a variety of sheep, goat, and cow cheeses. (Cheese plates are so new in most Manhattan restaurants that, not long ago, when Kaufelt asked forty students at the French Culinary Institute, in SoHo, if any of them knew how to serve a classic cheese course, not one hand went up.)

Thorpe usually sets aside a few days a week to visit clients, and recently I went along. Several years ago, restaurants would send someone by subway to pick up the cheese; now Murray's has a driver who makes two deliveries a day. Thorpe spends a lot of time on the phone. Some clients just call and say, "I have four hundred dollars to spend; pick sixteen cheeses."

The first stop that afternoon was Alain Ducasse, in the Essex House hotel. The kitchen is an ebony temple: cool and devoid of histrionics. The chef, Christian de Louvrier, who was introducing a new hundred-and-sixty-dollar prix-fixe menu that day, stopped for a minute to exchange greetings. "It's a busy day," he said. "Cheese—in and out." Sylvestre Wahid, a sous-chef, who was wearing immaculate whites, took two cheeses and vetoed the others. The exchange lasted seven minutes.

After an elevator ride in the new Time Warner Building, a few blocks west at Columbus Circle, we took the back entrance into Per Se, the restaurant opened by Thomas Keller, the owner of the French Laundry. In the private-dining kitchen, the staff was making truffle popcorn. For Per Se, Keller built a multimillion-dollar kitchen, and it has a separate refrigerator for cheese. He offers a composed cheese plate as part of a nine-course tasting menu. (Persillé du Beaujolais, a blue cheese made with raw cow's milk, is paired with carrot slaw, pickled Medjool dates, and French lentils.) A sous-chef, Jason Shaeffer, wanted a cheese that moves spring into summer. Thorpe nodded. She had new goat cheeses coming in on Friday.

Across the hall, Thorpe poked her head into Jean-Georges Vongerichten's new restaurant, V Steakhouse, which was scheduled to open the following week. At the front desk, a few tentative-looking waiters were learning how to pour wine. Thorpe said to me, "The restaurant doesn't know yet if it's doing a cheese plate."

The chef came out to say hello.

"You selling to Per Se?" he asked Thorpe.

She told him she was.

"They have one guy just to do the cheese?" He raised his eyes to Heaven.

The plate-glass window of Murray's announced sale prices for Spanish almonds, fig jam, candied walnuts. Kaufelt, opening the door, said, "We keep finding wonderful things to eat with cheese. You put a scoop of this and that on a plate, and it's nice." He glared at me. "But don't say the word 'gourmet.' It's a bullshit term. Say 'tasty.' Say 'delicious.'"

What to say about food—especially cheese—is a constant preoccupation of Kaufelt and his staff. Each cheese at the store is labelled with a description: Stinking Bishop is "running stinky, bound in wood and washed in perry"—a hard pear cider—"this is a Scottish classic for the cold weather." Vacherin Fribourg, from Switzerland, is "herbaceously full . . . luscious, mossy texture." Alpage Prattigau "tastes like popcorn butter, with age it develops a powerful aroma that screams to be noticed." This penchant for hyperbole, for the language of love letters, is not confined to Murray's. Adrian Murcia, the *fromagier* at the Tribeca restaurant Chanterelle, who buys his cheese from Kaufelt, described Tomme Crayeuse, a French washed-rind cheese, to me as "earthy, mushroomy, decadent—a killer."

One April morning, in the cold back room of the shop—Durando's old meat locker—where the cheese is stored, Kaufelt, with a few members of his staff, including Liz Thorpe and his friend Tamasin Day-Lewis, the Anglo-Irish food writer, whom he met two years ago at a food symposium in Ireland, were tasting products from Niman Ranch, the California-based supplier of all-natural lamb, beef, and pork. (The new store will have more room for charcuterie.) Day-Lewis, a tall, striking woman who keenly resembles her brother Daniel, the actor, lives on a five-hundred-year-old farm in Somerset. (Kaufelt says, "I should move to England, but I'm too nudgy.") She peppered the Niman representative with questions: Are the pigs free range? What breed are they? How did you kill them?

The rep, a small, tidy woman, took a deep breath, and said, "They're raised for fat," to which Day-Lewis replied, *"Brilliant."*

Then Thorpe said to Day-Lewis, "I went out last night and found my nightmare—the server didn't know what he was doing!" The restaurant had opened the week before. Thorpe was at the bar, and she spotted a friend, the *fromagier* at another restaurant that Murray's supplies. "He's grinning, and holding up a piece of cheese on a fork, and he says, 'Look, Sally Jackson!' The cheese he was holding up was hard, yellow, and obviously aged. So I said, 'That's not Sally Jackson.' He leaned over to me and said, 'I know, but I *ordered* Sally Jackson.'"

Thorpe paused and said, "The point is that Sally Jackson is one of the pioneer American cheesemakers. She lives in northern Washington. She makes only a few two-and-a-half-pound wheels each week, and a grape or chestnut leaf encases the cheese. It's one of the easiest cheeses in the world to identify."

What did you order? I asked.

"Bayley Hazen Blue, Poudre Puff, Constant Bliss—girl cheeses."

Bayley Hazen Blue and Constant Bliss are made in the Northeast Kingdom of Vermont by two brothers, Andy and Mateo Kehler, who began making cheese only a year ago. The first time I tasted Bayley Hazen Blue was last New Year's Eve, when Kaufelt and Day-Lewis arrived at my house with two of her children and a shopping bag of cheese. It was tangy, sweet, creamy, velvet on the tongue, the most delicious blue cheese I'd ever tasted. "Eat it," Kaufelt said. "I know where you can get more." Liz Thorpe, among others, already considers the Kehlers to be the best cheesemakers in America.

"Mateo Kehler's not the best cheese-maker," Kaufelt said. "He's just the best-looking. Liz bought his whole inventory without even tasting it! How can I run a store like that? He's the James Dean of cheese, and I've got him in my icebox!"

One of the things that Kaufelt hopes to do in the new store is to continue, on a larger scale, supporting local farms. This spring, when Thomas Keller opened Per Se, he called Kaufelt, asking for local butter. Kaufelt posted an inquiry on the Internet. "There were no replies," he told me. "Zip! But we can try to develop these sources, if we can insure a market."

We were so cold from standing around in the storage room that we went and sat on the bench outside the store. Kaufelt said, "O.K., now think of sexy words we can use in the new store to describe cheese." He ruminated, then looked sly. " 'Louche.' 'Thick, rampant blue veins'! I like older women! 'Unctuous'! 'Mousselike'! I'm the only one who likes these. Everyone else thinks they're over the top. But think of what you can do with just a few notes. What is cheese? Milk. Rennet. Salt. Cheese is Dylan, singing on 'Blood on the Tracks.'"

Day-Lewis looked at him. " 'Mousselike?' That's insane."

For the new store, Day-Lewis is developing recipes for prepared food—cheese pies, cheese straws, cheese tarts—which will be made on the premises. The dishes, at first, will be familiar but made with better ingredients. Frankie Meilak, who is thirty-five, has worked at Murray's for nineteen years, and is now the store's director of operations. (He started as a stock and delivery boy for Louis Tudda.) He says, "Who else is cooking with Montgomery cheddar? No one. But I know in the beginning people will say, 'I'm not going to pay for this.'"

The Montgomery family of Somerset make Montgomery cheddar by hand. It retails for twenty-two dollars a pound. When Meilak started working for Tudda (who had himself worked for Murray Greenberg), there was only one cheese in the store that cost more than seven dollars a pound, and that was the Parmigiano-Reggiano. When Murray's moved across the street, Steve Jenkins, then the cheese manager at Dean & DeLuca, came in to consult and help find purveyors. Kaufelt sold Brin d'Amour, a Corsican sheep's-milk cheese, for ten dollars a pound. "People were saying, 'You're kidding,'" Meilak recalls. "The old customers were looking for specials—two-ninety-nine a pound for yellow cheddar." Kaufelt started giving samples in the store. Meilak recalls, "Louis didn't give tastes. He said, 'There goes the profit!' But people go to restaurants, they go to Europe, and come here looking for the cheese." He smiles. "Usually, they can't remember what it's called, but they can describe it."

One answer that the store favors when asked why some cheeses are so expensive is that they don't really cost that much. A good leg of lamb can run to sixty dollars; if you serve three cheeses afterward, an ounce of each to six people—even very expensive cheeses—it might cost twenty dollars. Another is volume. Liz Thorpe says, "Last summer, I visited a woman high up in the Spanish Pyrenees. She has fifty goats. It's a solo operation. When her cheese gets here, it costs twenty-one dollars a pound. That's shockingly reasonable to me, when I know what goes into it. Part of the Murray's experience is that the counter people can convey the enormity of the journey when they show you a little piece of cheese."

Cielo Peralta has worked behind the counter at Murray's for nine years. One Saturday when I came by the shop, a man wearing aviator glasses walked in clutching a coffee cup. Peralta looked him up and down and said, "You want a couple hundred pounds of cheese, you let me know." By the register, there's a list of cheeses to push: Brie de Meaux, Crottin de Chavignol, Sechon de Pays. These are ripe cheeses that the staff knows have, at most, a week—they're "pre-bad." But often cheese is best—*à point*—right before it goes off.

Peralta gave a woman who couldn't decide what to buy a taste of Sechon de Pays, an aged cow cheese from Savoie. He murmured to me, "The trick is to say, 'Taste this, darling. It's very good.' Especially with difficult customers. They're the kind of people who like to feel special."

Meanwhile, a few feet down the counter, another staff person was telling a young woman shopping for a party to try balsamic vinegar and strawberries with the Brie de Meaux. She shook her head. "Does everybody but me know about this?"

She ended up spending seventy dollars. Peralta, at the register, suggested that she try the Crottin de Chavignol as well. "You want me to give you *more* money?" she asked.

Another part of the conundrum of price has to do with distribution. The cheese world is an inverted pyramid. At the bottom is the farmstead cheesemaker who milks his own animals. Next up are handmade artisanal cheeses, whose milk may come from several local farms. Then there are cooperative cheese factories, which pool milk from usually ten or fewer sources—in France, a coöperative factory may be a barn in the middle of a field—and the industrial cheese factories, which, in the case of Kraft, draw milk from several hundred producers. (Murray's does sell industrial cheese, behind the counter, primarily Havarti, sliced Swiss, and American.) By the late-nineties, Kaufelt was travelling in Europe extensively, tasting farmstead and artisanal cheeses that were sold at local markets but had no American or even European distribution. (In France, many cheeses are made within fifty miles of their point of sale.) He and Valérie Montbarbon, who was then Murray's wholesale manager, decided to import directly from France. Previously, they'd imported cheese the way everyone else does: from large distributors, who bought flats of cheese at the huge Rungis food market, outside Paris. Montbarbon researched customs and F.D.A. regulations, and Murray's began ordering on a small scale—forty kilos here, twenty there, which made trucking both difficult and very expensive. In 1998, Kaufelt met Hervé Mons, who is one of ten master *affineurs* in France. An *affineur* ages cheese. His work is built on relationships—he knows where the animals graze, and how each year's rainfall affects the feed. He buys young cheese from the cheesemaker, brings it back to climate-controlled caves, which are traditionally underground, stores it, turns and/or washes it, and generally coddles the cheese until it either reaches maturity or is ready to ship. It's finishing school for cheese.

Mons, a charismatic, deeply opinioned man, whose father was a local *affineur* before him, helped Murray's upgrade and consolidate its importing operation. (Valérie Montbarbon, who is from Provence, left Murray's two and a half years ago, and now works with Mons, in Saint-Haon-le-Châtel, near Auvergne, choosing cheese to ship back to New York.) With Mons's help, Kaufelt pulled off two things at once: he has cheeses that no one else has, and he has some control over shipping, which Mons now supervises, avoiding what Frankie Meilak describes as "cheese left sitting on the docks turning into crap."

• • •

In cheese circles right now, the buzz word is *affinage*. A year and a half ago, Terrance Brennan, who owns two restaurants in New York, Artisanal and Picholine, which used to order cheese from Murray's but doesn't now—opened a ten-thousand-square-foot cheese facility at Tenth Avenue and Thirty-seventh Street and announced that it was the first state-of-the-art *affinage* center in the United States. Some cheesemongers argue that, at least in the United States, where F.D.A. regulations forbid the importing of cheese under sixty days old, *affinage* pretty much means optimum storage, although Kaufelt points out that now that Americans are producing farmstead cheeses you can age week-old goat cheese made in this country. At Murray's, shelves holding unripe cheese are marked "Do Not Pull"; the most fragile of these—the bloomy- and washed-rind cheeses—are kept in garment bags plastered with hand-lettered signs that say, "DO NOT OPEN: A HUMID CHEESE IS A HAPPY CHEESE."

In the basement of the new store, Kaufelt, in consultation with Hervé Mons, is building five masonry caves, three with vaulted ceilings in which to store and age cheese. Questions of *affinage* aside, Murray's inventory at any given moment is worth about two hundred thousand dollars; good storage is imperative.

One sunny June morning, I met Kaufelt in a pocket park at the intersection of Bleecker and Sixth Avenue. He said, "The point is to care for these lightly perishable, young French things. See this?" He gestured to a square patch of rugosa roses. "Someone tends this. They feel *tenderly* toward it. Whey tends to sink to the bottom. Cheeses need to be turned over. The down side doesn't get air. What we want is controlled breakdown. Isn't that what we're all looking for, even in a cheese?"

He narrowed his eyes. "The most impressive *affinage* I've seen is in Switzerland. They age Emmenthal and Gruyère in enormous caves in the Alps. You go through vaults in the caves, like in an old James Bond movie, and way down, hundreds of feet away, there's an enormous robot, six or seven stories high, coming in your direction, very slowly. It takes out the cheese, washes it, turns it, and puts it back in its slot. It does this twenty-four hours a day, three hundred and sixty-five days a year."

• • •

The week before Kaufelt closed on the new store, he was perturbed. He had to see his accountant. He was in the middle of a divorce (his second); he had to see his lawyer. He had planned to go to England; now he couldn't go. And he was in mourning. Next door, Zito's bakery had closed, after eighty years in business. (One reason for the closing is that the neighborhood, which once housed large families who ate a lot of bread, is now home to people who like to eat out.) The shelves were bare. Julius Zito, who was born in the bakery's back room, in 1924, was staring out the window. On the street, a woman in a housedress was yelling to passersby, "Come look, this was a landmark!" Anthony Zito, Julius's son, took me downstairs to look at the bread ovens, which had been in use since 1864, when the building opened as a bakery.

Kaufelt arrived with coffee from Rocco's. He'd been talking to people. Couldn't Zito reinvent the brand? Re-merchandise the bread? He mentioned some entrepreneurs in the New York bread business: Amy Scherber, of Amy's Bread; Eli Zabar, of E.A.T. Kaufelt said to Zito, "You wouldn't have to do anything you didn't want to." Zito replied, "What's left?"

Kaufelt and I went outside. He said, "Some people would ask, 'Why bother?' The idea that New York may become like everywhere else is inevitable, or not. A real entrepreneur says about Zito, 'Great! Now I'll sell more bread.' But I want the things to be nice on my map of the world."

One late-spring evening, we ate at Chanterelle. By the end of a dinner for four, there were twelve cheeses on the table and twenty-four glasses of wine. Kaufelt said, "A meal like that is my tasty dream—the *fromagier* knows what he's doing, the cheese is in good condition, the sommelier knows how to match the cheeses." He paused. "But the best food is what the farmer unloads from the truck at market, *and everyone knows it*. A fresh buffalo-mozzarella burrata, filled with cream, in Campania. I've always been partial to dairy."

I Married a Restaurant Critic

by Nancy Grimes

from *Bon Appétit*

Somebody has to accompany the reviewer to all those fine dining rooms. This insider account by the former *New York Times* critic's wife tells the lesser-known side of dining out for a living.

Our cats would be pleased. It was early evening and the restaurant was almost empty. "Now!" I hissed at my husband, who deftly swept a large piece of foie gras into a Ziploc bag hidden in his lap. As he passed it to me under the table and I dropped it into my purse, we exchanged a look of triumph. Gorged on goose liver, our cats would, perhaps, sleep through the night and forgo their 4:00 A.M. snack and neck massage.

In truth, they had a right to complain. Ever since my husband, William Grimes, became the restaurant critic for *The New York Times,* we abandoned them four or five nights a week in order to sample the highs and lows of Manhattan's newest and, sometimes, finest dining rooms. Like all delinquent parents, we bought them off with gifts—satiny slices of scallop, glossy cubes of tuna tartare, shreds of savory beef cheeks. Fortunately, the cats never tired of their gourmet delights; unfortunately, we tired of ours.

Human beings just weren't made to eat out more than once— okay, twice—a week. We were committing unnatural acts and, although our cats might disagree, we discovered that, yes, you can have too much molten chocolate cake and Opus One. For most people, the job of food critic, like that of movie reviewer, travel writer, or mattress tester, sounds like a dream come true—a never-ending vacation on somebody else's dime. For those who actually do the work, however, the dream become a nightmare. When? In my case, about two years and two dress sizes after the first palate-teasing *amuse.*

Before he became a restaurant critic, my husband (known as Biff) would never have shoved foie gras into a baggie. In fact, he thought it was gauche even to ask for a doggie bag. Taking leftovers from a restaurant represented a severe slackening of his stringent code of public conduct. Of course, so did the use of fake names, bogus credit cards, and wigs, which, like baggies and tinfoil swans, he came to accept with the stoicism of the committed professional. His job required him to dine anonymously. The restaurants were determined to thwart him at every turn. The battle raged for the five years he held the job of critic.

Despite the demands and indignities of his job, Biff, for the most part, maintained his equilibrium. He always tried to be fair, never gained weight, happily took the bad table next to the kitchen door, and didn't mind the fact that his wig made him look like the provost of a community college.

I, on the other hand, became an overweight kvetch. If Biff, eternally uncomplaining and slender, was Dorian Gray, I was the portrait—my haggard face and swollen form an accurate record of every course on the tasting menu. Years of enforced gluttony transformed me from a starry-eyed, easygoing diner, happy just to be eating out, into a bellowing she-beast, enraged by lazy waiters and flat Champagne. As my standards for cooking soared, my tolerance for bad service withered. Legitimate accidents and mistakes I took in stride (like the time the seat of the toilet I was about to use crashed to the floor in a fashionable French bistro), but perennial misbehavior, often prompted by greed, inflamed me.

"No, I do not want a drink at the bar" became one of my most-used phrases. Even though most diners are wise to the ploy, restaurateurs still try to bully their customers into running up a bar tab while they wait for tardy companions. Is it really so strange that a woman alone may not want to sit on a barstool nursing a glass of mediocre Chardonnay? Or, even worse, stand in the freezing vestibule of a certain well-known steakhouse, surrounded by a crowd of half-drunk alpha males, just so the restaurant can create an illusion of convivial hubbub? My policy is: I'm on time, the table is ready—seat me. And the menu had better follow soon.

Another pet peeve was the logjam in the reception area. All too often, our fake names—Brooks, Harris, Johnson—eluded detection in the reservations book. With rising panic we would watch the maître d' scroll down the list of names and frantically flip pages in the book. "Smith, you say? Party of four? Seven o'clock? Mmmm. . . ." As my husband's upper lip began to bead with sweat, mine would thin with suppressed rage. Did he forget to make the reservation? Did he misremember the fake name? But no, "Smith" would suddenly appear, and we would, with luck, be whisked to our table with a sudden burst of efficiency.

Even worse than the specter of the lost reservation was the one that wasn't honored. Frequently, we would be asked to wait for our table, even though all of our party had arrived on time. This despite the fact that we almost always took an early reservation. The restaurant had all day to prepare our table. I came to the conclusion that the prospect of a hefty bar tab and the illusion of a covetous throng ("Look at that crowd! Wow, that place must be hot!") were just too seductive. You thought a reservation was a contract? Not so. A reservation merely allows you to be an extra in the percolating scene at the bar.

I used to be a forgiving diner who gracefully accepted most of what came her way. As time wore on, however, my dissatisfaction with certain restaurant practices and my willingness to voice that dissatisfaction grew. I love Champagne—my preferred aperitif—but if a restaurant offered just one sparkling wine, and a cheap one at that, I became irate. Ditto if they had a decent sparkler, but served it in the wrong glass. A certain Italian trattoria, that used to have its own TV show, served ironically retro food and poured Champagne into ironic Champagne coupes straight out of the 1950s. The waiter served mine with a twinkle in his eye. I sent it back. Even worse than flat glasses was flat Champagne, all too often served in the best restaurants. I developed a keen eye for counting bubbles in the glass, and if there weren't enough of them, the glass went back. Our breakneck dining schedule not only changed my attitude toward service, it also severely strained what I considered to be a committed, respectful relationship with food. Within the first three months of the job, I became disgusted with my own cooking. Yes, I'm a decent home chef, but after constant exposure to the likes of Mario Batali and David Bouley, decent wasn't good enough. My pleasure in cooking, like my enjoyment of the Food Network, shriveled. Our previously well-stocked refrigerator became a scene of desolation.

The dining pattern was heaven or hell. On our nights in, we actually took perverse pleasure in eating bad food. Pastas sauced with the bits the cats wouldn't eat whetted our appetite for the endless parade of three-course restaurant meals. These, for the most part, were superb, and often we would forget the pain as we toasted the restaurant capital of the world. Although I eventually tired of tuna tartare, seared foie gras, and flourless chocolate cake, the memories of certain dishes will forever sizzle, like the chicken Albuféra at Alain Ducasse, L'Actuel's *tarte flambé,* the truffled macaroni at Mix in New York, and Marseille's peanut butter tart. I'll salivate every time I recall the french fries at The Harrison, the baby goat with potatoes and artichokes at L'Impero, the fried eel backbones at Sushi Yasuda, or the Quark dumplings at Wallsé.

Of course, there were a few culinary duds, too, like white asparagus ice cream, peanut-lime-wasabi panna cotta, and duck tongues, which, by the way, taste like duck, but feel like tiny cartilaginous fins in the mouth.

It has been eight months since Biff stepped down from the critic's job. Do I miss it? Absolutely not. Now that my evenings are my own, I can work on my relationship with my cats and catch up on episodes of *Forensic Files.* Am I glad he did it? Absolutely! I returned to my neglected kitchen humbled but highly motivated. These days when I cook, I try to imitate the gnocchi at Craft, the vegetable lasagna at 71 Clinton, the heirloom tomato salad at The Biltmore Room, and the *sonhos* at Pico (now called Dominic). Dishes like these have become the guiding stars in my culinary universe. If I keep them in sight, I'm on the right course.

Now, if I can only drop those 15 extra pounds.

Diatribes for Dinner

by Jay Rayner

from *Saveur*

> There's nothing genteel about the way British dining critics are willing to roast a restaurant, as this member of the snarky London pack cheerfully admits.

It was the kind of story British newspapers love. A restaurant critic had written a caustic assessment of a long-established restaurant, and the proprietor had hit back with legal action for damages. "Restaurateur tells our reviewer: 'This is war,'" proclaimed the *Sunday Telegraph* last January, gleefully reporting that it was their man, the award-winning Matthew Norman, who had aroused the ire of veteran restaurateur Richard Shepherd.

Norman had described Shepherd's eponymous London establishment as being "among the very worst restaurants in Christendom" and "the eighth circle of hell." "Were it found today in a canister buried in the Iraqi desert," he wrote of the crab and brandy soup, comparing it to Saddam's missing weapons of mass destruction, "it would save Tony Blair's skin." Shepherd's lawyers were no less strident. This, they said, was a "vituperative diatribe."

American readers would be forgiven for wondering if this was really news. Aren't all British restaurant reviews "vituperative diatribes?" That was certainly the impression given in 2003 by a review of Jean-Georges Vongerichten's trendy New York Chinese restaurant 66 in *Vanity Fair* by A. A. Gill, critic for Britain's *Sunday Times*. Gill described Vongerichten's shrimp and foie gras dumplings as "fishy liver-filled condoms" and earned newspaper headlines of his own. One in the *New York Observer* suggested that Gill had been hired as a "hitman" by *Vanity Fair* editor-in-chief Graydon Carter—who allegedly had a less than high regard for 66.

A subsequent article in the *New York Times* by Warren St. John described Gill as "the unofficial ringleader of a pack of sometimes hilarious, astonishingly brutal restaurant critics who in the last few years have turned English food writing into a blood sport." As a member of that "pack"—I am the critic for *The Observer,* a national British Sunday newspaper—I can report that the piece contained one major inaccuracy: it stated that we critics never book tables under pseudonyms, and while it is true that film director Michael Winner (who writes scathing reviews for the *Sunday Times*) is hard to miss, the rest of us do always attempt to go incognito. But St. John's general point—that British restaurant criticism is a far more brutal business than the American variety—is indisputable.

The explanation lies in the history of both British newspapers and British restaurants. The first reviews in Britain generally turned up in guidebooks, like *London at Dinner: Where to Dine in 1858*. The author, whose name is now lost, set the tone with an assessment of dining rooms housed for the most part either in grand hotels or in gentlemen's clubs. "If business require attendance in the city, or pleasure to the Opera or theatre," the introduction announced, "a spot suitable to the neighbourhood will naturally be selected." For decades very little changed. Guidebooks of the early 20th century, like the 1914-vintage *Gourmet's Guide to London* by (as he signs himself) Lieut.-Col. Newnham-Davis, still focused on venues favored by the wealthy—among them the Savoy Hotel, Claridges, and the Criterion. These were books written by gentlemen for gentlemen.

Not surprisingly, it was a magazine for Britain's moneyed society, *Queen,* that in the 1960s ran our nation's first modern-style restaurant column—and it was a generalist who wrote it. Although Quentin Crewe—who suffered from muscular dystrophy and had been in a wheelchair since his late 20s—was to become recognized as an expert on gastronomy, at the time he was regarded as a jobbing writer who could turn his hand to anything from film to politics.

Later, Crewe was hired to review for the *Evening Standard,* the first British newspaper to run regular restaurant criticism. "Quentin Crewe started the whole business here by writing about restaurants as entertainments," says Fay Maschler, who took over from Crewe at the *Standard* in 1972 and who reviews for the paper to this day. "He was writing about the people and the room." In the early 1980s, Tina Brown, then editing the society magazine *Tatler,* hired novelist Julian Barnes to write her reviews. "In Julian's case, he is a major foodie," Brown says, "but what I wanted was his dry, funny point of view, so that people who didn't care about restaurants would find it a must read." In a country notorious for its suspicion of gastronomy, it made sense that other glossy magazines—the only publications apart from the *Standard* to cover restaurants for some years—would follow suit by hiring similarly renowned writers, including Kingsley Amis, rather than food experts.

The big change came in 1986 when Rupert Murdoch took on the all-powerful print unions, which were resisting the introduction of new technology, by shifting production of his newspapers to an enclosure in London's Docklands. British newspapers could now easily produce supplements, and editors needed something with which to fill them. Coincidentally, restaurants had become fashionable. "It was a very interesting time to be reviewing," says Jonathan Meades, who was critic for *The Times* from 1986 to 2001. "The River Café, Bibendum, and Marco Pierre White's first restaurant, Harvey's, all opened within a few months of each other."

Other British newspapers soon wanted critics of their own, so before long there were a lot of them: in addition to numerous tabloids, Britain has five major national dailies and four national Sunday papers, and each has at least one reviewer. The current crop generally know their subject, but they also know that authority isn't enough: if a column isn't engaging, there's always another guy working down the street for the readers to try. Matthew Fort, who recently stepped down after 15 years of reviewing restaurants for the *The Guardian,* put it the most acutely when he told the *New York Times* that "there is a competitive element to be the funniest or most vituperative or to find the most disgusting comparison."

The economics of the newspaper business also affects the way reviews are researched. With a meal in a midquality London restaurant now costing the equivalent of $250 for two and easily rising upward to $400 or $500, no British paper can afford to have a critic visit a place four or five times, as, say, Frank Bruni often does for the

New York Times. Then again, many of us wonder why we should. As Fay Maschler says, "You don't have to go five times to know whether a restaurant is good or bad. Anybody with reasonable antennae can work it out for themselves."

Others argue that there are double standards at play. "Frank Rich of the *New York Times,* the so-called Butcher of Broadway, became famous for closing theater productions overnight," says Giles Coren, the current restaurant reviewer for *The Times.* "And those are much more expensive ventures. So why get so upset if we put the boot in to a bad restaurant?" It's a good point. After all, Americans have whinged for years about the quality of the food and service in British restaurants. Isn't it a good thing that there are now aggressive critics patrolling the waterfront? Most British restaurant reviewers, this one included, genuinely believe they are there to perform a service. And if we happen to be entertaining while we're doing so, well, is that really such a crime?

DISHING IT OUT BRITISH STYLE

Here are some examples of modern British restaurant criticism, published in the past few years:

GILES COREN, *The Times* (the Court Restaurant at the British Museum) The pork was grey and grizzled. The gravy was Oxo-ish. It tasted like airline food. I'll take that kind of grub if I can swallow a couple of Temazzies [tranquilizers] afterwards and wake up in Sydney.

MATTHEW FORT, *The Guardian* (Opium) [What] looked like a sea mine in miniature was the most disgusting thing I've put in my mouth since I ate earthworms at school. . . . On second thoughts, I preferred the worms.

TRACEY MACLEOD, *The Independent* (Bistrotheque) Never before in my years of restaurant criticism have I had to apologise to someone for encouraging them to order fish and chips. As for the side dishes, that's exactly where they stayed—on the side. You can just about make a case for al dente green beans, but al dente new potatoes? No thanks.

JAN MOIR, *Daily Telegraph* (Deya) I'm choking on a really nasty amuse bouche, a kind of savoury, macaroon-sized bite flavoured with what tastes like dried shrimp. At least, I hope it's dried shrimp. If not, then it is some suspiciously fishy business of uncertain age and background.

A. A. GILL, *Sunday Times* (Fashion Café) I am prepared to stick my neck out and say that the Fashion Café is the worst restaurant that I have ever reviewed. It hit professional depths in every department. The dining room looks like it was decorated over a weekend for an art school. There really is very little point in describing the food in any detail. I didn't put a single thing in my mouth twice. It all went back.

MICHAEL WINNER, *Sunday Times* (Bibendum) I have recently had the worst meal I've ever eaten. Not by a small margin. Not "This is terrible but another one somewhere else was nearly as bad." I mean the worst! The most disastrous. The most unrelievedly awful! You don't need to be an atomic physicist to grill steaks, do you? They arrived so raw you could have drowned swimming in the blood. But the pièce de résistance was my persillade of tongue. Leathery, so hard it was difficult to cut and, as far as I could tell, not fresh. I picked away at it. What I should have done was tell everyone, then and there, very icily, that it was a disgrace.

MATTHEW NORMAN, *Sunday Telegraph* (Shepherd's) There is so much about Shepherd's that is wrong that it would, in a more elegant age, merit a pamphlet rather than a review.

JAY RAYNER, *The Observer* (Jaan) The food at Jaan is, by turns stupid, ill thought-out, or just plain nasty. I may not be able to call it the worst cooking in Britain, but that's only because I haven't eaten in every restaurant in the land.

Ingredients

Berry Bonanza

by Rick Nelson
from the *Minneapolis Star-Tribune*

Do blueberries taste better when you pick your own? In staff writer Rick Nelson's series profiling various Minneapolis food artisans, this piece on a family berry farm convincingly makes the case for getting close to your sources.

The tips of my fingers are stained a purplish-blue. Ditto my running shoes, now splotched with a hue foreign to the official New Balance palette. My lower back has been protesting for the past half-hour, despite the help of an overturned 10-gallon bucket, pinch-hitting as a chair. And I can feel that the effects of the SPF25 on my forehead are beginning to fade.

But the benefits of blueberry picking at Rush River Produce in Maiden Rock, Wisc., far outweigh those few minor hassles, because John and Terry Cuddy's farm is a playground for sensory-overload junkies. The grab-the-camcorder scenery could stand in for a Napa Valley vineyard; the neatly planted, football field-length stretches of leafy bushes cascade, one row after another, down a hill that abruptly drops into a gasp-inducing green valley. At any moment you expect to hear the thunderous overture of a certain Rodgers and Hammerstein musical involving a nun and a mountaintop. It's that gorgeous.

On this sunny midsummer morning, a cooling breeze rattles through giant cottonwood trees and coaxes cotton-candy clouds across the wide-open sky. Every so often the birds' cheery chorus is punctuated by the satisfying sound of a handful of berries rumbling into the cardboard box at my feet. A teasing blueberry scent hangs in the air. Adding to the overkill, every few minutes I recklessly sneak a few of the pert, sun-kissed berries for a taste test. They collapse in my mouth in tangy, juicy bursts.

In a word, paradise.

NEW ON THE SCENE

Twenty years ago, relishing a few idyllic hours at a blueberry U-pick operation was unheard of in the Upper Midwest, fallout from the region's harsh climate. Enter the Cuddys. John, a New Jersey native, and Terry, who grew up near Lake Nokomis in Minneapolis, were both laboring in northern California's wind-energy industry when they decided to relocate to the Midwest. "We decided to get married, buy a farm and make babies," said Terry. "And here we are."

After inspecting and rejecting dozens of rural properties, they fell head-over-heels for a dairy farm perched high above the spectacular Rush River valley. Their first agricultural impulse—growing ginseng—didn't work out. Then they heard about a Twin Cities nursery that was introducing a hardy and highly productive blueberry bush, developed by the University of Minnesota. It struck a chord.

"It was kind of like walking up to a shady character who says, 'Hey buddy, you want to buy a plant that will grow you a ten-dollar bill every year?'" said John with a laugh. "Of course, he didn't mention that the payoff would be 15 years down the road."

Enthusiastic but perhaps a bit naive about what lay ahead, they got to work, planting an acre of berries every year for four years. Their first crop wasn't enough to fill a cereal bowl; the next year, 1991, they harvested all of 150 pounds. Undaunted, they continued to add to and care for their burgeoning farm, patiently biding their time as the bushes slowly but surely inched to maturity. Now, 17 years into their venture, their faith in the blueberry has not disappointed them. This year the Cuddys are measuring their farm's berry output in tons.

"The exponential growth function has arrived," said Terry. "Finally."

Today the family—John and Terry and their sons Lucas, 12, and Joe, 15—tend nearly 10,000 half-bush and high-bush blueberry bushes spread across nine acres; if placed end to end, the long rows would add up to nine miles of plants. Nine varieties are under cultivation, timed to continually produce small, medium and downright zaftig berries from mid-July to late September.

Running a blueberry farm isn't just sticking bushes into the ground and then waiting to weigh the profits at the check-out stand (the Cuddys' going rate is $3.25 per pound for U-picks, $5.50 for ready-to-buy). Besides the warm weather's endless watering, mulching and weeding, each and every bush must be meticulously pruned, by hand, a process that can linger from late November well into early March. "It may be more of a lifestyle than a living," said John. "But it's a good lifestyle."

Naturally, this is a family of expert pickers. John leads the pack, estimating his top-speed output at two pounds of berries in five minutes. Beyond blueberries, the Cuddys also raise much smaller amounts of gooseberries and white, red and black currants. Over the years they've experimented with other crops, including lingonberries, apricots and hazelnuts. They're currently pondering the possibility of raising grass-fed cattle.

WEATHER ALL ITS OWN
Because of its proximity to Lake Pepin, the farm enjoys a microclimate all its own, with a growing season eight to 10 days longer than farms just a dozen miles to the north. The Cuddys consider the season a success if half of the farm's berries make it past the cash register, figuring that the birds fly away with about a third of the crop, another 10 percent falls to the ground and visitors probably eat the rest.

Not that they object to that last demographic. At Rush River Produce, the more is definitely the merrier. Fit, energetic and prodigiously outgoing, John and Terry Cuddy are enthusiastic advocates for the social side of U-pick farming. "Picking berries connects people," said John. "It's a place where anyone can come and connect with their families, and their food. And for us, we get to meet the people who buy our berries."

That's a major selling point for Terry. "In the winter we get out and visit other people," she said. "But in the summer they come to us, and it's one big party."

No kidding. A steady stream of repeat customers motor down the farm's long gravel driveway, some traveling from as far away as South Dakota and Iowa; one family holds their annual reunion at the farm every summer. Painters and photographers are frequent guests, and lots of folks come just to tour the farm's extraordinarily lush flower gardens. The Cuddys even bill their place as an ideal first-date destination. "We're a cheap date," said Terry. "It's good, clean fun in the fresh air, and of course you can eat all the berries you want."

And pick berries, too, although on this glorious summer day it would be a falsehood to refer to this activity as picking. The berries, hanging in heavy clusters like grapes, are so ripe that the slightest touch sends them tumbling. Their color is so mesmerizing that it's tough to tell where the indigo leaves off and the purple begins, that fine line further obscured by foggy blush. As I continue picking—correction, tapping—my imagination downshifts into overdrive, daydreaming about all the delicious things I'm going to make with, literally, the fruit of my labors.

Hello, reality check. Truth be told, aside from a modest stash destined for the freezer for the occasional smoothie or baked goodie, most of these beauties are going to disappear within days, scarfed, straight from the box, by the handful. And why not? Like all locally grown produce, the Cuddys' blueberries have the can't-resist farm-fresh flavor and sublime texture that their trucked-in counterparts just can't touch.

That goodness is amplified through the satisfaction that comes from participating in the food process, even if it's just a few steps beyond pushing a shopping cart through a store. So which would you rather eat: Rush River blues you picked that afternoon, or their tepid supermarket counterparts, which were probably on a truck longer than the average American family's summer road trip?

It's a no-brainer for Sherry Brevick of nearby Alma, Wisc., in the midst of treating her two young children to their annual berry picking adventure. "We love to come here," Brevick said. "You couldn't pick a more beautiful spot, could you? And the berries are wonderful. My son Andrew eats as many berries as he possibly can. Every time we move to a new bush, he says, 'These are the best berries, Mom.'"

Extending the Olive Branch

By Dai Huynh

from the *Houston Chronicle*

Harvesting olives and pressing them to make oil is a far more complicated process than we imagine when we casually drizzle olive oil on our salads. Houston-based reporter Dai Huynh traveled to Tuscany for a firsthand glimpse.

The second-floor window of the restored farmhouse where Carolyn Adair is staying overlooks the Arno Valley, a verdant sea of curving slopes and jagged edges blanketed by olive groves.

The moist early morning air hangs in wet sheets over the trees. Adair pauses, savoring a moment of silence before the sun pierces the fog and bounces off the droplets of dew, draping a shimmering veil over the landscape. Through the open window, the sound of girlish laughter grows louder and nearer. A group of women emerges from beneath an awning of trees in the ancient grove next to the stone farmhouse. The women carry ladders and bundles of netting. The olive picking is about to begin.

Inside, perched on a rustic bench before a roaring fire, Adair pulls on a pair of well-worn rubber boots. The hillsides will be slick with dew this November morning. Adair's face is lineless and glows with anticipation. At first glance, the former teacher, 65, resembles a native Italian, with her short, glossy black curls and milky skin made rosy by the frosty air.

Despite outward appearances, the Houston native didn't venture into the Tuscan hills until 1984, when her life unfolded like the pages of Frances Mayes' *Under the Tuscan Sun*.

But unlike Mayes, who renovated a neglected Italian villa, Adair has revived an ancient grove of olive trees planted centuries ago. Later, she began importing the grove's extra-virgin olive oil to Houston and Bryan-College Station, where she lives with her husband, Tom. I discovered Adair's brand, Amici Oil, while shopping at Leibman's Wine & Fine Foods on Memorial. "Amici" is Italian for "friends."

"Try it," Ettienne Leibman urged, "It's one of the best oils I've come across in years."

At home, I pour the oil onto a small white plate to judge the color. I slather the luminous golden-green liquid onto warm French bread I'd baked earlier.

The air blooms with the oil's fruity fragrance: clean and crisp, reminiscent of ripe Granny Smith apples. I bite into the oil-drenched baguette and, for the first time, taste good extra-virgin olive oil. Really good extra-virgin olive oil. Until that moment, I had never truly experienced the complexity of olive oil. Knowing that the producer is a Texan, the experience is even more significant.

When I met Adair, she invited me to come help harvest her olives near Reggello, a picturesque town 20 miles south of Florence in a region dotted with panoramic stretches of private vineyards, Medici villas, stone-and-brick farmhouses, Italian cypresses and chestnut trees.

Harvest starts in October, but Adair doesn't pick until November, after college football season. The former Texas A&M director of student activities and her husband, a professor, are staunch fans of the home team. They've never missed a homecoming game.

In Tuscany, locals say that olive oil greases the gears of life. The region's olive trees produce about 20 percent of the country's oil, which gets tossed, drizzled and stirred into wild greens, soups, stews and pastas. In Reggello's cozy, neighborhood restaurants a bottle of greenish-gold, peppery oil is on every table. Tuscans are so fond of their strong-flavored oil they even deep-fry in it, a luxury by our standards since a bottle of quality Tuscan oil can cost $25 or more in the United States. Here, a bottle sells for $4 to $8. Most families make their own oil, keeping enough to last through the next harvest. What's left goes to the local grocery stores. A fraction finds its way to the United States, hence the high prices.

The sun dodges in and out of misty clouds the first day I pick olives. Adair gets a head start a few days earlier with some visiting A&M students. We all sleep in the 12th-century farmhouse she rents during harvest season from Daniele Raspini, the Italian who changed her life.

Raspini, a handsome dark-haired Tuscan, met Adair in 1984 when she and several A&M seniors were hitchhiking through the Italian countryside. The then-17-year-old Raspini, who had lost his mother two years before, bonded with Adair.

She refers to him fondly as her son. To be near him, Adair lives part of each year in a restored stone gristmill house in the neighboring village of Ponte agli Stolli. In 1998, the Texan bought a two-acre olive grove from Raspini on Pratomagno mountain.

"I was sitting in my house in Italy thinking that I better have something to do when I retire, when Daniele walked in and said he had more land than he needed," she recalls. "It was fate."

Adair's grove is on a terraced sliver of land 1,600 feet above sea level. It offers an awe-inspiring panoramic vista of gentle slopes broken by peaked ridges eroded over the centuries by rainwater. Many of the stone walls restraining the terraced farm lands were built by the Romans.

Above Adair's farm, higher up the Pratomagno mountain range, are thickets of pine trees. Near the crest, a village church steeple pokes through the greenery. Throughout the day, while picking olives, we are serenaded by its tolling bells.

At the bottom of the mountain, shadowy oaks and steep ravines meander through inhabited settlements. The yelping of barking dogs or the rumble of a tractor engine occasionally drifts up the mountain's sloping face. When they reach the olive grove, the sounds are dreamy and far away. Scattered all about Pratomagno are the olive trees. In the autumn winds, they resemble swaying nymphs with riotous silvery leaves for hair.

"The *olivetto* had been abandoned because of a severe freeze in the mid-'80s," Adair says. "I simply wanted a sunny view and a little spot to put a garden. When I got to the mountain, I had something I'd never dreamed of: 100 olive-producing trees."

The trees must be severely pruned every March to keep them at a manageable picking height. Even so, by harvest time, you need a ladder to reach the olives, which hang in clusters, like grapes. There are dozens of varieties, varying in size and color. Adair's grove has fruity, piquant frantoio olives, oblong in shape and the color of merlot. Growing nearby are green moraiolo olives, fleshy, round, slightly bitter and rich in oil. Threaded throughout are greenish-yellow leccino olives, characterized by fruity, almost sweet notes.

Adair starts the harvest by spreading nets underneath the trees to catch the olives as they are raked from the limbs. Last year, she picked 70 baskets of olives, which produced 400 bottles of oil.

"Try not to step on the olives," she instructs. "And the higher the olives are on the tree, the better they are, so don't leave them behind, or you'll have to deal with the wrath of Gigi."

On cue, Gigi, Raspini's 70-plus-year-old father, strolls up the mountain to check on our progress. Adair and Raspini combine their harvests to produce about 2,500 bottles of organic oil. Gigi acts as foreman, making sure that everybody is doing his or her job -- Gigi's way.

"He's so cute," says Adair, watching the white-haired man trudging up the path. "He's as strong as an ox and very bossy. 'Bring me this; bring me that. We'll use these plastic rakes to harvest the olives.' Gigi is as tough as an old bird. He'll strip these olives off the vines with his bare hands. I can't do it. I would get a bloody hand."

It is difficult enough using the orange rakes that look like a large man's hand. Picking the olives one-by-one is counterproductive, so the olives literally are stripped from the tree with rakes. Working methodically, I comb the branches, pulling hard, like a mother combing an errant child's hopelessly knotted hair.

Sometimes I stand on the ground, tugging at the tips of willowy branches, pulling the fat, low-hanging fruit within easy reach. Other times I perch unsteadily in the branches, harvesting the elusive olives in the crown. The picking isn't hard. It is mindlessly and calmingly repetitive, moving from one branch to the next. Occasionally, I break to soak in a landscape lush with wild heather. We work continuously until lunch: fresh bread from a local bakery, stout Italian cheeses and a wide array of cured meats, all consumed picnic-style on the deep grass beneath the olive trees.

By the time the sun slides off the hill, we have cleared four trees and filled five baskets. Exhausted, we pack up and drive back to the farmhouse to clean up for dinner. Afterward, we visit a regional co-op called, appropriately, the *frantoio*, where local harvesters take their olives to be washed, pressed, filtered and bottled.

In the past, the *frantoio* used millstones to cold-press the olives. Today, it relies on a state-of-the-art machine with paper-thin stainless-steel blades that coarsely chop and press the olives. At the end is a large spout. A steady stream of oil pours from its mouth. It is a wonder to watch: a beautiful, gushing waterfall of extra-virgin olive oil the color of green-gold kryptonite.

"Notice how cloudy the oil is," Adair says. "That's before it's filtered. The Italians prefer it that way because they feel the oil tastes fruitier with a better body. I do, too. But Daniele said, 'No, Carolyn, you must filter your oil for the Americans or they won't buy it.'"

That evening, Adair takes her crew of volunteer American pickers down the mountain to a cozy family trattoria in Reggello. I order wild Italian arugula salad and a bistecca alla fiorentina chargrilled to juicy perfection. As instructed, I generously drizzle olive oil on the thick T-bone steak. I do the same for the arugula salad, along with a sprinkle of lemon juice and some salt.

Back in Houston, this is the only way I eat steak now, with an arugula salad and a bottle of Carolyn Adair's Amici Oil. I'm especially fond of the few bottles made with the olives I helped harvest. It's not only extra-virgin, it's extra-special.

⊸∝⊷

Polenta with Wild Mushrooms

Houston Chronicle kitchen-tested recipe.

> 5 cups chicken stock (canned or homemade)
> Kosher salt
> 1 ⅓ cups polenta
> Extra-virgin olive oil
> 1 ½ cups Parmigiano-Reggiano shavings, plus extra for garnish
> ⅓ cup mascarpone cheese
> 2 tablespoons fresh basil, chopped
> 2 tablespoons flat-leaf Italian parsley
> 2 cups wild mushrooms (or baby portobello), sliced or quartered

In heavy saucepan, bring chicken stock to a boil. Reduce heat to simmer and season with kosher salt to taste. Slowly pour in polenta, stirring constantly with a wooden spoon. Stir until mixture is thick and comes away from the sides of pan. Add ¼ cup olive oil, the Parmigiano-Reggiano and mascarpone cheeses, 1 tablespoon of the basil and 1 tablespoon of the Italian parsley; season with salt to taste. Set aside and keep warm.

In a skillet, heat 2 tablespoons olive oil. Add mushrooms, season with salt to taste and sauté for a couple of minutes until tender. Divide polenta between two warmed bowls and spoon mushrooms on top. Garnish with remaining 1 tablespoon basil, 1 tablespoon parsley and Parmesan shavings. Drizzle with olive oil and serve immediately.

SERVES 2

Gardens on the Mesa

by Eugenia Bone
from *At Mesa's Edge*

Transplanted to an isolated farmstead in Colorado high country, food writer Eugenia Bone gained great insight into how one's relationship to food deepens when you grow it yourself.

I flinch when better gardeners ask me questions about our plot. Is our soil high in acid? Low in alkali? What's the pH factor? Hell if I know. We never checked any of that stuff. It seemed evident there had been a garden behind the house once, and that was good enough for us. With a combination of rototilling and many, many wheelbarrows of old chicken manure from the coops Kevin had dismantled before I came into the picture, our garden grew to about twenty-five by forty feet of nice fluffy earth, ready for seeds.

We buy our seeds on our wedding anniversary in early May, over a bottle of champagne, from catalog sources such as the *Cook's Garden* and *Seeds of Change*. Since we get a little drunk, we order way too much. It's easy to have great ambitions at a fancy French restaurant. It's a different story when we are on our hands and knees under the Colorado sun.

I can never remember what seeds we put in, and since the little staked packages promptly disintegrate, I have to wait until they begin to grow. But around the second week of July, everything starts to come in. For herbs, we plant cilantro, sage, flat-leaf parsley, rosemary, and mint. We also plant a small amount of tarragon, thyme, and marjoram. And basil, of course, lots of basil. I learn from a cooking show to pile the leaves on top of each other, roll them up like a cigar, and cut them across, width-wise. This makes a thin julienne that, when used for a garnish, shows off the taste better than mincing.

I make bulk pestos from cilantro, basil, and arugula. I preserve pesto in two ways—by freezing and by packing it into a jar and covering it with olive oil. The downside of packing pesto with oil is that the pesto will ferment eventually, and quickly if you make it when the leaves are wet. Freezing is a sure bet, but you have to have room in your freezer, and I never do. I don't add any cheese to pesto until I am about to eat it. The cheese can turn rancid in the oil, and I don't like the way it tastes frozen. I sometimes replace pine nuts, which are expensive, with walnuts, almonds, or pecans. The word *pesto* comes from *pestle,* as in mortar and pestle, the hand-grinding system used to make herb purees back in the old days. Although pesto made from pine nuts and basil is the Genoese classic, anything you make in this fashion is a pesto.

Early in the season, the leaf lettuce comes in. It grows in a solid bank of tender greens, too tight for weeds to intrude. The leaves are delicious when dressed and mixed with spaghettini for a light lunch. But if I want head lettuce, I buy it. My favorite is iceberg, which is so nutritionally poor it is not even recommended for turtles, but it's perfect when you're dehydrated. I cut it into wedges and dress it with oil and vinegar that I put in a Ball jar with a couple of tablespoons of crumbled blue cheese and shake with all my might.

We plant climbing beans along the deer fence, and the tendrils wind in and out of the wires. In the garden are bush beans. By mid-August there are so many beans that I don't even lift the leaves, for fear I'll find more. We eat lots of them when they are juveniles and the flesh is shiny and wet and crisp. We plant eggplant because there is nothing more delicious than grilled slices dressed with garlic and olive oil, although the leftovers pureed with grilled wild porcini mushrooms, lemon, and salt make a pretty irresistible dip.

We plant too many zucchini plants, because I am greedy for zucchini flowers, but I don't realize our folly until Kevin and all the guests are gone and only the kids and I are left to eat them. I try to pick them when they are about eight inches long, but they seem to double in size overnight. Sometimes I make individual zucchini fritters, and other times I just make a huge skillet of the stuff and serve it like hash browns next to omelets filled with caramelized onions, Monterey Jack cheese, and cilantro. I make chocolate zucchini cake—a surprisingly aerated and moist local favorite. I cook grated zucchini with grated onion, garlic, and tarragon and mix the savory mash into a bowl of hot, buttery penne.

We also plant too many peppers. Just four jalapeño bushes produce hundreds of the fiery things. I make mint jalapeño jelly, but I need only one pepper per pint. I smoke and freeze bags and bags of them, in hopes that my Mexican food–loving friends will like them as gifts. Each year I promise myself: one plant next year. We put in bell, Hungarian, and Italian sweet peppers, which I throw into every stewy dish I make. Most spectacularly, I prepare a pepper condiment from Kathryn McCarthy's recipe and mix it with soft goat cheese, scramble it into eggs, or bake it into corn bread.

I roast a lot of peppers, too, placing them on a cookie sheet and broiling them until the skin blisters, turning them often. Or I put them directly on the gas burner, turning them often to blister the skin all over. (This also works on the grill.) I don't put freshly broiled peppers (red or otherwise) in a paper or plastic bag, since the steam will cook the peppers and they'll be too fragile or slimy to peel. Instead, I peel them as soon as they are cool enough to handle. I remove the seedpods but do not wash them, which would take away their smoky taste. We eat roasted peppers in salads and tarts, stuffed and fried.

We also grow cucumbers. There is nothing more refreshing than a cucumber straight from the garden. I serve them with every meal—cut into wedges, chilled, and salted. I throw them into salads and gazpacho, and I pickle them by the case. Of the green leafy vegetables, we grow collards and Swiss chard. Almost every day, I make a stew with chard, potatoes, garlic, and the wild purslane and dandelion greens that grow between the garden rows.

Tomatoes love our weather, and they ripen red and shiny, firm and juicy, despite my shabby attempts at pruning. I'm too shy to do the job properly, and the plants become unruly tangles. Kevin and some of his buddies from Colorado Springs made tomato plant stakes from twisted, spindly cedar branches. They give the garden a witchy feeling. With the first homegrown tomato of the season, I am transformed into a novice gardener cliché: amazed that it grew, astounded by the taste, proud as a new parent. We eat tomatoes, marveling, with a vengeance: raw in pasta sauces, broiled with slivers of garlic and rosemary leaves, as a base for countless stews and soups. I preserve as many as my energy allows, in pint jars with basil and salt, to be opened, blissfully, in midwinter.

I work in the garden in the very early morning, before the sun gets too hot. The children are usually asleep, and I've had my coffee and planned my day ahead. I walk across the backyard in my rubber boots, hoe in hand, stepping on the tiny white morning glories that blanket the lawn. I follow the shade in the garden, hoeing to aerate the soil. I can see how it loosens things up, creates more of a feather bed than a pile of heavy woolen blankets. One day I hoe up a tidy row of weeds that Kevin has painstakingly transplanted, thinking they were a vegetable. A shame: they were doing so well. When I hoe, I have to lift the skirts of the tomato plants to weed underneath. It's like changing a diaper, and I sympathize with the indignities the plant endures to stay weed-free. Often I hit a rock, and I grunt and moan and try to wedge the thing out. Almost always it turns out to be the size of a small potato.

While hoeing in the cool morning, my mind first empties, then starts to fill with words. It is as if the words come down from the mountains with the meltwater and rush through the little ditches straight into my head. I stay with the tide of articulated feeling, assuring myself that I will not forget a particular metaphor, until the bugs find me and I must go in and scramble eggs or make pancakes for the kids. By the time I leave the meditation of the furrows and am crossing the yard again, my inspiration, like the morning glories, has disappeared with the heat of the day.

When the opportunity arises, I buy a rustic table and chair and place it in the barren part of the garden. I bring my journal with me in the morning and take brief breaks to grubbily write down my thoughts as they come, before they fade away.

There are some beautiful gardens in this valley—rich red soil where the stones have been cleared for more than a hundred years. We see them everywhere: thick orchards, leafy vineyards, tall cornfields. If we allowed ourselves, garden envy would be easy. Kathryn McCarthy's herb garden sits in a circle on top of Sunshine Mesa, with very little between the tops of her plants and the stars. The herbs are huge and bushy, and the delicate leaves burst from woodier stems than my anemic specimens. Likewise, her vegetable garden is of such a fine caliber—such ripeness, such Jurassic hugeness—that I am always overwhelmed. She calls one day and encourages me to come and pick. "I planted too much this year," she admits in her husky, curvy voice, as I suspect she does every year.

After I pick my fill, Kathryn serves boiled sliced potatoes and beets, local goat cheese, raw scallions, and grilled slices of eggplant and zucchini with a Dijon mayonnaise. We wrap our choices in beet leaves; there is no bread. We drink Michael McCarthy's grassy homemade mead, chilled and slightly effervescent, and sit in a backhoe-dug kiva on the edge of the mesa. Once when I visited, there was a full moon, and the kiva filled up with spirits. It was very creepy and lovely.

I suppose my favorite garden is Mrs. Burritt's, atop Redlands Mesa, which rises out of the adobe lands. I follow a switchback road up, up, up, wondering how a farm could exist in such an arid, rocky environment; up, up, up, until we reach the mesa top and the wide farm. It is green and lush, with fields filled with tidy rows of corn, green beans, cantaloupes, cucumbers, potatoes, carrots, and tomatoes. We park near a huge barn with a sign that reads BURRITT PRODUCE. PLEASE HONK. We do.

Out of the house comes Ann Burritt, an elfin woman with callused hands and a sun-browned face, short hair and nifty blue eyes. She looks to be in her fifties, but she's twenty years older. Mrs. Burritt is very polite, in that courteous and careful Western way. She leads me into the barn, and I am met by the most amazing smell: cantaloupes ripened on the vine. They are so sweet you can smell them over the gasoline in the tractor parked nearby. "Oh, my cantaloupes have been in the paper," Mrs. Burritt says mildly. I buy half a dozen, each the size of a softball. I also buy lemon cucumbers. On the long, dusty ride home, during which we get lost because Mrs. Burritt suggested a shortcut, we eat a bag of the cucumbers, brushing the dirt off on our jeans and consuming all but the little dried stems at the end.

The truth is, once you have become accustomed to a vine-ripened cantaloupe or a summer tomato, it's a drag to eat the tasteless junk shipped from elsewhere in the world. But if you choose to eat seasonally, you can usually do pretty well using local producers. Who needs Tuscany or Provence when most of us have it all in our own backyards?

The best-tasting foods come straight from the wild, and nature's wild gardens are the greatest of all. But you have to hike to find them, and that's not something I have ever really cared to do. Kevin is a hiker. His first Christmas gift to me was a sleeping bag. I've always had a hard time separating the act of looking where I am going from the act of looking where I am stepping—a qualitative difference. But then I met Peggy Tomaske, a massage therapist who taught me that hiking in Colorado can be synonymous with mushrooming.

Mushrooming, for me, has always involved a certain kind of conjuring, not unlike the experience of hunting and fishing. That is, if I want a trout, a pheasant, or a chanterelle badly enough (and I've applied a little common sense), I can focus with extra intensity. By focusing, I have a chance to succeed. And the magic is that once you see one mushroom, you see dozens. Like an optical illusion, the mushrooms are always there, just not visible until you are in sync with nature.

In the dark, piney woods of the nearby Uncompahgre Plateau, I follow Peggy about, wishing to find a mushroom she can identify for me. And she wishes, too, because we are new friends, and the granting of our wishes would be a positive omen. It is early August, almost too early in the season to find anything, and as we tromp along, I feel, rather pettily, the undertow of disappointment—that without mushrooms, our newfound kinship will lose momentum. But Peggy can conjure, too. With a cry of delight, she finds one perfect porcini mushroom *(Boletus edulis)*, fat-stemmed and fat-headed, with a shiny brown cap and no gills. We continue—giddy, instantly bonded—and suddenly there are mushrooms everywhere. She points out chanterelles *(Cantharellus cibarius)*, and delicious milky caps *(Lactarius deliciosus)*. We find about two pounds of chanterelles that day, and once home we sauté them in butter and roll up the slick, fleshy nubbins in delicate crepes with *queso anejo,* a crumbly Mexican cheese.

At the end of the summer, after Kevin returns, I reluctantly agree to a hike up Bald Mountain. We have guests, and guests expect to climb mountains when they visit Colorado. Kevin, as always, is way ahead of me. I trudge up the trail in a grumpy fog—Douglas firs to my left and right—and almost bump into him. He is standing astride a mushroom with a cap as big as a salad plate. It is a king boletus, a great prize. No one in our party is as adept at finding these mushrooms as Kevin, who has used the initial magic. After gathering as many as I can carry, I return down the trail to wait by the car, poring over each individual in the hoard, while the rest of our party hikes to the summit they have come to scale.

Once home we cut cross sections of the stems to see if any are wormy, the sample each cap to make sure it is sweet (a sour boletus will spoil the entire batch). We cook some of the sliced caps with far-falle, chicken broth, and lemon zest, then throw all of the stems in a robust oxtail and hominy soup. I sauté what's left of the caps until they release their liquid, or blanch them in boiling water, then pack two cups at a time in freezer bags. During the winter, I just dump the frozen mushrooms directly into stews and sauces.

Kevin's desire has finally been fulfilled: now I enthusiastically hike with him. But while he forges ahead, his long strides covering the miles, his head held high, breathing in the view, I walk in circles, head down, and check the foot of every tree.

By mid-July the canning sections in the local hardware stores are full of every canning gizmo and gadget you can imagine. Everyone seems to have a bushel of fruit in the back of his or her truck. In New York, a jar of home-canned preserves is a novelty. In the valley, another family's jellies are a burden: just one more jar to find a place for in the cellar.

In July I can cherries: yellow Rainiers with basil or mint, which I roll up in crepes or dump beside pork chops; red Bings and the left-over cherry-flavored syrup, which we mix with soda water and pour over ice for the kids; and sour Montmorencies. We pack the small and wrinkled sour cherries into quart jars—enough for one pie. By mid-month the apricots come in, so ripe they practically fall into halves. I can them with brandy or puree them into a honey to pour over pancakes in the morning and ice cream at night.

The old fruit trees on our property don't produce much fruit, as they suffer from a variety of ills and years of neglect, but one little apricot tree manages to flourish along our driveway. It is full of fruit the size of eyeballs. I drive by slowly so the kids can rip the apricots from the branches through the car windows, then eat them in the back seat, grimacing at their tartness. I can a few pints of them as well, writing "ranch apricots" proudly on the labels.

The plums arrive in August. There are big red Santa Rosa plums, purple prune plums, Black Friar plums, and, most exquisite of all, red blood plums—intense, sweet, and tangy. What we don't gorge on at the table, I can as purees, jams, and jellies. Peaches and nectarines come in, too. Halved and canned in syrup, they'll nourish us all winter long, as we eat them with cottage cheese and freshly ground black pepper. I also send some to my grandmother in Memphis, who, at nearly one hundred, won't open her eyes but will open her mouth for their clean, tender taste.

Everything I feel confident canning, I do: tomatillos, red tomatoes, green tomatoes (for the Italian fish stew we make in the winter), pickles of all sorts, and jalapeño mint jelly. A batch of that jelly suffers from too much green food coloring and looks like something I imagine you'd find in a nuclear spill, but it tastes cool and snappy nonetheless. I also make jelly from the crab apples on our lone tree, flavoring them with spearmint. My brother, Cham, who comes for a visit, announces that it tastes like candy canes. The jars are beautiful resting on the kitchen counter, and at night I hear the lids pop as the cooling air inside creates a vacuum.

I have always loved county fairs, and the Delta County Fair, held at the Hotchkiss fairgrounds, is as good as it gets. All the towns compete in a variety of classes: livestock (llama, swine, goat, poultry, rabbit, cattle, sheep), horticulture (fruit), agriculture (grasses, hay), produce (including largest and oddest), pantry (canned, frozen, dried, and baked goods; soap, candy, and honey), needlework (sewing, knitting, crocheting, embroidery, afghans, and quilts—beautiful quilts that hang on rods, to be fingered by expert grandmas), crafts (such as pottery and doll-making), art, and flowers. There is a vegetable sculpture competition for kids, a dog obedience show (which is rather chaotic), a horse show, a demolition derby, and a rodeo.

With some trepidation, I enter my Candy Cane Jelly among the sixty or so other beautiful, glistening jars of preserves. The next day, when we return to see how the jelly has fared, there are lots of blue ribbons—the Crawford booth has done very well—but my jar is not to be found. And then a petite lady with a gray perm hands me my jar, hidden behind a tremendous multicolored ribbon. "Well, now, you're just going to have to give us the recipe," she says. My kids puff up with pride, but I feel a rush of gratitude: it is the first time I've ever won anything.

We leave for New York when the pears come in. Most of the canned and frozen goods are shipped back to the city, and we scramble to sort through the kids' stuff and pack our clothes and sheets and towels into big plastic tubs so the mice can't get at them. Projects are hastily completed, arrangements are made to keep the fields irrigated, and meals entail fewer and fewer ingredients as I try to use up all the perishables. I can feel the slightest hint of coolness in the air, and I wonder what it is like here in the winter. Is it lovely? What do the West Elks look like covered with snow? But there is no time for regrets. School—and all the rest of colorful, stimulating New York life—is around the corner.

Killing Dinner

by Gabrielle Hamilton
from *The New Yorker*

The gruesome art of butchering is something most of us would prefer not to experience firsthand. Gabrielle Hamilton—now chef-owner of New York's popular Prune restaurant—didn't like it either, the first time.

It's quite something to go barehanded up through a chicken's ass and dislodge its warm guts. Startling, the first time, how fragilely they are attached. I have since put countless suckling pigs—pink, the same weight and size as a pet beagle—into slow ovens to roast overnight so that their skin becomes crisp and their still forming bones melt into the meat. I have butchered two-hundred-and-twenty-pound sides of beef down to their primal cuts; carved the tongues out of the heads of goats; fastened baby lambs with crooked sets of teeth onto green applewood spits and set them by the foursome over hot coals; and boned the saddles and legs of rabbits, which, even skinned, look exactly like bunnies.

But when I killed my first chicken I was only seventeen and unaccustomed. I had dropped out of school and was staying in the basement of my father's house, in rural New Jersey, for very little rent. That fall, I spent a lot of time sitting outside on the log pile at dusk smoking hand-rolled cigarettes in my canvas jacket, watching the garden decay and thinking about death and the inherent beauty of the cycle of life. In my father's chicken coop, one bird was being badly henpecked. My dad said we should kill it and spare it the slow torture by its pen mates. I said I could do it. I said it was important to confront the death of the animal you had the privilege of eating, that it was cowardly to buy cellophane-wrapped packages of boneless, skinless breasts at the grocery store. My father said, "You can kill the damned thing when I get home from work."

From a remote spot on the back kitchen steps, he told me how to pull the chicken decisively out of the pen. I spoke to it philosophically about death, grasping it firmly yet calmly with what I hoped was a soothing authority. Then he told me to take it by the legs and hold it upside down. The chicken protested from deep inside its throat, close to the heart, a violent, vehement, full-bodied cluck. The crowing was almost an afterthought. To get it to stop, I started swinging it in full arm circles, as my dad instructed me. I windmilled that bird around and around the way I'd spun lettuce as a kid in the front yard, sending droplets of water out onto the gravel and pachysandra from the old-fashioned wire-basket spinner my mom used. He said this would disorient the bird—make it so dizzy that it couldn't move—and that's when I should lay it down on the block and chop its head off, with one machinelike whack. In my own way, not like a machine at all, I laid it down on a tree stump, and while it was trying to recover I clutched the hatchet and came down on its neck. This first blow made a vague dent, barely breaking the skin. I hurried to strike it again, but lost a few seconds in my grief and horror. The second blow hit the neck like a boat oar on a hay bale. I was still holding its feet in one hand and trying to cut its head off with the dull hatchet in my other when both the chicken and my father became quite lucid, and not a little agitated. The chicken began to thrash, its eyes open, as if chastising me for my false promises of a merciful death. My dad yelled, "Kill it! Kill it! Aw, Gabs, kill the fucking thing!" from his bloodless perch. I kept coming down on the bird's throat—which was now broken but still issuing terrible clucks—stroke after miserable stroke, until I finally got its head off. I was blubbering through clenched teeth. My dad was animated with disgust at his dropout daughter—so morose and unfeminine, with the tips of her braids dyed aquamarine, and unable even to kill a chicken properly. As I released the bird, finally, and it ran around the yard, bloody and ragged but at least now silent, he screamed, "What kind of person are you?"

It was a solid minute before the chicken's nerves gave out and it fell over motionless in some dead brown leaves. I wiped my snot on my sleeve, picked up the bird from the frozen ground, tied its feet, and hung it on a low tree branch to bleed it. The other chickens in their pen, silhouetted against the dusk, retreated inside to roost for the night. My dad closed the kitchen door and turned on the oven. I boiled a blue enamelled lobster pot full of water, and submerged the bird to loosen its feathers. Sitting out on the back steps in the yellow pool of light from the kitchen window, I plucked the feathers off the chicken, two and three at a time. Its viscera came out with an easy tug: a small palmful of livery, bloody jewels that I tossed out into the dark yard.

There are two things you should never do with your father: learn how to drive, and learn how to kill a chicken. I'm not sure you should sit across from each other and eat the roasted bird in resentful silence, either, but we did that, too, and the meat was disagreeably tough.

To Win A Cook's Heart, Butter Her Up

by Suzanne Martinson
from the *Pittsburgh Post-Gazette*

In the *Post-Gazette's* excellent food section, Martinson is an ardent advocate for preserving our authentic relationship to the food we eat. This memory of her childhood underscores why.

When cooks sing the praises of cream, they talk of the smooth satin of a sauce, the melt–in–the–mouth richness of a holiday cookie, the butter-slathered slice of warm homemade bread. I still feel the sandpaper tongue of a fawn–and–white spotted heifer as she rhythmically sucked my fingers while I enticed her wet nose into a pail filled with her mother's warm milk. The calf bunted the pail, sending the colostrums sloshing, splattering my shirt and sending me sprawling into the soft manure in the calf pen.

This curious calf with the velvety coat, which bunted me as if I were her mother, was the firstborn of Miss Fancy, the 4-H calf I bought when I was 9. I hoed bean for 35 cents an hour to earn the $25.

We named Fancy's baby May June because the heifer was born on Grandma Mayme's June birthday. The golden cream from our Guernseys went into the stuff of bakers' dreams—$25 today gets you 7 pounds of butter.

So much of a cook's taste depends on what she grew up with, so leave the Italians to their olive oil, the manufacturers to their margarine, the Canadians to their canola.

Butter's better.

A first-grade teacher I knew in Springdale, Ore., taught three generations of children to read. When she asked what they remembered, they said, "The day we made butter." Simplicity itself: Pour heavy cream into a glass jar. Every kid gets a shake. Butter!

Reality set in early. On a dairy farm, it's golden to be born female. Bull calves were sold at the Tuesday auction. My father lifted any newborn calf's back leg to check. "It's a heifer!" were magic words.

Country girls look at things differently. The animals ate before we did. Every choice had consequences, and even a Pollyanna learned that bad things can happen even to the best person—or animal.

When I grew up, cows had names and idiosyncrasies. Our Guernseys were smart. At milking time, we called "Come, Bossie, C'Boss," and they hurried home from the pasture. They ambled into the milking parlor, stuck their head into the stanchion and stood quietly while their udders were washed with warm water. They nosed a button in their bowls to make fresh cold water flow. They munched ground oats and corn while the milking machine was hooked up to their four teats. Dad said a dairy cow had more sense in one day of her life than a beef animal had in its whole lifetime.

In an afternoon, you could teach a calf to lead. After some practice, Fancy walked regally around the show ring, switching her fluffy tail washed in Surf and bleached with Clorox. My father suggested dehorning, but I begged him not to. So Fancy's horns stuck straight out, unlike the graceful, curved horns of Elsie the Borden Cow. With one toss of her head, Fancy could have gored me. She never did. She was a natural mother, giving birth, getting up to lick her calf clean with her sandpaper tongue, pushing the calf to the rear for her first meal.

Farming isn't so simple today. Today's dairy farmers get big or get out. Survival is a business of numbers and nameless cows with docked tails, and they seldom stroll in the sun.

Guernseys now make up fewer than 2 percent of dairy breeds, falling far behind Holsteins, which give more milk but less cream. The black and white Holsteins get the best press, although I contend they're on the labels of Ben & Jerry's Ice Cream because of their spectacular spots, not their cream. As teens, we teased the Holstein owners that their cows' milk was so watery that we Guernsey girls used it to rinse out our milk pails.

Once a week our milkman left a Grade AA pound block of butter when he picked up our four metal cans of milk. In the city, the milkman dropped off your milk, but our milkman took ours. I grew up thinking butter was free. We cut our blocks into half-cup squares, and I was amazed to discover oblong butter dishes. City people's butter was divided into premeasured quarters.

Butter went into everything except piecrust, because lard was the shortening of choice for ultimate flakiness. Butter contains saturated fat and margarine contains trans fat, and scientists are arguing not which is better, but which is worse. All fat, whether animal or vegetable, contains the same number of calories, and all should be eaten in moderation. I stand with the late Julia Child, who once told me a little butter goes a long way in creating a delicious, satisfying dish, "and you don't have to eat it all."

Farm profits twist and turn like butter prices. Farmers are paid only when they sell their crops, but we had The Milk Check, which arrived monthly.

Farms families are 1 1/2 percent of the population. They may use the same words as their city cousins, but the meanings are different. Our *fat cats* waited behind the cows for the milk filter to be flung into the gutter. They sucked down the cream-soaked filter whole—cats like fiber. Urban couples announce they'll *party till the cows come home*. After my senior prom, Dad spotted my date and me on his way to the morning milking. He quickly called it a night.

Our unpasteurized milk got slightly citified after Dad purchased a stainless steel milk tank. A large paddle agitated the rich milk so it would cool quicker. Where did the cream disappear? Homogenized. If we wanted to churn ice cream, we went straight to the cow.

So it goes. Many bakers remember stories of how their kin had to mix food coloring into naturally white margarine if they wanted it yellow like butter. Such was the power of the butter lobby. The dairy industry's first preference was pink, so there would be no mistake that oleo was a butter substitute.

Margarine, popularized during World War II shortages, now outsells butter 2 to 1, and no wonder consumers have lost track of which is heavier, milk or cream. Few have witnessed the lighter cream rising to the top of a glass quart, a sight as beautiful as the snow-capped Mount St. Helens before she erupted. Gram skimmed off the golden butterfat to brown her apple pies.

Most cream today is ultra-pasteurized, which extends its shelf life but renders it inferior to old-fashioned cream. And many people don't realize that whole-milk buttermilk is a modern concoction. True buttermilk is what's left after the cream has been removed for butter—buttermilk is skimmed milk.

Such observations seem as antique as metal milk cans. In Tennessee, where I once worked, a young reporter was proofreading recipes. She pointed to *whipping cream*. "What's that?" she asked. It's the creamy topping for strawberry shortcake, I said. She brightened. "Oh, you mean CoolWhip!" I'll admit I've used the Whipped Topping Not Found in Nature and it does have the stability of a stone, but I swear I imagine tears in Fancy's eyes. I also gave up trying to save a few cents baking with margarine after manufacturers replaced some fat with water and ruined many recipes. It can't be butter unless it has at least 80 percent butterfat.

Fancy left me her legacy, all right. I learned to use sandpaper to polish her horns. I learned to dress in all white and walk backward to lead my cow into the show ring. Fancy and I got last place without crying, and I once milked a Guernsey on daytime TV.

Farm life was always unpredictable. When Fancy was 4, she had twins. Twin bulls. Her insides came out with them. I stood by her wooden stall as the veterinarian dipped her intestines into a bucket and pushed them back into her body. "My, God, man, can't you work any faster than that?" Dad said and jumped in. The vet gave Fancy a 50-50 chance to live. "It could be worse," my aunt said kindly, citing the old farm lore of "better in the barn than the house."

Fancy lived but never had another calf. "Lefty," Dad said one sad day, using his nickname for me, "better go to the barn and say goodbye to Fancy."

The cycle of life continues on the farm, and in the spring there would be another little calf, Fancy's granddaughter, to teach how to drink from a pail.

To this day, when people pass me a spread they claim "tastes just like butter," I just shake my head. A cowgirl never forgets.

Where's the Nutella?

by Mort Rosenblum
from *Chocolate*

Delving into the world of chocolate, from the Swiss Alps to Hershey, Pennsylvania, Rosenbloom, a former editor of the *International Herald Tribune*, indulged himself in plenty of confections, some more exclusive than others.

During 2002, as terrorism stalked the planet, police in the Italian town of Pordenone tracked a mysterious man people called *il unabomber.* At first, suspicion settled on a thirty-five-year-old student, but a search of his home near Treviso turned up nothing. Tension grew among an anxious public. The terrorist had struck where it hurt: He had booby-trapped a jar of Nutella.

For uninitiated travelers, that ubiquitous jar of dusty brown hazelnut-flavored chocolate spread is just another item on the hotel breakfast buffet table. This is fine with the locals, of course, because then they can have all the more Nutella to eat.

As several dozen disparate European nations try to form a more perfect union, they fight an uphill battle. Statesmen decided a new currency, the euro, would hold them tightly together. When it was launched at midnight on December 31, 2001, however, it faced an uncertain future. Britons kept their pound sterling. Scandinavians were unconvinced. And there were all those central and eastern Europeans yet to join. At a distance, the answer was obvious. Europe should have chosen a common symbol more universally loved than money. Nutella, for instance.

For the tragically unenlightened, Nutella is chocolaty glop that comes in glass jars or plastic tubs. It is meant to be spread on bread, but more often than not, it is licked straight off the knife.

"The worst-kept secret in Europe is where mothers hide the Nutella from their kids," Cecile Allegra said, laughing aloud as she pictured her own mother trying nobly but in vain to secret away the family-size jar. High up, down at floor level behind forgotten canned goods, in the bedroom closet with the old shoes, it didn't really matter. About the most Signora Allegra could hope for was two days before one of her brood sniffed it out.

Cecile, a Paris-based foreign correspondent, grew up in Rome before moving to France for school. Her memories are of Italian-style Nutella, which is heavier on the hazelnuts and lighter on sugar than is the French variation. Another of those ill-kept secrets is that the president of Ferrero, the Italian company that owns Nutella and licenses it around the world, also prefers the French formula.

Chloë is an unapologetic Nutella nut. One Christmas holiday, her brother, Tristan, visited her while she was on a United Nations assignment to Haiti. The trip was a last-minute decision, and she found she had nothing to eat in the house. Both lived happily for a week on her reserve stock of Nutella. On the last day, they made a film: "Fatal Attraction."

For a backdrop, Chloë stacked jars of Nutella on an ironing board. And then, one at a time, they recalled their Nutella moments.

One tragedy was the Great Nutella Squander. Growing up in Mexico City, Chloë and Tristan lived for the economy-size tub that sat on their breakfast table, replenished only sporadically when someone managed to make the trip from Europe. Some stuffy Paris friends visited her parents and, as asked, brought a jar with them. They had no idea what it was or what it meant. Chloë's mother put it on the table. Good hostess that she was, she urged her friends to try some. With no enthusiasm or appreciation, both spooned great heaps onto their toast, seriously depleting the fresh supply. Chloë watched with horror she has yet to forget.

But nothing approaches the Great Airport Incident. Once Chloë's mother returned from Paris to Mexico City with the usual huge jar, and she was stopped at customs. An inspector refused to let it through. At first, she thought of the usual Mexican solution: a small gift. But the man was serious; food was forbidden. Suddenly,

Madame Doutre-Roussel had an inspiration. This was not food, she said. It was cosmetics. To make the point, she smeared Nutella generously across her cheeks and forehead. It worked.

Chloë and Tristan watched the scene from behind thick glass, unable to hear what was going on. All they could see was that their mother had lost her mind. Worse, she was wasting the family's precious Nutella. And all they could do was leap up and down, flinging themselves against the glass wall in helpless frustration.

Years later, a grown-up Chloë visited a Nutella plant and watched steel paddles mixing chocolate, ground nuts, and sugar in a giant vat. A friend who went with her watched with concern. Chloë seemed dangerously close to a swan dive.

The Nutella formula was invented out of necessity after World War II. Italy was short of chocolate, but it had plenty of hazelnuts and other non-chocolate fillers. Pietro Ferrero, an enterprising pastry maker who later built up a food empire, mixed toasted hazelnuts with cocoa powder, cocoa butter, and vegetable oil to make what he called *pasta gianduja*. In February 1946, he sold 660 pounds of the stuff. Soon after, he was in hot pursuit of more hazelnut growers.

In 1949, Ferrero came up with a more spreadable version of Supercrema Gianduja. Pretty soon, Italian food stores had a special counter for a Nutella schmear. Kids paid a few lire to have their slice of bread topped in the stuff. The new name was adopted in 1964, and Nutella oozed across Europe and beyond.

Today, the mix has changed. A thirteen-ounce jar of Nutella contains fifty hazelnuts, a cup and a half of skim milk, enough cocoa to make it brown, and a lot of sugar. Worldwide sales of Nutella amount to two million quintals a year, Ferrero reports. That is half a billion pounds of Nutella. The core market is Western Europe, but Nutella is just about everywhere.

For a while, I collected stories from friends and contacts by simply saying the word *Nutella* and seeing what came of it.

As expected, I got a rise out of Nico Jenkins, the son of my food-loving friend Nancy Harmon Jenkins and her ex-husband, Loren Jenkins, a foreign correspondent who came in from the cold. Nico grew up in Italy. Like his famous-chef sister, Sara, he loves to eat well. As a former maître d' at Le Cirque 2000, he knows how to go about it.

Nico and two friends once sailed a small boat across the Atlantic, headed for America. They thought they had carefully rationed their Nutella supply to make the trip. But the level dropped precipitously. Then on the night watch, the lonely man at the helm cracked under the strain. When Nico and the other guy found the jar licked clean, they nearly keelhauled the culprit.

Boris Vlasic, one of the finest and funniest journalists in Croatia, was thrilled with the breakup of Yugoslavia in 1992. "We could stop being dangerous smugglers," he said. "We had to make secret runs over the Yugoslav border for Nutella and jeans," he said, adding that he could have done without the jeans. "Nutella is not food; it's a medicine, a drug, a cure for anything. If you have any kind of problem, you just need Nutella. My wife gets mad at me when I buy two jars at the store, but when it is on sale, it is your sacred duty to buy it."

Boris is married to Snjezana Vukic, my level-headed Associated Press colleague. She rolls her eyes when her husband and Nutella appear in the same sentence. But she gave me his cell phone number. Weeks later, as she was about to give birth to their first child, I happened to reach him on his way to the hospital. At one point, I mentioned that Nutella was made with different recipes in each country. I could hear Boris stiffen.

"I'm living in darkness," he said. "It's not fair. Look, call Snjezana and tell her I've gone around the world to buy Nutella. She knows me. She'll understand."

In a globalized world, American kids have mastered the European trick of smearing the insides of a glass Nutella jar to disguise unauthorized raids. As any kid knows, this is no mean feat. If the cosmetics job is too thinly done, you are busted. But if done too well, your mother will not add a new jar to her shopping list.

My friend Franny Sullivan discovered Nutella as a young teacher in the Dominican Republic after graduating from Duke. She and her roommates survived mainly on peanut butter and jelly sandwiches. Then someone discovered Nutella.

"We had to ration ourselves to one jar a week," she said. "I'd get a jar and eat it for two days, and then they would hide it for a while. I did the same for them." When I asked what the attraction was, she gave me one of those "duh" looks. "It's chocolate. Spreadable chocolate."

Back in Greenwich Village, Franny's local grocer kept a steady supply. Except, of course, during 2003, when an unexpected run emptied his shelves. It seems that Los Angeles Lakers star Kobe Bryant had become a Nutella nut when his father played basketball in Italy. Ferrero hired him to appear on its jars in America. When he was charged with rape, he was taken off the label. But the Kobe Bryant jars that remained in circulation sold like, um, Nutella.

The Kobe Bryant scandal hardly dented Nutella's image in America. Nor is Nutella as unknown as I thought. A Google search produced 325,000 references. A company Web site devoted to it offers ideas on such things as Nutella hot dog (a regular bun, with a banana as the hot dog and Nutella as the mustard), Nutella pumpkin pie, s'mores, and a tortilla rollup with raisins and chopped nuts.

Italy remains the Nutella homeland. In Bologna and Genoa, a *Nutellaria* offers a dozen ways to indulge, including Nutella pizza, focaccia, cornflakes, and tacos. Gigi Padovani, born in the Nutella capital, Alba, wrote a whole book about it, entitled—what else? It ends with observations from well-known Italians, including this remark by the writer Luciano Ligabue: "I have three or four certainties in life, and Nutella is one of them."

Even such culinary chauvinists as the French have succumbed. Nutella France sells 80 million jars of the stuff a year. And, for me, nothing comes close to the Paris-street-corner specialty: a warm crepe slathered in Nutella.

When I visited Claudio Corallo in São Tomé, I found a jar of Nutella occupying a place of honor in his kitchen. His well-disciplined kids were above midnight raids. But just with the normal breakfast hits, the level dropped at a dizzying rate. Before I left, Claudio handed me a prized volume from his library. It was a small booklet, cleverly written in non-Italian by Riccardo Cassini, entitled *Nutella Nutellae, Racconti Poliglotti*. It began with the Creation, in far-fetched Italianate English. ("Na cifra," repeated often, is Italian slang for "in great abundance.")

> Once upon a time, many many, ma'na cifra of many years
> ago, at the beginning of the initiation of the mond, there
> was the caos. One day, God (God is the nome d'art of
> Dio), God, who was disoccupated, had a folgorant idea and

so God created the Nutell. And God saw that the Nutell was good, very good, very very good, good na cifra.

The mangiation of God was long, he manged one million of barattols of Nutell sfrutting the fact that God has not a Mamm that strills if you sbaf too much Nutell . . . And after this mangiation, God invented the Water Closed Run, the cors in the cabinet, and some Nutell's derivates like the red bubbons, the panz, the cellulit . . .

And so on. After putting Nutella on earth, God invented Adamo ed Eva. He placed them in a Paradise: "You have gratis restaurants, cinemas, theaters, all the Paradise is yours: air conditioned, autom riscaldament, moquette, parquet, tresset, bidet, omelette, eccet eccet . . . There's just one thing, remember, in tutt the Paradise just one thing absolutely prohibited." God showed Adamo ed Eva the Nutella tree and declared it forbidden "because I want all the Nutell, tutt the Nutell for me."

As expected, Adamo led Eva astray, and God gave them two choices. They could continue in Paradise without Nutella. Or, "you can take the Nutell, no problem, but for you is the cacciation out of the Paradise, you will soffer, you will have to lavorar with the sudor of your front . . ."

There was no contest, of course.

Cassini offers other *racconti*. A poem called "Weight Watchers Blues" bewails life without Nutella. A Quixote tale in sort-of Spanish speaks of Dulcinea. Her name, the text explains, means 50 percent sugar, 7 percent cacao, 12 percent hazelnuts, and the rest, soy lecithin and natural aromas. In a fractured fairy tale, with a title that translates to "The Dwarves Are Many More Than Seven," Sleeping Beauty has needle tracks. Only the strongest drug of all—you guessed it—can save her.

Essentially, the little book's message can be summed up by the end of the opening story of Creation: "But the final pensier of tutti noi is 'It's meglio faticar and soffrier with the Nutell piutost che the Terrestr Paradise senz the Nutall.'" In clear English: Everyone's final thought is that it is better to toil and suffer with Nutella than to live in earthly paradise without it.

Cassini was hardly exaggerating. During the American invasion of Iraq, early in 2003, an Austrian television crew found itself stuck in Baghdad, robbed of just about everything by a gang of roving looters. Editors in Vienna made an urgent appeal to the U.N. High Commissioner for Refugees office in Jordan. They asked the UNHCR to find some way to get them the barest essentials of survival: a sizable stack of U.S. dollars, a Thuraya satellite phone, and a jar of Nutella.

Cooks at Work

1 Tsp. of Prose, Recipes to Taste

by Judith Jones

from the *New York Times*

One of the deans of American cookbook editing, Jones has an unerring instinct for the difference between a good cookbook and a great one. Here she explicates the most important ingredients for a cookbook's success.

In the spring of 1960, as I turned the typewritten pages of a huge tome on French cooking written by a Smith College graduate named Julia Child along with her French cohorts, Simone Beck and Louisette Bertholle, I couldn't contain my delight at what I was reading.

I was a general book editor at Alfred A. Knopf, and here was the cookbook I had been dreaming of—one that took you by the hand and explained the whys and wherefores of every step of a recipe. It spelled out techniques, talked about the proper equipment, necessary ingredients and viable substitutes; it warned of pitfalls yet provided remedies for your mistakes. Moreover, although there were three authors, it was the voice of the American that came through, someone who was clearly a learner herself, who adored la cuisine française and was determined to dissect and translate it for an American audience. I was enthralled.

It so happened that I had spent three and a half years in Paris, about the same time Julia had been there, and had also fallen in love with French cooking. I had no cookbooks over there, so my husband, Evan, and I would talk to the butcher, the baker, the fishmonger or madame at the vegetable market and pick up a tip about how to roast a whole dorade or what the best fat was for frying frites.

But nobody ever told me how to make a boeuf bourguignon, and my beef boiled in wine was a far cry from the one described in what would become "Mastering the Art of French Cooking": "Carefully done, and perfectly flavored, it is certainly one of the most delicious beef dishes concocted by man."

Back in America, I had searched in vain for the book that would tell me exactly how to prepare it "carefully" and flavor it "perfectly." And here was everything I needed to know in Julia's precisely worded instructions. I quickly copied them and spirited them home.

I followed her advice on the best beef cut to buy for a stew, and how to create lardons with American bacon; I learned the importance of drying the beef cubes (damp meat won't brown) and of sautéing only a small batch at a time (it will steam if crowded in the pan). I braised the small white onions (following an eye-opening tip on fast peeling) separately from the mushrooms, so the nicely glazed vegetables maintained their identities. As to the cooking wine, only a full-bodied young red would do—the same that you would drink with this masterpiece of classic French cuisine.

And, of course, my boeuf bourguignon was a masterpiece. How could it not be?

So Julia really formed my idea of what makes a good cookbook, and I soon found myself searching for cookbook writers who would do for other cuisines what "Mastering" did for French. I was convinced that the more unfamiliar and exotic the cuisine, the more important it was to really translate the techniques and food-ways of the particular culture. When the home cook first sets out to make a Chinese stir-fry or a genuine Indian curry dish, we are really flying blind, creating something we may never have even tasted, and we need to know what to expect every step of the way.

Often the best teachers are not born cooks but late bloomers who were prompted to cook out of a yearning for the dishes of their childhood, to recapture in a new land the authentic cooking of their past: Claudia Roden with Middle Eastern dishes, Madhur Jaffrey with Indian dishes, Irene Kuo with Chinese. Because, like Julia, they were all learners, they understand exactly what we American neo-phytes need to know.

Technique is all-important: To attain the wonderful complexity of a genuine Madhur Jaffrey curry, we have to master the art of toasting spices, of blending flavorful pastes and then frying them; to make an Irene Kuo stir-fry with the proper texture, we need to "velvet" the chicken cubes to make them fluffy and tender or to "slippery coat" the little chunks of meat, to line up all the ingredients so we can work fast over high, high heat. Language is crucial to describe the action accurately and evocatively, and to seduce us and bolster our confidence, so we'll try anything.

Good recipe writing does not rely on clichéd terminology but creates a vocabulary of its own. We need visceral words that make us feel the texture of the dough in our hands before we "plop" (one of Julia's favorite expressions) it into a bowl. It is important to use the correct terms so we come to know what a batter is, a dough, a base, a roux, rather than calling everything a mixture. Now "slippery coated" means just what it says; you can almost taste the slippery, satiny finish that Irene Kuo intends.

I also welcome a good story along with the recipe—a bit of history, something about the author's connection to the dish, a helpful tip for the home cook. An old recipe for parkerhouse rolls becomes something special when we learn from Edna Lewis in "The Taste of Country Cooking" how they were a part of her family's Emancipation Day Dinner (which they celebrated instead of Thanksgiving Day). I particularly love Edna's advice about how to tell if the cake is done: "Pick up the pan and listen for any quiet noises in the cake. If you hear faint sounds, remove it from the oven." That is the voice of a born cook.

What most of us really want, though, is a collaboration with the cookbook writer, who becomes a comforting presence as we prepare his dishes. How often my husband and I would refer to our cooking mentors as friends: Julia says to salt the meat . . . Jim (Beard) salts the pan . . . Michael (Field) says don't salt at all before cooking, leaving us in the last analysis to make our own choices. The good writer, in fact, enables us. We should be encouraged to taste and adjust seasonings and, once we have absorbed the basic technique, to improvise.

With the development of the more personal cookbook and the need for marketing handles, the cult of the celebrity chef was inevitable, but it has taken its toll. Obviously a talented chef has a lot of creative ideas to offer, but too often his book is turned over to a writer who doesn't even watch the maestro at work in the kitchen, to have the chance to ask questions and capture his voice. The result is sterile formula recipe writing that is devoid of helpful instruction and the kinds of culinary secrets you hope will be divulged.

Moreover, restaurant cooking and home cooking are different experiences, and the professional tends to forget that he or she is writing for the home cook. Three or four different fresh herbs may be used in a simple stew (at least $1.99 each for a wilted package in the supermarket); the mushrooms must be wild; and saffron, truffle oil, aged balsamic vinegars and special liqueurs are de rigueur. The chef is intent on inventing a new spectacular dish. He's not interested in the rhythm of cooking through the week, thinking ahead, recycling leftovers (a dirty word these days) in creative ways, finding substitutes for extravagant items.

I have had young people say to me that they can't afford to cook from our kind of cookbooks—it's too wasteful. They don't want to purchase too many high-priced ingredients that they'll use once and let rot in the fridge. They also find it too time-consuming: a bowl for this, another bowl for that, all those pots simmering and reducing, and then everything to be cleaned up.

It doesn't have to be that way if you're in the hands of a responsible cookbook writer. We need writers who persuade us that cooking is fun and that there is a wonderful creative satisfaction in going home and making a good meal at the end of the day. Lidia Bastianich in her new book, "Lidia's Family Table," stresses the importance of cooking with all our senses. In her recipe for basic risotto, she interrupts the instructions with reflections on what you are doing each step of the way. She explains, for instance, why it is important that each grain of rice be coated with fat, and she makes note of the clicking sound when you stir it.

So as you pour in more broth, stirring rhythmically, you watch and you listen. And you relax, reflecting on what is happening. In about 20 minutes, you will have a warm bowlful of satisfying risotto, and you will want to raise your glass in thanks to Lidia for being there at your side.

Cool Cucumber

A New Dish Comes Together as Easy as a Summer Soup

by **Greg Atkinson,**
from *Pacific Northwest Magazine*

> With a poet's eye for the mysteries of cooking, Greg Atkinson—a Seattle chef turned culinary consultant and writer—ponders how ingredients and appetite and occasion serendipitously give birth to a new recipe.

Only occasionally do I make anything truly new, and when I do, I'm not entirely sure where it came from.

In her book of essays, *Small Wonder*, Barbara Kingsolver wrote a piece on poetry called "Stealing Apples." "I rarely think of poetry as something I make happen; it is more accurate to say that it happens to *me* . . . When a poem does arrive, I gasp as if an apple had fallen onto my head." Some recipes are like that, too. They simply happen.

I'm presented with tomatoes, basil and pasta, and suddenly I know. The basil leaves will be fried alone in olive oil and lifted out with a slotted spoon to be scattered later, like crisp, green flakes over angel hair, tossed with strips of seeded tomatoes warmed in the basil-blessed oil. It's not a recipe exactly, just a response to a certain set of ingredients and a certain vacancy in a menu.

Some dishes spring fully blown from the subconscious mind as if they had always been there, and I put them together without any dabbling or experimenting. The ingredients appear together because they naturally become available at the same time, or because they have a regional or cultural affinity for one another. Any technique applied to the ingredients must come out of my own experience.

Two years ago, I was entertaining a small group of women who were putting together a conference for a foodie organization called Les Dames d'Escoffier. I had promised them a light lunch, and without any conscious thought about what I would serve, I made some bread dough for French rolls, then I went to the cooler as if I had a plan. I reached for some eggs that came from a friend who keeps chickens. Then I grabbed a pound of applewood-smoked bacon that I happened to have on hand. I washed some Bibb lettuce delivered by a local farmer, and dutifully whisked together a dressing of red wine vinegar and walnut oil.

It wasn't until I sat down to eat with my guests, buttered a roll and plunged a fork into the poached egg on top of the salad that I was stricken with the uncanny similarity between this lunch and one I'd eaten at an outdoor café in a French town called Puy-en-Velay. I hadn't planned to serve the salad ahead of time. It just happened.

That salad was more like a spontaneous recollection, though, than a creation.

New dishes are those that emerge with no discernible connection to anything I have eaten before. Last summer, for instance, I was suddenly and perhaps unreasonably compelled to produce a cucumber soup with watermelon gelée. There was no call for the dish; no one was asking for chilled soup. I was under no obligation to use up any watermelon. But I knew I had to make it. I could picture the dish as clearly as if I had seen it in a photograph.

In all honesty, I had to wonder if I *had* seen it somewhere. But I have a pretty good memory for food, and for the life of me, I do not remember ever having eaten this cucumber soup or seen it anywhere in print. It was an apple falling on my head. And when I made it, it was exactly right. I was a child again. School was out and through an open window I could hear a lawn mower. A watermelon was on the counter and cold fried chicken was in the ice box. It would be a very good day.

Cucumber Soup with Watermelon Gelée

2 medium cucumbers
½ a sweet onion
1 tablespoon rice wine vinegar

1 teaspoon sea salt
¼ teaspoon ground white pepper
Watermelon Gelée, recipe follows

1. Peel the cucumbers and cut each one in half lengthwise. Use a spoon to carve out the seedy center section of each half cucumber. Discard the seeds and cut the cucumbers into 1-inch pieces. Pile the pieces into a blender.

2. Peel the half onion and cut into 1-inch pieces. Put the onion into the blender with the cucumber pieces and pour in the vinegar, salt and white pepper. Purée the cucumber soup and chill it.

3. To serve, invert one watermelon gelée into the center of four wide-rimmed soup bowls, then ladle about ¾ cup of the cucumber soup around each watermelon gelée. Serve cold.

MAKES 4 SERVINGS

Watermelon Gelée

3 cups seedless watermelon chunks, packed
2 tablespoons sugar
2 teaspoons lemon juice
1 (¼-ounce) envelope gelatin
4 pinches black sesame seeds

1. Put the watermelon chunks in a blender with the sugar and lemon juice and purée. Strain the purée to yield 2 cups watermelon juice.

2. Put ½ cup of the juice in a saucepan and sprinkle the gelatin over the surface. Allow the gelatin to soften for 5 minutes, then put the saucepan over high heat and stir until the gelatin is dissolved and the juice is beginning to boil.

3. Put a pinch of sesame seeds into each of four paper cups. Stir the hot gelatin mixture into the remaining juice and distribute the mixture evenly between the four cups, pouring the mixture over the sesame seeds.

4. Chill the gelée in the paper cups until it is firmly set, about an hour. To remove the gelée from the cups, dip the cups one at a time in hot water and then invert them into a serving bowl.

MAKES 4 SERVINGS

The Count and I

by Emily Kaiser
from *Gourmet*

> Fresh out of college, Emily Kaiser wrangled a job as private cook to Provençal aristocrats— and discovered that what she didn't know about cooking far exceeded what she knew.

When the Countess greeted us, she apologized for the luggage strewn in mid-pack in the halls. She had been preparing for departure to their château, but she hardly looked flustered. A woman in her sixties, with hair restored to a jet-black hue, she looked ready for *Hello* magazine in a red sundress and matching pumps, with a cigarette trailing smoke in her wake.

She led us into the sunroom, followed by Lulu, the terrier. A small but princely creature, he gave me a cursory sniff before curling up at the Countess's feet. Then the Count marched in, a stocky, white-haired man clad in his favorite olive silk suit, singing a Breton folk tune. *"Chant, Lulu, chant,"* he called. Lulu scrambled to his haunches and began to howl along with his master.

The concert completed, Lulu settled back in and the Count got down to business. He listened attentively as our mutual friend Judy aggrandized my CV. Then his round blue eyes lit up and his face broke into a wide grin. He almost shouted, "Does she know how to make an *omelette baveuse?*"

I mustered a shy *"Oui,"* and the Count shook my hand. I was hired. *"Elle est très jolie, oui, ça marche très bien."*

I was 22, a month out of college, with a degree in American history. Beyond *omelette* and *oui,* I spoke no French. Though I was inter-
viewing for the post of summer cook, I'd cooked professionally for
only six months, if I rounded up generously: one month flipping
flapjacks at a sleepaway camp, three making Shabbat dinners for a
family in New York, and two as a *commis* in a London restaurant. But
I'd fallen in love with the métier and I was determined to learn
cooking at the source. A few days after graduation, I'd flown to
France with the secret wish that I might find an apprenticeship.

Grace à Dieu, I had been given the phone number of a woman
who might be able to help. The afternoon I arrived at Judy Boullet's
apartment, she prepared a sumptuous lunch and teased out of me the
extent of my hope. By coffee she'd mapped out my cooking career,
starting with a summer as a private chef. Her friends Monsieur le
Comte and Madame la Comtesse were kind and good-humored,
and had reassured her that they did not need someone with much
experience. They had just hosted a wedding for their son, with 900
guests, and were looking forward to a modest summer.

At their Paris apartment, the Count and Countess had a guest
room where I stayed for the two weeks until we departed for Brittany. I divided my time between cooking classes in the morning,
French classes in the afternoon, and evenings watching the Coupe
du Monde with the housekeeper, Najiyah.

Najiyah was a Moroccan woman in her forties who had worked
for the Count and Countess for nearly a decade and whose quiet
manner belied her influence over the household. She knew their
tastes and habits, and would watch me carefully to see that I understood them, too. Whatever I could not comprehend, Najiyah would
show me by gesture. The day after Bastille Day, the two of us
boarded the TGV to prepare the château for their arrival.

From the train station, we zipped along twisting roads past clusters
of stumpy houses cobbled from brown Brittany stone. Long open
fields of grass and wheat lined the roads, with occasional signs for
moules and *cidre,* Muscadet, crêpes, and *coquilles St.-Jacques.* The Breton air was clean, and gusts blew clouds across the wide blue sky. We
turned off the road at a rusty gate, crunched along a gravel drive surrounded by trees—and out popped a magnificent redbrick castle.

The estate came complete with field, forest, pond, vegetable garden, chapel, and small barn; the main house had turrets and dungeonlike cellars.

The servants' rooms were on the top floor of the west wing. I took the one in the south turret, round and snug with bright blue and yellow wallpaper, a soft double bed, and a door that led straight to a spiral staircase down to the cavernous kitchen.

There, Najiyah walked me through the daily routine. Pointing to the hours on the kitchen clock, she explained that breakfast would be served every day at 8:30. Pointing to twelve, she said we would eat lunch at noon, followed by their lunch at one. We would eat dinner at seven, and they would eat at eight. For them (*"pour eux"* was a frequent phrase between us), and for us (*"pour nous"*), lunch and dinner consisted of an appetizer, a main course, salad and cheese, and dessert.

Najiyah moved over to the coffee machine. Each morning, I was to start two pots: one for us, extra strong, and one for them, milder but with fancier beans. She extended her hands long for the three baguettes that would arrive: one for us, two for them. At 7:30 Najiyah and I would prepare the breakfast trays. If there were guests, we would serve them in shifts. I would follow her with any additional trays, and then circle back to meet with the Countess in her *chambre* to plan the day's menu.

Next, Najiyah led me outside, where the gardener, Monsieur Madiot, had started radishes, lettuce, chives, onions, garlic, shallots, green beans, beets, and turnips. Now he was planting squash, pumpkins, and potatoes. For Madame, who was a talented flower arranger, he provided a range of blossoms. Najiyah showed me where to find the artichoke plants, the blackberry bushes, and the strawberry patch. It would be my responsibility to make sure we used as much as possible, reminding the Countess of what was ripest when we planned the menus. The three of us then packed off to the supermarket to get our sundries. The Count and Countess were to arrive later that night.

The next morning, the summer began in earnest. At seven, I let in the gardener, and together we enjoyed strong coffee and fresh baguette. We then set off, he to the garden, I to visit Madame and Monsieur in their room.

When I came in, Najiyah was raising the curtains, while the Count and Countess nibbled on breakfast in their pajamas. I had stayed awake late coming up with dishes for their approval, but I quickly discovered that when the Countess asked what they were going to eat today, she was speaking rhetorically. She and the Count knew well what they wanted. My suggestions were politely dispatched. *Coq au vin?* "Peasant food!" the Count chirped. Green beans with veal scallops? "You serve spinach with veal scallops, my dear," he said, shaking his head at my American ignorance. "I'd like a steak for lunch. Did my wife tell you? We have guests coming!"

The Count had already called a local fisherman to come to the house with his catch. "The sea is full of sea bass!" he laughed. If the fisherman arrived, dinner would be poached sea bass with hollandaise and boiled potatoes. Carrot soup to start, lemon tart for dessert. For lunch, veal scallops with spinach. A platter of crudités to start, and perhaps a fruit salad for dessert.

And for tomorrow? Well, come back tomorrow morning and we'll plan tomorrow, they said. It was time to get dressed.

Najiyah walked out with me to make sure I understood everything. "Four today," she said. Their son and daughter-in-law would arrive that morning. "Get the potatoes from the garden, and get a beef tenderloin for dinner—that fisherman might not come," she said.

When I returned from the supermarket, I found the Count with the fisherman in the kitchen, surveying a large bucket of flopping sea bass. The fisherman was tall, profoundly sunburned, and had wide blue eyes that seemed permanently focused on a distant horizon. He'd brought three dozen, and was smiling softly at his catch. Najiyah came in and started to gesture that I should begin skinning and gutting them, to prepare them for freezing. But lunch was in two hours, and I didn't see how I could fit it in. I thought I might throw up.

As she walked out, I ran to the garden to get the potatoes, along with beets, radishes, and lettuce. Monsieur Madiot chastised me for not taking enough beans: there were thousands, and they would go bad if I left them too long. I'd read Alice Waters; I knew that I was supposed to love this garden. But that morning I silently cursed it. "Tomorrow!" I promised, as I raced back with arms fully loaded.

Back in the scullery, I hid the fish in the refrigerator to be dealt with after lunch. I tossed the beets in a pressure cooker and filled the sink with water to clean the mud-coated greens. After what felt like a half day of washing, I was ready to start chopping. Najiyah stopped by to tell me the Countess liked hard-boiled eggs with her crudités, so I set those to boiling. The gardener came in to ask when his lunch would be ready, and he suggested I watch Joël Robuchon's noon cooking show to help me with my knife skills. Even he could see I was slow.

At noon he came in and I was still chopping, though now finally just the shallots and chives for the salad dressing. Salad done, I set out ham, *cornichons,* Brie, and a bowl of beets left over from the crudité platter. He looked pleased. He clicked on the Tour de France and I started in on dessert.

I'd bought peaches and apricots for the fruit salad, so I pitted them and tossed them with sugar and some mint the gardener had brought from home. Najiyah said she was not hungry, but noticed that the fruit hadn't been peeled, and clicked her tongue. No peel *pour eux.* I set to work peeling the halves. I wanted to serve the veal Italian-style, with butter and lemon. The pan was too hot and the butter scorched. I started over and remembered they wanted plenty of parsley, too. I hadn't gotten enough from the garden, so I started digging some out from the salad. The veal started to curl in the pan. Najiyah sounded the buzzer. The gardener had stopped watching the television and was now watching me with his mouth slightly open.

I spoke aloud in English, slowly, to get it all straight: veal on platter, butter, lemon, parsley. The platter was warming in the oven. I burned my wet fingertips taking it out, burned the other hand scooping the veal out barehanded. I squeezed the lemon over it and fished out the seeds. I tried to spread out the scant parsley. The veal had not browned, so the scallops looked like pale, green-flecked shoe inserts. I averted my eyes as the platter rose up the dumbwaiter.

The next two weeks I did not improve. More guests arrived, so for a week I made similarly botched meals for six and eight instead of two and four. My mistakes doubled and trebled. The Countess started to notice unusually high bills from the Super U, for the extra eggs, butter, and olive oil needed to mend my mistakes. Najiyah came in four and five times before each meal to make sure everything was covered. The guests, other aristocrats, were charmed by the idea of *"une jeune américaine"* working in the castle. But I was afraid to ask what they thought of the food.

Gradually, though, I came to see that I was more nervous than I needed to be. My food was not great, but it was good enough. Even when it wasn't, help appeared. For the first leg of lamb I roasted, Julia Child's timing actually worked, and a dinner guest who had come to the kitchen to practice his English insisted on demonstrating the proper way to slice it. Another night, when I mistook green peppercorns for capers and served a tremendously spicy beef tongue, the Count laughed it off, saying that the men all loved it, it was just the ladies who found it *"trop piquante."*

My hollandaise started to improve. I realized if I whisked it twice as fast, in a container twice as large, I ended up with twice as much. Even the Count was impressed. "Very nice and lemony," he remarked.

I actually started to enjoy the daily treks out to the garden, and though I couldn't find time to make jams as the Countess had requested, I was able to make vats of pumpkin soup for the fall, and introduced them to zucchini bread with the excess squash. I didn't even panic when I found my first feathered ducks in the refrigerator's crisper drawer.

Every night, the Count took Lulu and his hunting dog, Olga, on a stroll by the duck pond, bringing with him an antique pistol in case any fur or fowl crossed his path. He'd bagged a rabbit but hadn't been able to get any ducks for weeks. Finally, he got two, and tucked them into the fridge for supper. I figured they were awaiting the taxidermist, until Najiyah informed me of his expectations.

Since I didn't know that the wings should be cut off, not plucked, and they take the longest, it took an hour and a half. But I got all the feathers off in time, and roasted the birds in butter with thyme and turnips from the garden.

Every day, I found myself thinking more with my hands than with my head. Instead of having to write out each meal in 15-minute increments of prep time, I could feel in my fingers what work needed to be done. I still didn't know to judge doneness by touch, but I could now hear when the roast beef sizzled just so, indicating that it was near medium-rare. I could see what a well-roasted chicken looks like. I started to improve on little things: adding garlic cloves to the french fries, caramelizing the boiled turnips, peeling the baked apples halfway since the skin was so troublesome to eat. No longer in a state of steady panic, I had time to think things through.

My last week, the Count and Countess arrived home from a wedding hungry. I offered to make them an omelet.

"Une omelette baveuse?!" the Count roared, smiling, as he removed his coat.

"But of course!" I teased.

While browning the lardons of bacon, I whisked the eggs vigorously and heated the skillet. I knew to get it plenty hot to keep the omelet from sticking. In went the eggs. Before the inside had a chance to finish cooking, I scattered the bacon over it. Then I ran a fork along the edge, and the omelet's outside rim peeled off like it wanted to come out on its own. I folded it over and slid it onto a plate. I cleaned up and went to bed, not waiting for their response. After eight weeks of cooking, I knew myself that it was good.

Omelettes Baveuses aux Lardons
BACON OMELETS

This omelet is meant to be runny (baveuse) in the middle.

> 2 (¼ inch-thick) slices slab bacon (¼ lb; rind discarded if necessary), cut crosswise into ¼-inch-thick lardons
> 4 large eggs
> ⅛ teaspoon salt
> Pinch of black pepper
> 1 tablespoon unsalted butter

Put oven rack in middle position and preheat oven to 200°F. Cook lardons in a well-seasoned 8-inch steel omelet pan or nonstick skillet over moderate heat, stirring, until well browned, about 8 minutes. Transfer to paper towels to drain and discard fat from pan.

Whisk eggs, salt, and pepper vigorously in a bowl until foamy.

Put 2 ovenproof plates in oven to warm, then heat ½ table-spoon butter in omelet pan over moderate heat until foam from butter subsides. Pour ½ cup egg mixture into pan and cook, lifting up cooked egg around edge with a heatproof rubber spatula to let raw egg flow underneath, until bottom of omelet is set but top is still runny, about 1½ minutes. Scatter half of lardons over omelet, then fold omelet in half using spatula and transfer to a heated plate. Keep warm in oven.

Make another omelet in same manner, then transfer to other heated plate and serve immediately.

COOKS' NOTE:

The eggs in this recipe will not be fully cooked, which may be of concern if salmonella is a problem in your area.

SERVES 2

A Question of Taste

It's Not Easy Accepting Who Gets to Lick the Spoon

By Monica Bhide

from the *Washington Post*

Every cook instinctively learns to rely on his or her own senses to navigate the challenges of the kitchen—and, as freelance food writer Bhide discovered, these techniques differ from cook to cook.

I t started out as a perfectly normal workday. A food writer by night, I was working at a consulting firm, out of my lonely cubicle, on the seventh floor of a suburban D.C. office. I worked alone, since most of my teammates were all over the United States, part of what is called a virtual team. It sounds glamorous but translates into being very lonely at work. So imagine my surprise when the receptionist called me to say I had a visitor. I could hear her giggling on the other end of the phone. "Who is it?" I demanded to know. "Well," she hesitated, "it's a gentleman in a chef's uniform and he has a picture of you holding your cookbook. Says it's from the *Washington Post*."

A chef here in my office? With my picture in hand, no less. If you live long enough you see everything, my grandmother used to say, and sure enough here it was—a chef asking for a novice writer at an HR consulting firm.

And there he was, a young man in uniform, chef's hat and all. He extended his hand toward me, saying, "Hi, I am Jonathan Krinn and I have just opened a new restaurant downstairs in this building. It's called 2941. My mother saw the article about you in the newspaper and told me to check you out. She thought we might enjoy meeting each other."

Those were his exact words. I thought his mother was match-making. It must have shown on my face. "Since you write books and I cook," he quickly added.

I wasn't sure how to react. He invited me to his kitchen, to learn more about him and his cooking. And I agreed, reluctantly, not knowing what would be expected of me.

We set a date and he left.

I took the day of our meeting off from work and arrived armed with nothing more than anxiety, for now I had Googled him and knew who he is. What on earth would we talk about, I wondered.

The interior of the restaurant looked like a new bride: perfectly adorned, a bit coy and yet very inviting. He met me at the door and led me into the kitchen. It was huge, almost as big as the restaurant. I was in awe of all the gadgets. As we chatted, a chemistry began to develop. His passion was French American food and mine was Indian, so vastly different, and yet the soul behind them was the same.

He muttered something about showing me how to make a perfect sauce. I was completely ill at ease, my knowledge of French stopped at "*oui*," and he was talking a mile a minute about ingredients and techniques. We were standing over the pot. And then it happened, that bewildering incident.

He took a spoon, dipped it in the sauce and then proceeded to ... dare I say, lick it. I was stunned. Completely horrified and stunned. He offered me some and I shook my head. "Are you okay?" he inquired.

I stuttered, "You tasted the sauce. . . . How could you do that? Don't you know you are not allowed to taste while you cook?"

Now it was his turn to look stunned. "I have never heard of that," he said. "How would you know when to season?"

When you least expect it, culture shows up. I had learned to cook by sight, smell, sound and texture. In our kitchen we were not allowed to taste.

My father would teach me to roast spices and learn that coriander whimpers, cumin smolders, mustard sizzles and cinnamon roars. I learned to cook by sight as the colors of the spices turned and then by smell—sweet, earthy, heady, sharp if they are roasting correctly, or the unforgiving acrid smells if they burn.

My mother taught me to make curries by hearing how onions sing in oil, from a slight sizzle to a glorious harmony as they get perfectly caramelized. I learned to watch the tomatoes marry the onions. The sign the union was complete and ready for spices to be added was when the oil separated from the mixture.

Roast, sizzle, temper, broil, boil, bake, simmer, saute, fry—we had to do it all by watching and listening.

The reason, I was told many years later, was that in our house the first offering of the food was for the gods. If you tasted while you cooked, it made the food impure. My grandmother would carefully take the first piece of bread she cooked each night, place it on a plate along with a helping of all the other vegetables and lentils, and set it aside before the meal for the family was served. After we all ate, she would go outside and set the plate in front of the cows that used to hang around our neighborhood. Cows are considered sacred in the Hindu religion and feeding them is said to be akin to feeding God.

Jonathan listened carefully to my story and nodded. Then he held the spoon to me and said, "Here, taste it. There are no cows in D.C."

Pucker Power

by Dara Moskowitz
from *City Pages*

Moskowitz's lively reviews and essays in this Minneapolis alternative weekly magazine always make entertaining reading. Her enthusiasm and curiosity about food make this piece — one of a series on the elements of flavor — particularly insightful.

When I got together with Thomas Keller recently, that French Laundry dude, that Einstein and omega of American chefs, he told me that in his mind, an ideal cookbook would have no recipes, none, not one. Why, how lovely, I purred, because I have been working on just such a loosey-goosey thing all year, pursuing how various local chefs manipulate the most basic elements of flavor, the sweet, the salty, and such, to present the ideas to you, Dear Reader, so that you might use them yourself, without a single burdensome recipe! And here I had felt sort of guilty at focusing on "ideas" and not "news you can use," when I shouldn't have felt guilty at all, but in fact sort of blindingly forward. I mean—ideas! Ideas are so much more convenient than recipes, not least because you can fit them into practically any head at all and carry them into airplanes without paying the excess baggage fee. I mean, what about the idea of "sour"? It's one of the elemental tastes, but one that almost never gets top billing. Sour is considered a good thing in sauerkraut, lime curd, and certain pickles, and a bad thing in nearly everything else, from sourpusses to sour milk to sour notes. So why is it that restaurant chefs use so much more sour than home cooks do? Go to a Thai restaurant and you might find lemon juice, lime juice, and vinegar in a single sauce, and the resulting sauce doesn't make you gag, it makes you smile and ask for more. An ingenious chef in a four-star hotel in downtown Minneapolis might top a preserved lemon with balsamic vinegar and place that doubly acidic thing in a vinaigrette-covered salad beside a fourth sort of acid, goat cheese— and the whole thing doesn't taste sour at all, but merely sweet and delicious.

Why, Seth Bixby Daugherty, head chef at Cosmos, the high-end hotel restaurant I just mentioned, why do you do it? What do you know that I don't? I phoned him up to get just that answer. "When my chefs and I get together and talk about building a dish," he said, "we want at least three of the four components of sour, sweet, salty, and bitter." For the sour part, the restaurant stocks as many as 30 different vinegars (including four sorts of sherry vinegar and seven grades of balsamic) and relies on a variety of both house-made and purchased sour stuffs, like preserved lemons, preserved tomatoes, or even vats of house-pickled yuzu, the Japanese citrus fruit. Why such an expansive pantry? "If you want a particular flavor, you need a particular acid to get there," says Daugherty. That and the fact that no one who cooks at Le Meridien ever seems to go home or get a day off—the working motto in the kitchen these days is "Breakfast, lunch, dinner, forever"—and the deep Le Meridien pantry is what the restaurant uses to motivate and inspire the various chefs who fulfill the various hotel functions (like the dawn till after-bar bar and restaurant, the bustling ballrooms and banquet halls, and the elaborate room service).

"We're incredibly lucky," says Daugherty. "Where most restaurants today are 'Cut, cut, cut,' we're 'Push, push, push.' Oh, a couple weeks ago we did the coolest thing—took the inside of a preserved lemon, took the pulp and flesh, dried it, put it through a Vita-Mix so it was pulverized and we got this nice, fine, silky powder. You could smell it when you put it on the warm plate, as a garnish, and it just tasted great." Preserved lemon dust? How on earth did that idea come up? Daugherty couldn't quite say, but I think I can: Genius is what happens when you take some of the most talented chefs in the state and strand them, sleep deprived, in the presence of the *Tyrannosaurus rex* of blenders. Still, talking about the sour ideas at Cosmos is as nothing to experiencing them, so I zipped in for a dinner with the idea of ordering only dishes with the sourest elements layered on one another. What I found was revelatory: A duck confit salad with a poached quail egg that strikes the palate as nothing but rich, warm, wonderful and wintry, if built with a peppery structure, and yet is revealed to be made of practically nothing but layers of sour: bitter frisée, spicy watercress, acidic roasted red bell peppers, and acidic preserved tomatoes coated in a citrus vinaigrette.

How does this work? The secret is the way the acid from all of those sour things cuts through the richness of the duck meat and the egg. "If you've got the double richness of duck confit and quail yolk, you need a double tart and sour to balance it out," explained Daugherty, on the phone again, later. Ditto for the fantastic lamb chop dish that has been on the menu since the restaurant opened. Here, two gorgeous Summerfield lamb chops loll beside a watercress salad which conceals warm shreds of lamb shoulder braised in duck fat, tossed with strips of preserved lemon, tart and creamy lumps of Humboldt Fog goat cheese, sweet currants, and puckery roasted red peppers, all of it sauced with Malpighi balsamic vinegar (which costs about $25 an ounce). That the sweet, rosy lamb chops are like ripe raspberries of meat goes without saying. But the combination of lemon, vinegar, and goat cheese is the shocker: it's a lush, rich, and full taste, like a box of chocolate truffles in which each little dome was filled with an entrée. Amazing! How is it done? "If you take out the Humboldt Fog, it's too tart," explained Daugherty. "Even though the goat cheese by itself is tart, it's also creamy, which makes it all okay. There's a lot of fatness in this dish, from the lamb shoulder, which means you have a lot of room to work with on the sour side of the equation." I'll also mention that Daugherty makes a stunning vinaigrette by juicing fresh oranges and cooking that juice down with a vanilla bean until it's a syrup, and then whisking in extra-virgin olive oil. It makes salad greens taste as though they're floating; something about the plush texture of the emulsification of the oil, and the unusual vanilla-orange edge that makes the herbal qualities of greens stand out. (Cosmos; 601 First Ave. N.; inside Le Meridien Minneapolis; Mpls.; 612.677.1100.)

So there we have some acrobatics of sour in the hands of a master in the Western tradition, but how do they do it in Thailand? I dropped in at the former Sawatdee in Lowertown St. Paul, where

Thai cooking instructor Supatra Johnson (www.supatra.com) recently took over the kitchen and has renamed the place Supatra's Thai Cuisine. I sought out a number of sour dishes: An Erawan steak salad, potatoes in a tamarind sauce, and a daily special of a garlic seafood soup. Each was sour, and delicious, in a completely different way: The salad was sour like late morning sunlight, piercing and utterly clean; the potatoes were a sweet, deep sour, like a half-sad smile; the soup was hot and fiercely sour, like a dense jungle of noise.

Of course, I had to call up Supatra and find out how she did it. All of these sour flavors, she explained, were achieved through different methods. The steak salad had lemon juice, lime juice, and white vinegar in the sauce, and was made with a minced sour herb. The potatoes were sauced with three sorts of sour, ripe tamarind paste, vinegar, and vinegar-laced puckery sri cha hot sauce. The soup had at least five sorts of pucker in it, including green tamarind powder, ripe tamarind paste, tomato, lime, and pickled garlic.

"Sometimes when I'm teaching my students about Thai cooking, they complain, 'It's too many ingredients!'" she told me. "I say, if you want the perfect taste, you have to combine all the right things. For one dish, if you combine lemon, lime, and vinegar, now that is the right taste. For another, it can only be tamarind, tomato, lime juice, and a little rice vinegar—not apple cider, or any other kind. Every sour has its right place. When you go to a Vietnamese pho shop you always have sri cha sauce, vinegar, fish sauce, and lime on the side for sour balance."

And for that matter, Supatra told me, what any of us ever see on a Thai menu is just the tip of the iceberg, vis-à-vis the life of sour in Thai cooking. Many of her favorite dishes are not on the Sawatdee menu because she thinks they're just too sour for the common taste. Why, just last night for dinner Supatra was dunking homemade pickled mustard greens in a dip made of lime juice ground with chiles. Now that's authentic Thai. And sour power to burn. (Sawatdee; 289 E. 5th St., St. Paul; 651.222.5859, and six other locations.)

Soon, I was seeing subtle manipulation of pucker everywhere I turned. At Surdyk's cheese shop they just started carrying verjus, that hard to find green-grape juice winemakers make and chefs love. Marianne Miller, the former chef and soon-to-be-owner of Red, that mercurial but dazzling French and Russian restaurant in the Foshay Tower, recommends that if you learn only one new sour trick this year, it should be this: Sauté a white fish, such as halibut or sole, with a little oil or butter in a very hot non-stick pan. Once the fish is toasty brown on one side, flip it, add a shot of verjus, cover the pan, and let the fish finish in the verjus steam for a moment.

"Brightening: We call adding a little acid at the end brightening a dish, and it's one of the most important things you learn as a chef in Western kitchens," Miller told me on the phone as she worked on trying to get the furniture and everything back so she could reopen Red (which closed last month and, cross your fingers, should reopen in late January). "In Florida, where I'm from, layering of acids is a key to 'Floribbean' cooking: You put lime juice on mango, for instance. But in a Western-kitchen mentality, you start with fat, and finish with acid. When I was cooking in London, it seemed like we deglazed every braised meat pan with malt or apple vinegar. Learning to deglaze a sautéed white fish with verjus is probably one of the more important things you can teach yourself."

That noted, you can also note that verjus is what most chefs make vinaigrettes with for wine dinners. Since it's not vinegar, it doesn't destroy the taste of wine. Sour secrets everywhere!

Last weekend, I dropped by the newly renovated Auriga to find out what it's like to have chef Doug Flicker's delicate cooking in a restaurant space that feels grown-up and luxurious. Well, it's wonderful. And do I need to mention that there were secret sour touches everywhere? I tried an appetizer of teensy deep-fried artichoke hearts coated in the most subtle, buoyant golden batter; each was like munching on the perfect cross between a State Fair minidonut and a wee seaside cloud. Later I learned that the itsy-bitsy darlings had been misted, from a spray-bottle, with Italian apple cider vinegar. "If we drizzled it on, it would make the batter wet and mushy," Flicker explained to me on the phone.

And if I liked sour, I should have been there the season he was making his own version of verjus, with a home-brewing kit and green table grapes. After that, he made wine from fresh beets, and then from red bell peppers, and used it for sauces. (What separates the chefs of note from the rest of us? Well, when was the last time you thought of making bell pepper wine or pulverized preserved lemon dust?)

But it's not the beet wine that gets his line cooks teasing him, says Flicker, it's his constant harping on the Holy Trinity. No, not that Holy Trinity: "It's olive oil, salt, and lemon juice. It's something people pick up from working with me, they're always asking, 'What does this need, what does this need?'" The answer, says Flicker, is almost always one of those three. "Virtually everything and anything can take a little lemon juice. Even mashed potatoes. When we reheat a bit at a time for service, we're always adding a little salt or a little lemon juice."

Lemon juice? On the mashed potatoes? The palate doesn't read it as lemony, Flicker explained, just as correct. I pestered him until I got this further chef's secret out of him: At his station at Auriga he always keeps several lemons. He cuts off the far ends, so that he's exposing the flesh, and uses that to squeeze over the dishes that are about to head to the tables. If you cut the lemons in the middle, that's where the pits are, and you don't want to spend five minutes searching through the spinach for a lost lemon pit, he explained. The juiced lemons then are used in reducing sauces, to add a hint of lemon oil and the depth of pith. (Auriga; 1930 Hennepin Ave. S., Mpls.; 612.871.0777.)

And that, Dear Reader, is everything I learned in a month of pursuing the idea of sour. If I hadn't talked to Thomas Keller I'd probably end here by enjoining you to try filling spray bottles with vinegars, or to try boiling orange juice with vanilla beans, or at least to try finishing your mashed potatoes with a squirt from one end of a lemon.

But since I now have permission to run rampant with mere ideas, I'll say just this: After a month of sour thoughts I have come to think that sour, or more generically, acid, is the essence of almost everything we eat. It's the essence of wine, of coffee, of dairy (with its lactic acid), of most bread (with its ferment of yeast or sourdough starter), and of almost everything. If, as the Buddhists say, life is suffering, then the rough culinary equivalent may be that food is sour. Or at least acidic. And if that doesn't rattle your bones more than a recipe, I don't know what will.

The Pantry Forager

by Pete Wells
from *Food & Wine*

This weekend's cooking challenge? Base all your meals on the odds-and-ends in the back of a not-too-well-stocked cupboard. Wells, a frequent *Food & Wine* contributor, put his cooking skills to the test, *Survivor*-style.

Saturday morning, I woke up and decided not to buy any food until Monday. In warm weather this would be reasonable, because the refrigerator would be crowded with fruits and vegetables that my wife, Susan, and I had lugged home from the farmers' market. But this was January, at the front end of a searing cold snap, and the fridge, cupboards and freezer were exhibits in a museum of oddities. A cloth sack of rice. A nearly complete set of chicken giblets. Two rolls of film. Marmite. There could have been a rack of wildebeest under the icecube trays. Honestly, I had no idea what was in our kitchen. Cooking six meals straight without leaving home was one way of finding out.

I also hoped that my self-imposed performance of *Survivor: Brooklyn* would push me into uncharted reaches of my cookbook shelf. The problem of what to cook when the pantry is bare is one that every culture on earth has wrestled with, as have some of the best food writers. For years, I've read and reread certain recipes for squeezing sustenance and even pleasure out of severe hardship, and wondered about them. When hunger looms, though, my curiosity slips away. Now, if I was going to last the weekend without reinforcements, these books would have to talk me through it.

So: Breakfast! *How to Cook a Wolf,* M.F. K. Fisher's book of idiosyncratic advice for weathering the rationing and shortages of World War II, prescribes "some brown nutty savorous porridge." No problem—I reached above the microwave for a can of Irish oatmeal. I was out of the maple syrup and chopped dates Fisher recommends, but in the back of the refrigerator was a bottle of sorghum I'd brought back from Tennessee two years before. All my days should start so well.

After breakfast my eyes settled on a half-empty jar of peanut butter, and I determined, for no rational reason at all, to fashion lunch around it. I remembered a chapter on cheap Chinese noodles in John Thorne's *Outlaw Cook.* I'd always had *dandan* noodles made with pork and sesame paste, but Thorne had a meatless variation using peanut butter. He seemed to know just what I lacked and to have a fix ready. Out of Chinese black vinegar? Try balsamic. No fresh egg noodles—or, for that matter, eggs? Spaghetti will do fine, Thorne promised. I made one unauthorized switch, adding heat with Thai chili-and-garlic paste rather than chile powder. What I wound up with bore little resemblance to the *dandan* noodles at my favorite Manhattan Sichuan restaurant, but Susan and I agreed it was far better than peanut butter and spaghetti had any right to be.

This corner I'd painted myself into was feeling more and more comfortable. Susan and I once spent a winter in Provincetown. When the summer people left with their summer money, the farm stands closed, then the bakery, and finally the fish shop. The last loss really hurt. We were in a fishing village, surrounded by water on three sides, on a piece of land called Cape Cod, and the only place to get a fresh cod fillet was a 45-minute drive back toward the mainland. Our meals that winter grew out of basics from the town's sad, understocked A & P: pasta, eggs, lentils, kale, Portuguese sausage. It should have been depressing, arranging the same plain items in new patterns night after night, but we found it rewarding. Paradoxically, with fewer choices you think harder about the possibilities. If your meal turns out well, you feel like a magician slipping out of a straitjacket. For our dinner in Brooklyn, then, we ate lentil stew with sausages from the freezer. But the lentils never relaxed; even after two hours they kept a hint of crunch. They came from a box dated 2003.

That was Saturday: oatmeal, noodles, lentils. Grains and beans. Without even thinking about it, I'd fallen back on the same foods that people with no money have relied on forever. (Lentils were among the first cultivated crops.) The Italians call this kind of cooking *la cucina povera,* a lyrical phrase that almost makes poetry out of poverty. Many Americans now study Italian cuisine the way Renaissance thinkers pored over ancient Greek manuscripts, with the same sense of reclaiming lost wisdom. Like most cults, this one gets absurd at times. It is one thing to smack your lips in wonder at the powerful flavors of *cucina povera.* It is quite another to spend $40 for Laudemio olive oil and imported beans. And by the time you find yourself in a Tuscan village taking the seven-day cooking course on *cucina povera* that one Italian-vacation packager offers for about $2,000—well, you are some distance from the peasants, spiritually if not geographically. The lessons of *cucina povera* are elsewhere.

Sunday did not start well. I returned to *How to Cook a Wolf,* but this time the wolf bit me. Fisher merrily urges "piles of toast, generously buttered, and a bowl of honey or jam." She continues, "You *can* be lavish, because the meal is so inexpensive. You can have fun . . ." My piles of toast were all right, but no fun. A slice of ham would have helped, or some eggs, but by this point our protein stores were running perilously low. I sat down to think my way into a decent lunch and decided it was time for one of those recipes that fascinated and frightened me: the onion *panade* in Richard Olney's *Simple French Food.*

Panades belong to a set of European peasant dishes built on the unpromising foundation of stale bread and water. The Portuguese have *açorda;* in Italy, there is *acqua-cotta; panade* is the French version. In darker days, this was merely dried-out bread baked with water. Onion *panade* is a less dismal variation, ancestor of the beloved French onion soup. It can be made out of practically nothing—or, to be exact, stale bread, cheese and onions.

A month before, Susan had hosted a baby shower, and after the shower we were left with a sliced-up baguette and a big knob of cheese. Olney demanded sourdough and insisted only Gruyère or Parmesan would do. Our orphan cheese had no label, no name. It was covered with inexplicable scratchings and tiny nibbles, as if it had been left with a bored gang of mice. Olney also called for white summer onions or Bermudas. I had one of those orange mesh bags from the supermarket; inside I found exactly one decent mid-sized specimen and enough spongy, smelly, sprouting onions to start a compost heap.

America gives us more choices than we need: too many channels, too many Benjamin Moore paint chips, too many ways for Starbucks to overcharge you. Eventually you learn to shop first and ask questions later. This is how you find yourself buying a $40 bottle of olive oil when what you are really hungry for is a plate of beans. There are cures. You can drive to Provincetown or another remote place. You can run out of money, although in my experience that rarely helps clear your mind. Or you can simply pay more attention to what you've already got. If I'd been doing that, my lentils would have been ready in half an hour and my onions wouldn't have had green tails.

I had another bag of onions. About 30 small ones, the size of Atomic FireBall candies. Slicing them into rings was a job for a surgical laser, not a chef's knife. Running across the street to the supermarket for a few fat yellow onions would have been easier and faster. I didn't do it.

This is what I did. Peeled and sliced 30 tiny onions. Caramelized them for two hours. Layered stale bread, caramelized onions and mystery cheese; bread, onions, cheese; and finally, just bread and cheese. Funneled salty water into the casserole. Baked it for an hour and a half.

Susan and I were a little freaked out by how delicious it was. We were so proud of our something-from-nothing triumph that we decided it would be okay to buy a skirt steak for dinner.

Baking Up a Storm

New Loaves Rising

by John Kessler

from the *Atlanta Journal-Constitution*

Kessler has a special gift for tracing the cultural values underlying every food choice he and his fellow Atlantans make. Here is a rich profile of how a local bakery became a beloved institution.

Wherever there is a Jewish grocer or delicatessen, you are almost certain to find an excellent loaf of bread.
  —HENRY MILLER, "THE STAFF OF LIFE," 1945.

Savannah—Broughton Street may traverse the historic district of this lovely city, but it has none of the charm of the camellia-lined squares that flank it on either side. Instead, it faces the world with that depressed, glassy, stuck-in-the-'60s blankness of Main Street, Anytown, USA. Some storefronts sit empty and begging for tenants, while others provide the too-large shells for hermit-crab consignment shops or $6.95 lunch joints. Still, there are signs of comeback—high-end restaurants, chain clothing stores for putative hipsters and that ubiquitous latte palace.

Yet on a cold pre-dawn morning, all the dark storefronts look equally, eerily vacant. All but one. Even as Starbucks slumbers, the light is on at Gottlieb's Restaurant and Dessert Bar on the corner of Bull and Broughton. Press your nose against the plate glass, and you'll see straight through the chic, spare dining room to the open kitchen in the rear. There, the day's baking lesson, spotlighted in fluorescent chiaroscuro, is under way.

"Watch," the towering, dough-faced Isser Gottlieb says to his middle son, Laurence, as he slaps a stainless steel prep table in the kitchen with something that looks like an octopus made from pliant yellow dough. He twists the six strands of dough into a multi-furled braid that would be beyond Princess Leia's grasp. "This is what my father taught me: The only school for this is 'Watch.' "

Laurence, 31, a trained chef with an A-plus résumé, twists his own dough octopus. "It always takes me three or four times. If I get started and don't stop, fine," he says, hands flying. "But if I stop, I have to undo it and start again."

The morning's challah now braided, it is time to learn about croissants, cheese Danish, seeded rye . . .

For more than 100 years, Gottlieb's was one of Savannah's best-loved bakeries. Isser's grandfather Isadore Gottlieb, a Russian Jewish immigrant, opened the business in 1884 with a little knowledge of Old World breads, a pushcart and a lot of drive. The bakery flourished, moving from the old Jewish quarter, to downtown's Southside, to its suburbs. It grew and changed as the city grew and changed. At first, it supplied 5-cent loaves of bread to new immigrants, then doughnuts and Danish to the midcentury middle class, and eventually its famous chocolate chewie cookies—more than a half million per year—to the suburbanites who had fled the central city.

And then in 1994, Gottlieb's was gone—beaten by the Krogers and Publixes, the Krispy Kremes and the Keeblers. Savannah no longer had a place for a homegrown bakery.

Now it's back. Sort of.

Isser Gottlieb's three sons—two chefs and a retailer—joined forces, and a year ago opened an ambitious restaurant where the rack of lamb costs $39, the waiters push foie gras, and the Brunswick stew contains rabbit loin and wild mushrooms. With a recent profile in *Gourmet* and a prestigious Four Diamond Award from the American Automobile Association (Savannah's only recipient), Gottlieb's has made a national splash.

And the locals? Many are thrilled. "It's a beautiful restaurant with gorgeous food and wonderful service, in keeping with the family's tradition," says Julius "Boo" Hornstein, a lifelong, old-family Savannahian. But others grumble this restaurant is too expensive.

Besides, what many really wanted back was Gottlieb's—the real Gottlieb's, the chocolate-chewie Gottlieb's.

So in December, the family began testing the waters. Four days a week, Isser, 67, meets Laurence at 5 a.m. to bake. They prepare a small assortment of breads and pastries, set the pans hot from the oven on two wood-laminate folding tables just inside the door and tape a bakery menu to the window. If the response is good, the family hopes to carve a corner of the restaurant into a full-service bakery.

The history of Gottlieb's Bakery—its growth, demise and resurgence—tells a story of Savannah. This is not the oddball enclave of antiques dealers, paganists and white-gloved nibblers of tea sandwiches portrayed in "Midnight in the Garden of Good and Evil." Less the exotic flower of the South than a mirror of the Northeast, this Savannah is a city fueled by the scrappy vitality of successive waves of immigrants, challenged by the demographic changes of the '60s and '70s and only now beginning to recover.

FAMILY BONDS

As executive sous chef at the Inn at Little Washington in Northern Virginia, Laurence Gottlieb ran one of the country's most famous kitchens. He even oversaw a Relais & Chateaux dinner held on the Champs-Elysées in Paris.

And he thought the French were demanding . . .

"Laurence, I just got a hernia picking up that babka," Isser Gottlieb reports dryly on his way through the kitchen with the offending pastry in tow.

"If it was too light, he'd complain, too," Laurence says with a roll of his eyes, turning his attention to a long strip of croissant dough.

Isser stands nearly a head taller than Laurence, with massive forearms and hands, epic jowls and a gut still round despite having lost 30 pounds on Weight Watchers. His droll, martini-dry demeanor contrasts to the go-go energy of his bounding, curly-haired son.

The babka in question looks like an edible emissary from another time—a high, yeasty loaf bursting with furled ribbons of chocolate. It sits proudly on a folding table that, by 8:30 a.m., has started to fill up nicely. Almond and cheese Danish, butter-flake rolls, caramel rolls, cinnamon rolls, rye loaves and challah, now puffed and burnished with egg glaze, crowd side by side on warm aluminum sheet pans. And, of course, there are chocolate chewies galore.

As the sun rises, the other Gottliebs make their appearance. Michael, 27, inheritor of Isser's laconic mien, peeks in to say hi before changing into his chef's whites. Richard, 33, arrives with an ever-furrowed brow, a cellphone pressed to his ear and the bottomless stack of order forms and bills that will accompany him all day. Their mother, Ava, 58, joins the scene. She sets up a station at the granite bar to slice stale cinnamon rolls up for coffee crisps and fret about her three unmarried sons. These five people seem to share an intense bond of filial industry. Hard work defines them.

As they move through their paces, they move through ghosts. Everywhere hang pictures of bakery sites long gone and Gottlieb's past. In one, a young, handsome Isser poses with his father, Elliott, and his uncles Irving and Buster, their arms crossed over an ample display case. "The Jewish mafia," Laurence calls it.

Customers begin to wander in, tourists and locals, and are all enchanted by the abundant show of pastry. Isser gets everyone's story.

One young woman explains she is visiting her in-laws, mentioning their name.

"I know your father-in-law," Isser says, leveling her with a gaze that only family members recognize as playful. "Big guy, right?"

"Right," the woman answers.

"Ugly guy, right?"

"Uh . . . right."

"Your husband looks just like him, I bet."

"No!" she sputters.

Just about every morning, an old-timer wanders in to see if it's really true that the bakery is back.

"Ahhhhh! A return to the past," exclaims an excited Joan Levy, 62, the owner of Joan's on Jones Bed & Breakfast. "I never thought I'd see another Gottlieb's cheese Danish again!"

GETTING SETTLED

As long as there has been a Savannah, there's been a Jewish community. You need only consider Joan Levy's family.

Levy's ancestor, Benjamin Sheftall, arrived in 1733, one of 42 Jews who set sail from London to escape persecution. They were the first Europeans to arrive in the 5-month-old colony of Georgia after James Oglethorpe settled on this naturally protected parcel of land on a bluff overlooking the Savannah River, 13 miles inland.

Levy echoes the oft-repeated canard that Oglethorpe "allowed Jews but no lawyers, Catholics or slavery." History shows Georgia's founder may have been motivated to accept this boat, the *William and Sarah*, thanks to the presence on it of one Samuel Nunez, who became Georgia's first Jewish doctor and handily curtailed the colony's outbreak of yellow fever.

The passengers set up residence and that year established a house of worship, Mickve Israel, the third synagogue built in America. All the same, Savannah's Jewish population remained tiny for the next century until the great influx of German-Jewish immigration in the 1840s. Educated and industrious, the Germans grew into a wealthy merchant class—enough to commission a new home for Mickve Israel. Since 1878, it has occupied a neo-Gothic sanctuary that fronts Monterey Square along with another famous Savannah structure—the Mercer House of "Midnight in the Garden of Good and Evil."

The next great wave of Jewish immigrants came in the late 1800s, when Eastern Europeans arrived in droves at Ellis Island, N.Y., and made their way to points North, Midwest and South. Savannah's German-Jewish burghers established a benevolent organization, the Jewish Educational Alliance, to assist arrivals. The alliance, says Hornstein, "was a haven and a beacon for immigrant Jews who were getting started in life."

These new arrivals—more rural, less educated—settled alongside other immigrant groups in a rough-and-tumble area called the Yamacraw district, just west of the present-day City Market. There, Jewish and Irish street kids faced off in legendary turf fights.

This was the Savannah into which Isadore Gottlieb arrived, having booked passage from New York and mistakenly believing he would find a relative from Russia. Instead, he found Jennie Hurwitz, also Russian-born, married her and set up a small basement bake shop in 1884.

At first, Isadore delivered bread to other immigrants by horse and buggy, along with the day's news translated into Yiddish. Before long, he moved the business to a site near Franklin Square, then the center of life for the Yamacraw district's Jews, with two newly opened synagogues nearby. Jennie always had a cookie for the neighborhood children.

Isadore moved the bakery twice more before settling, in 1928, on the Southside location where it would remain for more than a half century. He, Jennie and their eight children lived upstairs. This is the Gottlieb's that everybody—everybody—in Savannah remembers.

SWEETS FOR GENERATIONS

Levy recalls the Gottlieb's of the '40s and '50s as a bare-bones joint with a stuffed-full display case and bakery boxes suspended from the ceiling with string. She recalls her parents stopping by to pick up boxes of miniature cheese Danish to serve for dessert after oyster roasts on Tybee Island.

Harriett Meyerhoff, 58, another lifelong Savannahian, remembers going with her mother to pick up bread—raisin pumpernickel or corn rye, the dense, dark, deeply soured Old World rye that has since all but disappeared from America's bakeries. Isadore's sons Elliott and Irving, behind the counter, would, like their mother, always have a free cookie for children.

During this period, Meyerhoff says, "the whole of Broughton Street, east to west, was filled with Jewish merchants." At first they were mostly pawnbrokers, but "they realized that they couldn't all survive selling pawn."

Between the '40s and the '60s, Broughton turned into a shiny, modern commercial thoroughfare, filled with department stores, jewelers, haberdasheries and shoe stores.

Over on the other side of Forsyth Park, Gottlieb's continued to grow, eating up its block, as other local bakeries like Swartz's and McCorkle's petered out. Set in the midst of a clutch of churches, it was where kids ran for doughnuts between Sunday school and services.

It was where Savannahians raised on Gottlieb's brought their own children. Decades later, Meyerhoff remains mortified about the time her 3-year-old wandered up to a rotund customer by the display case and asked, "Why are you so fat? And why are you in the bakery?"

Turnaround Never Came

In 1974, Isser Gottlieb, now in charge of the bakery, attended a professional conference in Jacksonville and demonstrated his technique for decorating a "bikini cake."

Modestly, he describes it as "just a sheet cake with two Easter eggs for the boobs, the waist cut out on either side and a frosting cover for the bikini."

Afterward, an attendee, whose name he never got, came up to thank him for the demonstration and shared a recipe for "Come Back Cookies," so called because customers always came back for more.

While these cookies had a short shelf life, Isser sensed they would move fast. With a slight, proprietary tweak to the recipe, the chocolate chewie was born.

In truth, the chocolate chewie isn't even that chocolaty. It in no way offers today's post–Mrs. Fields chocolate fix—that gooey, chunky drug dosage. No, it's a gentler thing. A texture thing. A cookie that says get it while it's fresh. A cookie that seems baked just for you. A cookie that always tastes like a treat passed across the counter.

Regularly copied, never duplicated, the chocolate chewie became as quintessential a fixture in Savannah life as the Forsyth Park fountain.

Around the same time, Isser began to see the writing on the wall. Savannah's Jewish population had by and large moved to the suburbs and taken two of the three synagogues with them.

If Gottlieb's were to survive, he'd have to stake out territory in the relocated center of commerce—the new Oglethorpe Mall. Other satellites followed.

Isser kept the main store open through the early '90s, even as other retailers abandoned the increasingly dangerous Southside neighborhood. He waited for the promised turnaround:

"'It'll be back, it'll be back,' they kept saying, but it kept going down, down, down."

He pulled the plug on the downtown store in 1992, and with the urban pipeline severed, the company went belly up soon thereafter. Suburban supermarket shoppers didn't need a bakery.

Return of the Chewie

Laurence says that he and Michael talked of reopening the family business when they were both at culinary school at Johnson and

Wales University in Providence, R.I. They found the Northeast stressful rather than exciting, and they missed home.

Laurence believes there were cosmic signs, like the time two years ago he got the urge to call his mother and reached her in the car, moments after a horrific accident. He still can hear Ava screaming, "Isser, wake up! Wake up!" Both were in the hospital for more than a month.

Then again, there was some not-so-subtle pressure. As Ava pointed out, she and Isser had bought a 40-quart Hobart mixer "just in case" the kids decided to reopen the bakery.

When the family announced their plans in late 2003, the Savannah *Morning News* tellingly headlined its coverage with "Return of the Chocolate Chewies." Never mind the paradigm-busting restaurant in the works; there was an off chance the bakery would make a comeback.

A year later, it did, without advertising or advance word, just a note on the door.

In a matter of weeks, Savannah's famous food writer, Damon Lee Fowler, was enthusing in the pages of the *Morning News* that its Danish pastry was "so sumptuously good it almost brought tears to my eyes."

One lady, who arrives in the early morning while the pastry is abundant, does seem a little moist-eyed as she surveys the goods. "I had heard you were back," she says to Isser, not able to rip her eyes away.

What she sees is the immigrant bakery of her childhood—of so many American childhoods. The dense sandwich breads. The cinnamon rolls dripping sticky frosting. The crumbly little spritz cookies that your grandmother set out on gilt-edged plates in the living room. The big cookies you ate straight from their crinkly paper bags.

After the woman comments on the challah, the babka, the rye, she finally makes up her mind and orders a dozen chocolate chewies.

"Anything else?" Isser asks.

She bites her lip and darts her eyes. "I think perhaps I'll take one chocolate chewie to eat now."

Isser hands it across the table, saying, "This one's on me."

Chocolate Chewies

When the Gottlieb family first printed the recipe for their signature chocolate chewies in a self-published 1983 cookbook, they warned home bakers that the cookies wouldn't be exactly the same. Why? "There must be a magic ingredient in the Gottlieb's Bakery air!" the cookbook surmised.

In reality, Laurence Gottlieb says, there is a small proprietary secret not divulged. At the current-day bakery, only he, his brother and his father can mix the batter.

For what it's worth, the cookies from this recipe come mighty close.

HANDS ON: 10 Minutes   TOTAL TIME: About 2 hours

12 ounces powdered sugar

1 ¼ ounces cocoa

2 tablespoons all-purpose flour

3 egg whites

8 ounces chopped pecans

Preheat oven to 350 degrees. Line cookie sheets with parchment paper. Place sugar, cocoa and flour in mixer bowl and beat until well-blended. Beat in egg whites one at a time, scraping bowl as necessary. Beat at high speed for 1 minute. Beat in pecans. Drop by tablespoonsful onto sheets, leaving 2 inches between cookies for spreading. Bake 1 sheet at a time for 15 minutes, turning sheet around halfway through baking time. Remove from oven; cool on paper. Place cookies on paper in freezer; freeze for 1 hour. Remove from freezer; peel paper off cookies. Store in airtight container. These don't keep very long, so eat quickly—as if that's a problem.

Per chewie: 126 calories (percent of calories from fat, 44), 2 grams protein, 17 grams carbohydrates, 1 gram fiber, 7 grams fat (1 gram saturated), no cholesterol, 7 milligrams sodium.

MAKES 2 DOZEN

On the Side

by Rick Nichols

from the *Philadelphia Inquirer*

Inquirer columnist Rick Nichols uses food as a springboard for musing about what gives meaning to our lives. Case in point: this wistful essay about a specialty food supplier at a crossroads.

Dark-eyed Gilda Doganiero offers me her biscotti-maker's hands—"bricklayer's hands," she calls them, the calluses waxy to the touch despite her application, on this particular morning, of olive oil and lemon. Later she will be off to Berwyn on a sales call. But for the moment we are having coffee in the Italian Market, not far from her home, and chewing over what she has decided is her suddenly looming future. She is 33 now, eight years into her one-woman biscotti business and already—if "already" doesn't minimize the grinding years in a back-alley bake shop in Chestnut Hill, hand-mixing and hand-cutting and hand-packing the city's finest biscotti—she is facing the question.

Sooner or later it surfaces on the outer edges of artisanal production—for chocolate-makers who vowed never to freeze their candy (until demand soared), for handwork patissiers seduced by the dough to be made with mechanical extruders. So Gilda Doganiero has poured out her soul on a yellow legal pad, gone through the sorting and visualizing exercises that someone told her they teach at a Wharton short course. Should she keep on keeping on—inching up production of the classic, crackling lemon-fig and chocolate-hazelnut biscotti (no oils, butter, shortening) that have made Gilda's Biscotti the toast of coffee shops across town and local Whole Foods Markets? Or while she's hot, should she spin the wheel, go for investors, do the industrial park thing, bring on staff, do the dance with Williams-Sonoma? Or finally, seeing that she is deep into a serious relationship, should she listen to the various clocks ticking inside and do what Colonel Sanders did: Look for a buyer and, she says, sliding her fingers down a strand of dark hair, "move on to the next chapter in Gilda's life?"

For every move, she sees a check, if not a checkmate. What if she invests in a factory and becomes "exactly what I was trying to compete against?" What if she plugs on and ends up shackled for life to an aging Hobart mixer? Or sells—even in a few years—and finds she has sold off the identity that has come to define her? For others who care for her, the choices are not so murky or painful. Her boyfriend, who is in corporate sales, favors full speed ahead: "He thinks I'm sittin' on a pile of gold." Her friends the high-end coffee roasters told her they'd buy the business—but only if she stays on. ("How do you sell a business that's just you?" she asks.)

Then, before Doganiero finishes her second latte, another quarter is heard from. Emilio Mignucci, who owns DiBruno Bros. cheesery nearby, spots her from the Ninth Street sidewalk, swoops in, and gives her a hug. The choice is a no-brainer, he insists. Doganiero has come too far to falter. Look at Metropolitan Bakery, he says. It has expanded but kept the integrity of its old-world breads. "Systems," he intones. "Time management. Reinvent yourself, not your product." The Mignucci solution? Add new horses to her stable—meringues, individual panettones, amaretto cookies.

Doganiero brightens. Mignucci's scenario is so positive, so relentlessly unconflicted. What biscotti making has done to her hands is on the minus side of the ledger she is keeping on her legal pad. But there is a long plus side, as well—the rush she still gets, for instance, when her biscotti come out of the oven just the right color, their sugary sheen twinkling.

She has "tiptoed up," as she calls it, doubling production, tripling it, then more than quadrupling it until, now, she makes each day the almost 1,000 biscotti she once made in a week. She bills 10 times the

$760 she billed her first month in 1996. She has reclaimed weekends for her own. She has a new love in her life. Her world is changing shape.

"O Sole Mio" rises across the marble cafe tables, soaring full-throated and passionate. Gilda Doganiero is 33 now, and the question is so much larger than biscotti.

When French Women Bake

by Dorie Greenspan
from *Bon Appétit*

Like this year's bestseller *Why French Women Don't Get Fat*, this in-the-know essay by a Paris-based expat reveals the brilliant shortcuts that allow chic Parisiennes to entertain effortlessly.

Here are some of the reasons I think Frenchwomen are worthy of admiration (okay, envy). They can negotiate cobblestone streets in stilettos; get a smile out of snooty waiters in chic cafés; tie scarves without benefit of mirrors or handbooks from either Hermès or the Boy Scouts; and hold down demanding jobs while married with kids and still never be seen tossing out the trash in anything less attractive than Chloe jeans, a little cashmere tee, and just enough Chanel blush to fool anyone into believing they're either fully made-up or healthier-looking than any busy person has the right to seem.

And, they can cook.

In the seven years I've lived in Paris, I've yet to meet a woman who can't cook or who, at the very least, can't talk a good game of food. Even women who say they don't cook much still know the addresses of the best butchers, bakers, and, yes, if not candlestick makers, then makers of candles. For sure, they own a shopping basket and pull it out a couple of times a week when they go to the outdoor market in their neighborhood—even now-and-then cooks must have a regular supply of freshly made goat cheese and a stash of oil-cured olives.

And those women who do cook *really* cook, and cook really often, not just for family because they must, but for friends because they want to. I've never been invited to so many dinner parties, cocktail parties, and Sunday lunches that stretch into dinner (one came dangerously close to ending in time for a midnight snack). Few of these were planned much in advance, many were on "school nights," and all of them were fun, because there was plenty of good food and wine and lively conversation.

How do they do it?

I've spent a lot of time thinking about this and have come to the conclusion that *les Françaises* don't know anything we don't already know. The big difference is, they actually do what we all know is smart: They keep it simple, while we Americans—especially we Americans in Paris working to live up to the culinary standards of our adopted country—are always trying to do just a little more. Particularly when it comes to dessert. And here, I speak from experience.

Let me back up a bit and tell you about the first dinner party I had in my Paris apartment. Call me neurotic, but no sooner had I invited everyone over than I began to feel responsible for producing a dinner that would bring glory to America's reputation for gracious living and measure up to whatever expectations I imagined my French friends had of me as "a food person." *Quel* pressure!

So, I knocked myself out. I had Champagne and piping-hot little homemade cheese puffs to welcome my guests, and I finished, four courses and 18 wineglasses-to-wash later, with a sleek, dark, dark chocolate cake layered with a fresh raspberry and chocolate ganache and topped with an all-chocolate ganache.

In a French meal, the main course is called *le plat de résistance,* and it's meant to be the biggest deal in the lineup. But I was pinning my hopes for hosannas on dessert—and I got a pretty great response, which at a Paris dinner party means a lot of ooh-la-la-ing. I got enough ooh-la-las to mention, as casually as possible, that I'd made the cake myself. You could have knocked me over with a cream puff when the first words out of a friend's mouth were, "Why'd you do it? I mean, it's great, but cakes like this are the reason pastry shops were invented."

There was the key: French women leave fancy restaurant food to fancy restaurants and fancy desserts to the *pâtisseries.*

. . .

Of course. Had I thought back to the desserts I'd been served over the years at French friends' homes, I'd have seen the keep-it-simple rule played to the max. No matter how chic the hostess, her home-made dessert invariably looked as rustic as if it had come from a farmhouse *grand-mère*. And at some point it probably had, since the majority of desserts my friends make are drawn from a repertoire of home-baking recipes that includes standards like rice pudding, tarte Tatin, *quatre-quarts* (the French version of pound cake), chocolate cakes in simple round layers and long loaves, mousses of many flavors, and hundreds more—among them the six recipes here that have become my own keep-it-simple classics.

The recipes are often centuries old, with techniques French women learned from their mothers, who learned them from their mothers, back through generations. In fact, the recipes are so true and so tried, many French women make them without recipes, or *au pif*. (I love the sound of this exression—*oh peef;* literally, it means "by nose," but it's used for stuff you just do, by second nature, feel, or guess work. In cooking, it's often a case of a-little-of-this-and-a-little-of-that.) My first *far Breton,* a custardy prune cake, was made *au pif* by a young French woman staying with us in New York. *Au pif* is also the way lots of seasonal fruit tarts are made and why they are often nothing more than crust, a layer of ground nuts or some crumbled stale cake, and sliced fruit sprinkled with sugar and dotted with bits of butter.

Since it took me years to perfect my own tart crusts, seeing tart after perfectly crusted tart served by endless French hostesses—even those who said they hardly ever cook, let alone bake—just made me even more convinced that my Gallic friends are goddesses. What it should have made me was suspicious! While I was ready to believe that every French woman was born with a scarf gene, I should have been a little less likely to accept that they had a crust gene, too. What they actually have that most of us don't are grocery stores offering cut-to-size, impeccably rolled-out all-butter crusts—*pâte brisée* for quiches, sweet *pâte sablée* for tarts, and puff pastry for everything from savory canapés to those tarte Tatins my friends turn out *au pif*.

In Paris, stores are filled with high-quality ready-to-pretend-they're-your-own products—and French women have no compunctions about using them. Although, just as with fashion, mixing it up is key. Only runway models wear head-to-toe Dior (stylish mortals add something from Gap) and only pros or not-so-very-assured hostesses make everything haute and from scratch.

The really stylish French hostess will mix store-bought with handmade for dessert and do it judiciously and with flair. Like my friend Paule Caillat, who teaches French cooking to Americans visiting Paris, many of my friends make excellent pear tarts, a true classic, using homemade almond cream for the filling and premium canned pears for the fruit; but, unlike Paule, many of my friends never fess up. (Which might explain why French women look so good at the trash bins—they go minutes before their guests arrive, so they can ditch all "incriminating" evidence.)

The same air of mystery can waft around the simplest desserts, the way it seemed to when my dear friend Martine just smiled after I'd complimented her on her chocolate mousse. It was perfect—dark, rich, not so light that it was unsatisfying, not so dense that it was puddingish—so I asked for the recipe. Martine, normally accommodating and always super-efficient, could never seem to get around to giving it to me, though I nagged her for weeks. Finally, she turned it over at the end of a meal at which I, a friend of 30 years, was the only non-family member. She took me aside, handed me a bar of Nestlé chocolate, and told me she used the recipe on the back of the wrapper.

When her cousin heard Martine's admission, she clapped her hands gleefully and said, "I never knew you used that recipe! I use it all the time, but I add grated orange zest to it." Then an aunt piped in and said, "I add coffee—but I thought I was the only one who used that recipe. I didn't know you used it, too." To which Martine replied, "Why would I mention it?"

Add to the growing list of qualities I admire in French women—the fact that they can really keep a secret.

Yogurt Cake with Marmalade Glaze

Like so many homemade French desserts, this pound cake, tenderized with yogurt instead of butter, is utterly simple and versatile. Enjoy a slice for breakfast with a steaming cup of coffee, or serve it after dinner with fruit coulis or whipped cream.

1 ½ cups all-purpose flour
2 teaspoons baking powder
¼ teaspoon salt
1 cup plain whole-milk yogurt
1 cup sugar
3 large eggs
1 teaspoon (packed) finely grated lemon peel
¼ teaspoon vanilla extract
½ cup vegetable oil

¼ cup lemon, orange, or grapefruit marmalade (for glaze)
1 teaspoon water

Position rack in center of oven and preheat to 350°F. Generously butter 8½ × 4½ × 2½-inch metal loaf pan. Sift flour, baking powder, and salt into medium bowl. Combine yogurt, sugar, eggs, lemon peel, and vanilla in large bowl; whisk until well blended. Gradually whisk in dry ingredients. Using rubber spatula, fold in oil. Transfer batter to prepared pan. Place pan on baking sheet.

Place cake on baking sheet in oven and bake until cake begins to pull away from sides of pan and tester inserted into center comes out clean, about 50 minutes. Cool cake in pan on rack 5 minutes. Cut around pan sides to loosen cake. Turn cake out onto rack. Turn cake upright on rack and cool completely. *(Can be made 1 day ahead. Wrap and store at room temperature.)*

Stir marmalade and 1 teaspoon water in small saucepan over medium heat until marmalade melts. Brush hot mixture over top of cake. Let glaze cool and set. Cut cake crosswise into slices.

BAKING TIP: To dress up this cake for a party, bake it in a nine-inch round pan and cut the cake horizontally into two layers. Fill with lemon curd and brush the top of the cake with the marmalade glaze.

8 SERVINGS

—∞∞—

Bittersweet

by Melanie Thernstrom
from *Food & WIne*

When a family jealously guards a favorite recipe, how can an outsider get hold of it? Thernstrom, a *New York Times* reporter with a sideline in food writing, recalls the delicate negotiations involving a certain toffee.

They said no. It was the first thing I'd asked my boyfriend Mark's parents for, and I'd thought of it as a rhetorical request—more a compliment than a question. Surely they wanted to share the special English toffee recipe I had so nicely expressed admiration for? I was spending Christmas at their house in Amherst, Massachusetts, for the first time, and I was anxious to make a good impression. So were they. We all seemed to be succeeding—at least until that moment.

"It's my special thing," Mark's father Bill said. "What would I have without toffee?" he joked—or at least I thought he was joking. But he wasn't.

Besides feeling hurt and confused, I was piqued; I actually wanted the recipe. Toffee draws on two qualities not usually associated with baking triumphs: It is burnt and it is broken. What makes toffee truly memorable is the way the butter and sugar (or maybe just the sugar) have been boiled past the point of pure sweetness. There's a fairy-tale surprise to the first taste of the shattered sugar. It's not bitter, certainly, but it carries the slightest suggestion of wintry darkness, like the walls of the witch's cottage.

Bill's toffee had the perfect triad of textures: a crystalline burnt-sugar base, a coating of creamy semisweet chocolate and a light sprinkling of toasted almonds. Every Christmas my boyfriend's father made dozens of batches and sent them to friends, neighbors, colleagues and co-workers with notes written by his wife, Kathy. A homemade sweet has a touching humility, an old-fashioned quality that's perfect for the Christmas season. "Although I'm a busy professional the rest of the year," it seems to say, "I took this time to cook for you." It's a personal gesture on the part of the giver, but it doesn't require a personal knowledge of the recipient's taste, so it suits both intimates and acquaintances.

When Mark first brought me a tin of his father's toffee, I hid it behind some dusty vases on top of a kitchen cabinet. A great sweet has a hold on me, like the grip of bourbon or unfiltered cigarettes, but nicer—or sweeter, you might say. A longing for a sweet is such an innocent, easily satisfied desire. If you're overcome by temptation, you can tell yourself that you're just going to have a broken, burnt piece—the kind of thing you do with Christmas cookies. Of course, toffee is *all* burnt and broken, but when it's gone, you can always make more. Except in this case I couldn't.

The family had coveted the recipe themselves for a long time before they finally pried it out of their live-in babysitter, Jan, whose mother had given it to her and told her not to spread it around. Friends had asked for the recipe—which they'd adapted and improved—but they had always guarded their secret. Even their close friends had to settle for making Christmas toffee from their own recipe, which everyone knew was not nearly as good. (Their first mistake, Mark said, was using Hershey's chocolate.)

I had some idea of the method: Bill would chat freely about temperature and humidity—how it had to be just the right kind of winter day for making tofee, or else it wouldn't set right when he put the pan outside to cool. But what were the ingredients? I questioned Mark to no avail. Burnt-sugar essence scouted in the Carribean grocery? Lyle's Golden Syrup from England, perfect for gingerbread and who knows what else?

"Mmm," Mark shrugged. "Nothing unusual."

As with so many things, the trick was getting the ordinary things right.

The following May, we visited Mark's parents to celebrate Bill's retirement and announce our engagement. In the gaiety of the moment, I mentioned the secret toffee recipe again, and Bill intimated that after the wedding would be a more appropriate time to bring it up. The wedding was almost a year away. I bit my tongue.

A few nights later, Mark and I were sitting at the kitchen table while his parents tidied up. Tired and talked out, I sipped bourbon and idly flipped through a cookbook from Greenwich, Connecticut, where the family had lived when Mark was a baby.

I love old cookbooks—the way they show how swiftly food culture evolves and improves. Within my lifetime, intelligent women in Greenwich truly believed that cream of mushroom soup was a reasonable base for a homemade dish.

And then I saw it: On two small scraps of paper, tucked between recipes for chipped and boiled beef, were penciled instructions: water, butter, sugar, salt, Nestle chocolate chips . . . The Recipe.

I looked up, smiled at no one in particular, looked back down and memorized the ingredients. I continued to browse through the cookbook, periodically flipping back to the recipe to memorize the steps, which were few and simple. I got up and poured myself another bourbon in celebration.

"I found the recipe," I gloated when we finally went up to bed. "Do you want to hear it?" I recited it over and over against Mark's chest until we fell asleep.

I can't explain why I didn't write it down or think about the effect of alcohol on memory. I couldn't explain it to myself the next day, when, on the train home, I realized I no longer had the details right. Three and a half cups of water and two cups of sugar. Or was it two cups of butter? Water, sugar, butter. Three and a half and two—what?

I looked online, trying to jog my memory. None of the recipes I found seemed right—maybe it was my comeuppance for sneakiness. I'd get the recipe after the wedding, I reassured myself. But, as it happened, there was no wedding. By the following Thanksgiving, the engagement was over.

"I'll still give you the toffee recipe," Mark joked, one of the many sad, sweet jokes we made about all the things we'd still do for each other even though we weren't going to be life partners. But although we have kept our promises—he still edits my writing, and I still lend him my car—I still don't have my recipe.

"Neither do I," he said. He could get it, of course, but he didn't want to go against his parents' wishes. One day, he pledged, when the recipe passed to the next generation, it would be mine.

It seems a long time to wait.

When I e-mailed my best friend, Cynthia, to complain, I expected sympathy. "I agree with Bill," she replied, much to my surprise. "I regret giving away my Christmas biscotti recipe. I wish I'd had the courage to say no!" Cynthia, my most generous friend, never says no to anything. But she didn't find my boyfriend's parents' attitude peculiar; she thought it was prudent.

It isn't easy, she told me, to find "a reliable edible-gift recipe." Cookie-cutter cookies are pretty, but absurdly time-consuming and fraught with pitfalls; the tiny reindeer antlers snap off in the transfer from cookie sheet to rack, she pointed out, or Santa's thin mittens burn before his round tummy is golden.

Biscotti, on the other hand, look difficult to make but aren't. When Cynthia sent out her biscotti in antique Christmas candy tins she collected at flea markets, everyone thought she'd slaved in the kitchen—or possessed superior domestic powers. Or they did until she told everyone how easy it is to make biscotti and offered to show them how. By the next Christmas, biscotti were an obsolete gift. Teach a man to fish, and he won't buy a cow.

Since Cynthia's secret is out, I'm going to pass it on. Her recipe is adapted from the one for Almond Crunch Biscotti in *Biscotti,* Lou Seibert Pappas's delightful little cookbook. For Christmas, Cynthia adds shelled pistachios and dried cranberries, so the biscotti are studded with red and green, then drizzles them with melted white chocolate.

Cynthia used to tuck a handwritten copy of the recipe inside the tin, but you may not want to follow her example. When people ask how you made the biscotti you sent them for the holidays, smile and stay silent. They'll think you can't be serious. They'll try to re-create your recipe and fail. They'll argue that the beauty of a recipe is its communal nature and that refusing to share it is contrary to the Christmas spirit. They'll complain to all your mutual friends. When the gift box arrives next year, they'll taste the treat with a pleasure cut by envy and rich with resentment. But since bittersweet is the most interesting sweet, they'll never tire of it, and you can give it to them forever and ever.

---·∞∞·---

Pistachio-Cranberry Biscotti

ACTIVE: 20 MIN; TOTAL: 1 HR, 30 MIN

This recipe was adapted from Biscotti by Lou Seibert Pappas.

1 cup shelled raw pistachios
2 cups all-purpose flour
1 teaspoon baking powder
¼ teaspoon baking soda
¼ teaspoon salt
1 stick (4 ounces) unsalted butter, softened
¾ cup sugar
2 large eggs
1 teaspoon pure vanilla extract
1 cup dried cranberries
2 ounces white chocolate, melted

1. Preheat the oven to 350°. Spread the pistachios in a pie plate and bake until golden, about 6 minutes, let cool. Turn the oven down to 325°.

2. In a small bowl, whisk the flour, baking powder, baking soda and salt. In a medium bowl, beat the butter with the sugar until light and fluffy. Beat in the eggs, 1 at a time, followed by the vanilla. At low speed, beat in the dry ingredients. With a wooden spoon, stir in the pistachios and cranberries.

3. Butter and flour a large cookie sheet. Pat the dough out on the sheet into two 14-inch-long logs 1 inch wide and 1 inch high, leave 3 inches between them. Bake in the lower third of the oven until golden, about 20 minutes. Transfer the cookie sheet to a rack, let the logs cool for 5 minutes. Using a serrated knife, slice logs on the diagonal ½ inch thick.

4. Bake the slices for 7 minutes on each side. Transfer the biscotti to a rack to cool completely. Drizzle with the melted

white chocolate and refrigerate until set, about 10 minutes.

MAKE AHEAD The biscotti can be kept in an airtight container for 1 week.

MAKES ABOUT 3 DOZEN

The Gentle
Rise of (Real) Cake

by Lisa Yockelson

from *Gastronomica*

A highly skilled baker, Yockelson is a double threat: she not only precisely conveys technique, but also has a poet's sensibility for the transformative magic of what happens in her oven.

An heirloom collection of beat-up baking pans is propped against the back shelving of the open cabinets in my kitchen. Some are imprinted with brand names, such as Calumet ("The World's Greatest Baking Powder Double Acting—Makes Baking Easier"), and others are nameless. I imagine the silky-smooth batters that a progression of home cooks poured into them, which baked up into handsome, fine-grained cakes.

Real cake.

Gently springy, with a melting texture defined by careful measuring and mixing. Turned out of the pans, those buttery, satiny layers offered honest flavor, lingering on cooling racks just long enough before becoming obscured by waves of frosting.

If the recipes from generations of bakers in my family are a valid reference, these cakes consisted of a pivotal ingredient, namely cake flour. In 1896 a certain Addison Igleheart developed and manufactured Swan's Down Cake Flour, and in 1928 he published a booklet to emphasize the product's potential appeal. Entitled *Cake Secrets,* this slender work offered, for ten cents, a taxonomy of cake in all of its basic forms (including tips on cake making and my favorite recipe title, Regulation Butter Cakes). The following sentence appears at the end of the booklet, and it could very well be the mission statement for my own baking ethos: "Cake is not really cake unless it is light, tender, moist, of even-grained texture, and delicate flavor."[1]

Whenever I think of cake, a classic butter cake comes to mind. Not the now-fashionable type of "cake" that flows onto the dessert plate when a fork breaks through it. This alleged cake presents my most beloved flavor, chocolate, in a partly cakey, partly liquid state, usually from a submerged little ball of dark chocolate ganache, which, when baked, turns molten in a batter that bonds around it. When you dig in, the center trickles out like silt from a backed-up storm drain. A cake that leaks its contents is, admittedly, so of the moment, so oddly swank. But it lacks technical finesse. The whole thing is neither properly fudgey like the best brownie nor voluminous and springy like a downy slice of layer cake.

The 1-2-3-4 cake—impressive for its delicacy—is my dictionary definition of real butter cake. Feathery and moist, the batter, which rises gently but purposefully, can be baked in a rectangular pan for a sheet cake or in several layer-cake pans. It forms just the right support for frosting, preferably thick, preferably confectioners' sugar based. (Be advised: a fancy French butter cream would be lost in this setting.)

One of the recipes I inherited for the cake calls for 3 cups sifted cake flour, 2 cups fine sugar (superfine in today's baking language), 4 eggs, and 1 cup milk.[2] This rundown accounts for all of the numbers in the title. The batter is put together in the traditional way, by creaming the butter until pearly and softened, incorporating the sugar by degrees and beating well after each addition, adding the whole eggs or yolks alone, and integrating the flour, sifted with baking powder and salt, alternately with the milk. If the eggs are separated, the whites are folded into the batter at the end of the mixing process. An indulgent pour of vanilla extract, along with the butter, becomes the primary flavoring agent. What you spoon from the

---

1. Francis Lee Barton, *Cake Secrets* (Evansville, IN: Igleheart Brothers, Inc., 1928), 49. Regulation Butter Cakes appeared in an earlier, 1925 version of *Cake Secrets* by Mary Jean Hart, director of the Domestic Science Department at Igleheart Brothers.
2. Numerous versions of this recipe exist with variations centering on the type of flour and amount of leavening and vanilla extract.

mixing bowl is a luminous mixture, buoyant as can be, already revealing in its unbaked form the guarantee of something fine grained and light.

When I want to recall the past in a sentimental way, realign myself after cooking some pretty complicated things, or please a band of sweet-starved friends, I take out a set of mismatched cake pans belonging to my late mother or a rectangular baking pan that's worn from my own life's work of baking. (Both boast slick interior patinas that only time and a particular amount of babying can guarantee.) I assemble the ingredients for the vanilla cake, leaving the butter to soften and the milk and eggs to ease out of their chilled state and then put together the batter. It spoons into the pan in cloudlike swells. I smooth over the top with a few quick strokes of a spatula. The individual layers that emerge from the oven are like soft, springy pillows, the sheet cake a nice plump cushion. I wait—impatiently—for the layers to cool in order to swirl a frosting between and about the individual layers or over the surface of the sheet cake.

Drawn to the barely set elements of cake and frosting, I then commit an act that is anathema to what I instruct (read: preach) in my baking recipes: "Let the cake stand for one hour before slicing and serving." Cake as authentic as this entices with its texture and teases all those tasty emotions that lurk within. My childlike impulses surface, and I cut a still-warm slice.

High-flying pastry chefs take note: you can have your confections that dribble, seep, and trickle. I'll take the light bounce, the silkiness, the utterly dissolving quality of genuine cake.

Essence of Vanilla Cake with Chocolate Frosting

Variations of this cake abound, using all-purpose flour or cake flour, fluctuating amounts of baking powder, salt, and vanilla extract, and eggs in whole or separated form. This version is designed for baking in one large single layer. It profits texturally from folding in beaten egg whites and reducing the baking powder from the typical 1-tablespoon amount. For the silkiest weave to the internal crumb of the cake, be sure to use the freshest baking powder, beat the egg whites until just firm rather than rigid, and take care not to overbake the cake. The frosting is creamy and softly accented with chocolate, appealing to both children and adults. For a more complex chocolate flavor, omit the bittersweet chocolate and use 6 ounces unsweetened chocolate.

Softened unsalted butter and all-purpose flour, for the baking
    pan

Vanilla Cake Batter

3 cups sifted cake flour
2 ¼ teaspoons baking powder
½ teaspoon salt, preferably very-fine sea salt
½ pound (16 tablespoons or 2 sticks) unsalted butter, softened
2 cups superfine sugar
Seeds from 1 plump vanilla bean, cut lengthwise and scraped
    clean
4 large eggs, separated
1 cup milk
2 ¼ teaspoons vanilla extract
¼ teaspoon cream of tartar

Luxurious Chocolate Frosting

12 tablespoons (1 ½ sticks) unsalted butter, softened
large pinch of salt, preferably very-fine sea salt
4 ounces unsweetened chocolate, melted and cooled to tepid
2 ounces bittersweet chocolate, melted and cooled to tepid
4 cups confectioners' sugar, plus more as needed
⅓ cup heavy cream combined with 2 tablespoons milk,
    warmed to tepid
3 teaspoons vanilla extract

For the cake batter preheat the oven to 350°F. Prepare a 13 × 9 × 2 inch baking pan by filming the inside with softened butter. Sprinkle a haze of flour over it and tap the pan from side to side to lightly cost the buttons and sides. Thoroughly tap out the excess flour and set the pan aside.

Resift the cake flour with the baking powder and salt onto

a sheet of waxed paper.

Cream the butter in the large bowl of a freestanding electric mixer on moderate speed for 4 to 5 minutes. Add the sugar in 4 additions, heating for 1 minute after each portion is added. Mix in the vanilla bean seeds and 2 egg yolks, beat for 30 seconds, and then add the remaining yolks and heat for 20 seconds longer. Scrape down the sides of the mixing bowl with a rubber spatula to keep the batter even textured.

On low speed alternately add the sifted mixture in 3 additions with the milk in 2 additions, beginning and ending with the sifted mixture. Scrape down the sides of the mixing bowl often. Blend in the vanilla extract.

In a clean dry bowl beat the egg whites until just beginning to mound. Add the cream of tartar and beat until firm and moist (but not stiff) peaks are formed. Stir about one-quarter of the beaten whites into the cake batter and then fold through the remaining whites. Keep the mixture light, but do take care to engage any and all little humps of unbeaten whites into the batter.

Spoon the batter into the prepared baking pan, leveling it lightly to all sides and into the corners. Gingerly sweep over the top to even the surface. Do not linger over the batter any longer than it takes to fill the baking pan and smooth the batter.

Bake the cake in the preheated oven for 40 minutes, or until golden on top, risen, and a wooden pick inserted 1 to 2 inches from the center withdraws clean or with a few stray crumbs attached. Here and there the cake will pull away ever so slightly from the sides of the pan. Cool the cake in the pan on a rack.

For the frosting beat the butter in the large bowl of a freestanding electric mixer on moderate speed for 3 to 4 minutes. Blend in the melted unsweetened chocolate, melted bittersweet chocolate, and 2 cups of confectioners' sugar. Blend in the heavy cream and milk mixture. (In cold, dry weather the frosting may require beating in an extra 1 or 2 tablespoons of milk to arrive at a creamy texture.) Scrape down the sides of the mixing bowl. Add the remaining 2 cups confectioners' sugar and vanilla extract. Beat for 2 minutes on moderate speed to blend. Scrape down the sides of the mixing bowl. Beat on high speed for 3 to 5 minutes longer, or until quite smooth and creamy. On a damp day or in a humid or warm kitchen, it may be necessary to beat in up to 6 more tablespoons of confectioners' sugar to bind the frosting.) Use the frosting immediately. If the frosting stands for any length of time, it will turn spongy; to restore it add 2 additional tablespoons of confectioners' sugar and reheat slowly.

To frost the cake spoon dollops of frosting onto the surface and then spread it from side to side. Lightly swirl the frosting, using a flexible palette knife. Let the frosting firm up for 1 hour before cutting into squares for serving. Serve the cake very fresh.

Drinking Again

Bitter Alchemy

by Deirdre Heekin

from *Gastronomica*

The elaborate months-long process of creating a home-made liqueur became a quest for Heekin; what she writes about it is not just a recipe, but a distillation of poetry in a bottle.

This is a Sicilian recipe, they say. Gather roses in perfect bloom during the hottest hours of a June day when their perfume is at their headiest. They say, pluck the roses and separate the petals from the flower. Trim the white moons from the base of the petals; these will be too bitter. They being those who knew, Sicilians recording a family recipe at the end of the nineteenth century. Steep the rose petals in a grain or fruit alcohol for a fortnight with a vanilla bean. Prepare a simple syrup of sugar melted in water on the stove. At two weeks strain the liqueur and remove the rose petals and vanilla bean. Add the simple syrup. Set aside in a dark corner of your pantry for another fortnight. Filter and bottle. Serve after a good meal. The drink will be quite strong, but quite nice, they say.

This recipe is for *rosolio,* a sweet yet bitter liqueur once enjoyed by young ladies and grandmothers in the nineteenth century and in *mangia e be' i* (eat 'n' drink), light beignets filled with *rosolio* and sold at country fairs one hundred, two hundred, three hundred years ago. *Rosolio* is still had after a lengthy meal or late in the afternoon or before going to bed. This particular recipe was found in the musty pages of an old cookbook in a dark, narrow used bookstore in Spaccanapoli, the old center of Naples, where the cookbooks were sandwiched between Italian Victorian erotica and a stand for old postmarked postcards. I wrote the recipe down in a little notebook, and chose two postcards, yellowed watercolors of towns in Campania with faded spidery ink on the backs, "sunny and warm, with much love— . . ."

So many months later, in Vermont, it is now late August. I should have been gathering my roses in July when our roses are at their fullest and most obscene, but I have had difficulty procuring the grain alcohol. I've been trying since July, but my local liquor store does not stock grain alcohol, a 190-proof distillation most widely used in this country for college parties where the hosts mix garbage cans full of fruit juice and Everclear (the trade name of a certain grain alcohol) and the guests drink the cocktail like water. Grain alcohol has very little flavor when mixed with other things, making it easy to go down, easy to forget you're drinking a cocktail, easy to get drunk. If you drink too much too fast, it can kill you. An adaptation of my recipe tells me I can use vodka if I'm unable to get the grain alcohol, but I've had *limoncello,* another Italian after-dinner cordial, made with vodka, and the taste is all wrong, the vodka imparting too much vodka despite its generally clean flavor.

So I wait for my three bottles of grain alcohol to arrive at the local state liquor store, a special order I have to discuss with the owner. He knows I'm well over twenty-one, and I've explained to him my plans. No garbage-can parties for me. I'm playing at alchemist. I'm making *amaro.* I'm making *rosolio.*

Amaro, which means "bitter" in Italian, is a kind of after-dinner cordial, a *digestivo.* Like a good espresso it settles a good meal. *Amaro* is particular to Italy, and *rosolio* is particular to Sicily and Calabria. Each region in Italy has its own style and recipe, and these *digestivi* can be made from herbs or walnuts or roses or lemons. They have antique, floral-sounding names or monikers said with an almost-religious fervor: *Amaro Lucano, Ramazotti, Rosolio, Vecchio Amaro del Capo, Jannamaro, Padre Peppe.*

I go to pick up my order two weeks later, and no one can find my three bottles of grain alcohol in the stockroom. I wonder about the young clerk, and summer parties, and place the order again. A few weeks later my husband picks up my order for me, but the young gentleman working, his skin still pocked with high-school acne, will only let him take one bottle at a time. Maybe if the manager was here, he could take all three, but the young gentleman doesn't want to take any chances. My husband, who is also well over twenty-one, gets carded frequently.

At the end of August, I am picking the last of my rose blossoms during the hottest point during my day, peeling the petals away from the flower, and trimming those white bitter moons. I'm preparing my concoction on the dining-room table that my husband and I made six years ago on Thanksgiving Day before friends arrived to feast. I'm wondering how I got here, at the end of August, picking the last of my roses, obsessed like a perfumer to pick the most fragrant, most luscious, most velvety of roses—one and three-quarters ounces of them, to be exact. After I have trimmed their pale crescents, I stuff them with a chopstick down the neck of a bottle of grain alcohol. Yes, I have to ask myself, how did I arrive here?

I arrived at this bit of alchemist's pleasure on circuitous roads, all of them stemming from Italy, a place with which I have long had a love affair. I have written this before, and I'll write it again: Twelve years ago, my husband and I flew on one-way tickets the day after our wedding for what became a year-long honeymoon in Italy. For twelve years now I've been living, learning, cooking, leaving, and returning from and to Italy. Each time I return, which is now once a year, I fall down another floor of her culture.

When my husband and I first lived in Italy, we were introduced to *vin santo,* holy wine, the traditional Tuscan after-dinner drink served with *cantucci,* those little almond biscotti that are dipped into the thick, mead-like wine. From there we became enamored of *grappa,* the Italian *eau de vie. Grappa,* a distillation made from grape skins, can be either sublime, smooth, and scented of saddle leather or rough and tasting like lighter fluid. We became collectors of *grappa,* fascinated and infatuated with the shapes of their bottles and the out-of-the-way vineyards that took the effort to make them. From here we made the leap to *amaro.*

Although we had always been curious at those brightly labeled bottles we saw on café bar shelves, as well as the old gentlemen in their tweed jackets and squire's caps standing at the bar with their heavy, elegantly shaped, and tall shot glasses of dark liquid, it wasn't until we traveled south that we were introduced to the father of all *amari* in the hauntingly beautiful cave city of Matera.

In the deep heart of Basilicata, the anklebone of Italy, Matera beckons. Once a condemned, impoverished city, once called Italy's shame for its inhabited malarial caves, Matera is, has always been, noble. Now, the city has been energized with the *Materese* pride; it is thriving and in a constant state of rebuilding. Our hosts there sent us out on an unusually foggy night to a little place serving some of the best of the local food. It was here, at the Trattoria Lucana, that we became members of the transformed. At Trattoria Lucana the lights were warm and bright, and the room was noisy. The tables were full. The walls were lined with black-and-white images of *Materese* sitting in front of their cave doors, photos from the fifties, and before. These are the non-Christians Carlo Levi once wrote about in his book *Christ Stopped at Eboli,* the ones UNESCO removed from their caves in 1956.

After a brief conversation with our waiter, Enzo, we decided to ask him to order for us. He is a consummate professional, wearing a white shirt, black bow tie, and a red vest. He poured us Aglianico, the kingly grape of the south, dry, big, elegant, and less than ten American dollars. Then the food started to arrive.

In order to tell you about the *amaro,* I must tell you about the food, as *amaro* almost always follows the food and its power lies as the final note to the orchestration of a meal.

At least nine dishes of antipasti came to the table. We ate fresh *ricotta* and *sformate,* wedges of egg and herb or rice tart. Enzo delivered plates of little fried things: slices of eggplant, zucchini, olives, and roasted red peppers, the edges of the slices black with roasting.

Then there were *orecchiette,* little handmade ears of pasta, tossed with braised *cima di rapa* and seasoned with hot *peperoncino.* We ate simple roasted meats: lamb, beef, chicken, sausage flavored with only salt, pepper, olive oil, and wood smoke. Then *dolci,* but I don't remember exactly about the dessert. I do remember the richness of this table. I have come to understand that, when I'm in Italy, true wealth is in the food of the poor.

Enzo asked if we wanted espresso to finish, or *amaro.* Because we like a good adventure, we chose *amaro,* but there was a further question from Enzo: "Fernet-Branca, or Padre Peppe?"

Fernet-Branca is a ubiquitous national brand. We didn't know Padre Peppe. Our momentary silence as we tried to make a decision was all Enzo needed. "Padre Peppe it is then."

This Padre Peppe is made by Franciscan monks in the plains of Altamura, only forty kilometers from Matera. It is an elixir of walnuts, so the label says. It is hot and sweet and medicinal and goes down with ease. We experienced a conversion, a glow of warmth radiating from our windpipes and stomachs.

Amaro, or drinks like *amaro,* have been made for a long time. Their origins include the practice within convents and monasteries of steeping herbs in alcohol, usually wine, as a means of preserving the medicinal properties of the herbs, as growing seasons can be short and winters long, especially in the many mountainous places to which religious orders had fled to practice their faith undisturbed.

Among some of the earliest writings on the subject of flavored alcohols are those found in the journals of Catalan Arnold de Vila Nova, an alchemist in Spain and France who was born in 1240. He wrote in his *The Book of Wine* of the distillation of wine into *aqua vitae* and the flavoring of those spirits with various herbs, fruits, and spices. In particular, de Vila Nova wrote of *aqua vitae*'s healing and restorative powers. It was even believed by one of de Vila Nova's students, a certain Raymond Lully, that these flavored *aqua vitae* were so powerful and vital that their crafting was an inspired gift from Heaven.

During the Middle Ages these distillations were primarily known as alchemical potions and made only among alchemists, especially those belonging to religious orders. It wasn't until a much later date that they were enjoyed as secular drinks. By the fourteenth century these drinks had become popular cordials in Italy and France, a popularity often attributed to the court of Catherine de'Medici, the Italian aristo who married into French royalty. It is said she brought the recipes and use of these liqueurs to France from her native Tuscany. But there is also some evidence of an earlier diffusion of this type of drink or an independent outgrowth of these distillations prior to their introduction by Catherine. There is no doubt, however, that the Medici court, so focused on food and the pleasures of the table, increased the interest in these *amari* among the nobility of France.

Between the fourteenth century and the early seventeenth century, monastic orders and village alchemists became the primary producers of *amari*. In the Abbey of Fecamp, around 1510, Don Bernardo Benedictine created the drink called Benedictine. The recipe for Chartreuse was originally called an *Elixir de Longue Vie* (an elixir of long life), given to a Carthusian monastery near Paris by the Maréchal d'Estrées, a captain under Henri IV, husband to Catherine de'Medici. Cusenir Mazarine, a French anise liqueur, dates to a 1637 recipe from the Abbaye de Montbenoit. Recipes, too, for herbal liqueurs like the Pugliese Padre Peppe were also originally monastic in origin. But it would be a mistake to claim that all production of liqueurs was limited to monasteries and convents. By the middle of the sixteenth century, several secular distilleries throughout Europe had been formed and were producing commercial quantities of *amari* and cordials. These included the Dutch distillery of Bols, founded in 1575, and Der Lachs, a German distillery that began producing Danzig Goldwasser in 1598. The first liqueur that Bols turned out was made from anise collected wild in the fields.

Commercially prepared and sold *amaro* didn't make its appearance in Italy until the mid- to late 1800s, Fernet-Branca began producing its line of cordials in 1875; Padre Peppe, in 1835. Prior to that, *amaro* was a home brew. Fortunately, it still is.

The word liqueur comes from the Latin *liquefacere,* to "melt" or "dissolve," and refers to the method used to flavor whiskies, brandies, and grain alcohols to make the base of any liqueur. And there are several ways to *liquefacere:* maceration, distillation, and percolation. The end result of any of these methods is the same, not unlike the process of making a perfume: the flavor/scent of the fruit, spice, or herb is dissolved into the alcoholic base. The choice of method depends on the properties of the fruit, spice, or herb, as well as the particular flavor desired in the final liqueur. Some additives will flavor differently, depending on which process is followed.

For the home cook maceration is the most typical process and the most simple. The aromatic flavoring, be it rose petals, lavender, violet, cherries, or strawberries, is bruised and then steeped in the alcohol for a period of time in order to extract the essence from it. Then this essence is added to the final base of the liqueur.

Distillation refers to the distillation of the desired flavor that has already been macerated. The process is often repeated several times to reduce the flavor to its essence, after which it is added to the bulk of the alcoholic base. In percolation either water or alcohol is allowed to drip through the flavor ingredient, or else it's heated, and the steam of the alcohol or water passes through the flavor before it recondenses. Simple maceration is just right for a juicy fruit. Liqueurs using citrus obtain the flavor not from the juice, however, but from the oil in the skins, and this is usually done through percolation.

When using different methods, different flavors can be extracted from the same source. In many spice-flavored liqueurs a more bitter or astringent flavor will result if an alcoholic base, rather than water, is used in percolation. Depending on the taste and the taste of liqueur desired, the process and base liquid should be carefully considered.

Once any of these three processes has been used, the remaining steps in production tend to be the same: mix the final blend of the aromatized base and, if necessary, age. Or mix the blend and add any desired sugar and/or water, followed by a generally short period of aging to allow the marriage of aromatics to alcohol. Then there is coloration, cold stabilizing, and finally bottling. In the fourteenth century coloration and cold stabilization would not have been considered in the same way we do now. These are modern inventions for large commercial products. When you make an *amaro* at home, you don't need to worry about altering the color or providing cold stabilization. Leave it to nature and alchemy, and follow in the footsteps of medieval alchemists, or monks, or baroque royal chefs.

This is what I like about making something that has existed for hundreds of years: I taste history. This is why my husband and I have collected *vin santi, grappe, eau de vie,* and now, ever since Enzo introduced us to the pleasures and varieties of Italian regional *digestivi, amari.* It is why, when in Italy, we walk into little wine shops and groceries and ask the *padrona* about the local brew. This is why we follow directions to out-of-the-way *osterie,* country cafés, to eat and then partake of the *rosolio* table, a tasting of five different *rosolii* prepared by the kitchen, liqueurs made with coffee beans or violets or rose petals or nuts and anise or a mixture of saffron and spices.

I have the great bonus of a rose garden. Along a stone wall to the south of the house is a hedge of mixed roses, here long before we bought the property, planted, I'm told, by the elderly lady who originally built our house and had a fantastic rose and wildflower garden. The owners between her and us destroyed much of her efforts through blindsightedness and neglect, and I work hard to resurrect the few things that are left. I've tried to classify her roses, looking in gardening books, asking knowledgeable friends. No one really knows what they are, except for a local man whose family has been here since the French and Indian War. He tells me that the pink roses with six petals and the yellow center are seaside roses brought to our mountain by a transplant. She transplanted not only herself but also a part of the place from where she came, and these roses do give our open field and wide-view landscape a decidedly seaside look. On a moonlit summer night, walking home from the neighbor's house, the wind in the trees sounds a lot like the ocean.

My old lady's roses inspired me. I have many others in a more formalized garden: Seafoam, Mother's Day, Madame de Bourbon, and Gene Bruner. This is the mixture of roses that I use to make my concoction, my *rosolio, ros solis,* "sun's dew" in Latin. I pick at high noon just like my old recipe says. I've got my bottle of Graves grain alcohol, and I've trimmed the white moons from the petals and stuffed the rose petals down the neck of the bottle with a chopstick, as I don't have a jar with a lid and mouth big enough to do it any other way. I wait. Two weeks later, I make my simple syrup. I strain the pale, now colorless petals, fragile like a moth's wings. I remove the vanilla bean. I add the simple syrup and set the jar aside again. I wait.

It is a cold, rainy October day when we first taste the *rosolio.* The rain falls horizontally, and the National Weather Service has issued a High Winds Alert. We are in the middle of a house renovation, and because the roof is off, with only our cedar ceiling and a large tarp between us and the elements, leaks have sprouted around the windows and in certain places in the roof. There's no reason this should be happening—the house has been amply protected from weather—except that the wind is so strong, it blows its way behind the window trim and insinuates itself beneath our roof tarp.

The bottoms of the windows and French doors are lined with plastic and newspaper. A few plastic buckets are positioned throughout the house to catch steady drips. We've finished eating a lunch of grilled ham and cheese sandwiches and leek soup I made from the last of the leeks I pulled from the garden yesterday. A plebian lunch that we decide needs an elegant finish. We get out our cut-crystal decanter and Georgian sherry glasses, petite stemmed glasses with a fluted bowl that I found in a junk shop north of here. We pour ceremoniously, the color of the *rosolio* a pale, almost tea-stained hue in our glasses. The scent is intense and alcoholic. I am pleased and surprised that the taste is multilayered, essence of rose, almost like a perfume, then the vanilla and sweet behind that, with a fiery finish. I feel it in my throat and down my windpipe. The recipe did say it would be strong, and the recipe is also right in that it is nice. My husband and I discuss possible refinements: Can I cut the fervent alcohol taste? Can I tame it just a little? We decide that tomorrow I will make another simple syrup of a half cup of sugar dissolved in a cup of water and add that to my brew to see if it softens the brawny structure.

That night we dine at a friend's house. In their dining room on a side table are jars full of *liqueur rouge,* a southern-French style of *rosolio* made of brandy, raspberries, red currants, and cherries. They made this batch of liqueur in July when they, in great fortune, found cherries, red currants, and raspberries ripe and available all at the same time. After forty days of maceration, they add their simple syrup to taste. They've been making *liqueur rouge* for years after trying their hand at an old southern family recipe of peaches steeped in bourbon and sugar, started in July when the peaches are in season in Maryland and ready by Thanksgiving.

We taste their *liqueur rouge* after a dinner of Cambodian curry flavored with peanuts, coconut milk, basil, cilantro, mint, and a hot-pepper fish sauce. The *digestif* is red in color, but clear, like a cranberry juice, and I taste all three elements of the fruit, the raspberry and currant the strongest. It is slightly sweet, and our host tells me this bottle may have had a cinnamon stick added. We compare recipes and tastes and talk of an orange liqueur made with a handful of coriander seed, and I think if I start now, it would be ready by Christmas.

This is why I've spent the last four months preparing my *rosolio,* why I carefully cut the white moons off my rose petals before steeping them in pure alcohol: this is part of my philosophy of taste. Taste is connected to history, the history of the table, which is, after all, a narrative history, an oral history. The tongue experiences, the mouth tells a story. At the table we share these stories. My husband and I, alone in our leaking house, tasting and reminiscing about the *rosolio* tasted in the mountains of Calabria, at our friends' table talking of the myriad versions of after-dinner liqueur and how our stashes will get us through the fall and the long, cold Vermont winter. I remember the generosity of other hosts, new and old friends in Italy, plying us with their regional, or family, concoction. I remember an Easter dinner at the seaside near Rome where we stayed up late and tasted *nocino,* a green walnut liqueur, *limoncello,* and a home brew so potent, made by the caretaker of our host's Rome apartment building, that it defies explanation. I wrote the recipes on the back of a paper napkin.

Yes, this is why I do this. To experience, to connect, to make two things at once, a recipe and a story, both shared at the table.

Recipe for Rosolio

Pick roses at the hottest point of the day, red roses, if possible, as they will impart more color and flavor to the alcohol. If you do not have your own rose garden, I recommend procuring your roses from a friend or a local grower so that you can be certain that the roses have not been treated with any chemicals. Separate the petals from the flower. Trim the white edge at the base with a knife or scissors. Weigh out 1¾ ounces of petals, and then steep the petals and a vanilla bean in a large canning jar filled with 190-proof (95 percent) pure grain alcohol. Close the jar and set aside in a dark place for two weeks. At two weeks strain the liquid and remove the rose petals and vanilla bean. Prepare a simple syrup from a pound of sugar and 3¼ cups of water. Add the simple syrup to the alcohol and return the mixture to the jar. Store for another two weeks. At the end of those two weeks, filter and bottle. After your first tasting more simple syrup can be added to suit your taste.

Big and Beautiful: Lafite for 12

by Eric Asimov
from the *New York Times*

For those of us who may never have the chance to taste a really valuable wine, there's vicarious pleasure in joining *Times* wine and restaurant reviewer Eric Asimov as he and a group of fellow gourmands do justice to a special vintage.

N ot just any bottle of wine can compel eight people to fly thousands of miles to drink it. But this was not just any bottle. When my friend Jason's father died last summer, he left behind what seemed to be the predictable assortment of possessions: his Seattle apartment, a beat-up old car, books and papers. But Jason's father also kept wine in an air-conditioned closet in his un-air-conditioned home. When Jason, a wine lover himself, pored over the bottles, he found one huge surprise: an impériale of 1986 Château Lafite-Rothschild.

Really, you don't just find an impériale. It grips you the way the view of Mount Rainier strikes people here on a clear day.

An impériale is as big as it gets in Bordeaux, big enough to hold six liters of wine, the equivalent of eight ordinary bottles. And Lafite is no ordinary wine. It's one of the great wines of Bordeaux and of the world, and 1986 was an exceptional vintage. Stumbling over an impériale is a free trip to wine heaven, with a first-class upgrade. It just does not happen, except that it did.

Like taxes on a lottery prize, any treasure carries hardships. An impériale cannot be doled out a bit at a time, like eight bottles. To uncork an impériale is to open eight bottles at once. It requires appreciative mouths and plenty of planning. It also requires courage.

Anyone who has ever owned a wine the caliber of an '86 Lafite will appreciate the agony involved in choosing just the right time to open a bottle. Is it too soon or, God forbid, too late? Is the occasion worthy enough of such a wine? It's one thing for a rich collector to break out a bottle, just for kicks. But for wine lovers of modest budgets, who may taste a world-class bottle once or twice in a lifetime, it's a momentous decision.

Fortunately, Jason and his wife, Lisa, who live in New York City, were not stymied by the big bottle burden. They proposed a dinner party at Jason's mother's house in Tacoma, practically on the shore of Puget Sound, where the bottle had been stored in the cellar. The guests would prepare and serve a dinner that would flatter the Lafite. They would toast Jason's father, and celebrate friends and family with a bottle that they hoped would be spectacular.

And so seven people from New York and one from Washington flew to Tacoma on Columbus Day weekend to share a bottle of wine with Jason's mother, his brother and two more friends from the Seattle area. Twelve people seemed just the right number to do justice to the Lafite.

Three days before we arrived Jason's mother, Patty, had the bottle brought up to her kitchen from her cellar. A remnant of purple tissue paper clung to the label, resembling a broad stain, or perhaps a mark of distinction. This was, after all, one of only 400 impériales produced by Lafite in 1986, and the chateau typically keeps 50 to 100 of them for its own use. By some estimates this impériale might be worth $5,000 now.

The bottle was placed upright in a cool, dark spot and left to settle, an important detail when dealing with an older Bordeaux. Wines like the Lafite, made primarily from cabernet sauvignon, produce sediment as they age. Drinking a wine full of sediment is like getting a mouthful of fine coffee grounds, not at all pleasant. When the bottle was standing upright, the sediment would settle to the bottom, where it would remain after the wine was decanted.

The wine needed to be decanted not only to leave the sediment behind, but because it was so young. An ordinary bottle of '86 Lafite would just about be rounding into shape now. But the bigger the bottle, the less the wine inside is exposed to air, and the slower the wine ages. Decanting it would aerate the wine, softening the still-young tannins and allowing the flavors to open up. A bottle this big would need quite a bit of air. We decided to decant the wine six hours or so before we drank it.

But where do you put six liters of wine? We scoured the cabinets for carafes, pitchers and flagons, managing to assemble a motley assortment of vessels that would do the job. The moment of truth had arrived.

Nothing about an impériale isn't big. The cork was practically as wide as a gas cap and presented a daunting challenge to the typical waiter's corkscrew. Jason pulled gradually at the cork, pausing to wipe the rim. Finally, with a soft pop, it emerged and the bottle was open. Slowly, he poured the wine into the decanters. Gritty sediment clung to the interior of one side of the bottle, on which it had been resting all these years.

As the wine flowed, I tried to banish my fears. Had we opened the bottle at the right time? Had it aged enough, or were we killing a baby? There was no going back now.

We poured one glass. I was struck by its elegant aroma, and relieved that the bottle was not corked. It was beautiful, though very young, with a smell almost like grape juice mixed with the cedar scent typical of a fine Pauillac. We shared a quick taste and could sense the depth and intensity of the wine, but the flavors were locked away in a vault of tannins. Would six hours of air be enough?

As Lisa and another friend, Rafael, spent the late afternoon in the kitchen preparing dinner. Anticipation built. The Lafite required a dramatic buildup, and so we started with duck terrine and Champagne as the final touches were put on the dinner. Then we began the meal in earnest.

First came a plate of scallop dishes: piquillo pepper stuffed with scallop, shallot and chorizo; scallop ravioli topped with a butternut squash purée, and a sliced, seared scallop with duck magret, superb with a pure, crystalline 2002 Pouilly-Fumé from Didier Dagueneau. Then tagliatelle in a cream sauce with truffle shavings, rich but delicate and delicious with a rough, fragrant 2001 St.-Joseph from Rochecourbe.

Then finally the main course, roasted lamb with garlic and rosemary, with figs, potatoes and onions, and haricots verts. The Lafite was poured into big goblets, leaving plenty of room for the fragrance to rise.

The wine had evolved beautifully in the seven hours since we opened the bottle. The grape juice quality was gone, but the elegance was all there: intensity and concentration combined with a light, velvety texture, the hallmark of great French wine. It was still a little closed and tannic, but the lamb smoothed out the tannins, leaving the seductive core of the wine in all its glory. The flavors seemed to last forever.

With the luxury of plenty, we savored each mouthful, paying attention to nuances even after the food was finished. Plates pushed away, last crumbs of cheese consumed, we realized we had finished only four of the seven pitchers of Lafite. Perhaps we overdid the buildup. Still there was another night. Given how young the wine seemed, even at dinner, we decided to leave the uncovered pitchers of wine on the cool kitchen counter, exposed to the air.

The next night, encore du vin. We poured it with grilled steak, and darned if it hadn't gotten even better. The tannins were softer, the fruit was clear and sedate and the cedar scent had developed into a complex tobaccolike flavor. Rafael said he had tasted all these elements individually in one Bordeaux or another, but never all together in one wine. The Lafite still seemed young, though, and we debated when this wine would hit its peak. Ten years? Twenty? Properly stored, we decided, this is a hundred-year bottle, perfect for celebrating the turn of the next century.

But could there have been a better time for this bottle than this Columbus Day weekend? We were friends and family, drawn from different parts of the country by the novel allure of this huge bottle. We were healthy and happy in one another's company. We drank to Jason's father, we drank to our friends and families, and we drank to ourselves. This is the point of a great wine. It was the perfect time to drink it.

An Ode to Hangover Cures

by George Singleton
from *The Oxford American*

From this Mississippi-based magazine's rousing special issue on Southern food, South Carolinian Singleton—author of a novel titled *Novel*—gives us this wry take on morning-after remedies.

Hangover theorists—evidently there are but a few profession-ally, but a whole crash of them working nonstop on an ama-teur basis—don't talk much about congeners and cytokines, at least not publicly. But anyone who has ever ingested more than 1.5 ounces of good bourbon per hour knows that he or she will suffer the classic symptoms right about daybreak: inflammation of the head, queasy stomach, and slight tremulousness. Personally, I don't get that 1.5 ounces per hour quota. Did a scientist make a typo? Did Dr. Moderation really mean 5.1 ounces per hour?

Here in South Carolina, where the hangovers come quickly and often, the cures are mind-numbing and questionable. Every good booze glutton has probably tried the standbys: two gallons of water, enough Goody's Powder sleeves to construct a life-size origami swan, Krystal hamburgers, hair of the dog, and a slew of over-the-counter, sure-fire remedies usually sold next to condoms, batteries, playing cards, and scratch tickets at the local convenience store.

What I suggest may only work for me, but it works. Without trudging through a stream of techno-medical babble involving dilated blood vessels and acetaldehyde, let me leave you with these words: embrace the endorphin-inducing hot peppers.

In the past—yeah, yeah, yeah, I just went through rehab, so trust me that I'm clearheaded and slightly rational on the following recipe—I started many a day with what I called Poor Man's Pâté Surprise. I minced a can of Vienna sausages as fine as possible (a blender would work best, but remember, the damn noise could kill you) and threw them into a blue-speckled, enamelware mixing bowl. Then, recklessly and without rubber gloves, I minced one medium jalapeño and one orange habanero, then threw them on top of the Viennas, seeds and all. During particularly vile, rabid, tenacious hangovers, I always hoped that the pepper seeds would lodge in my intestinal tract, cause diverticulitis, and kill me.

Then I added about two tablespoons of mayo, two squirts of yellow mustard, and a couple teaspoons of sweet-pickle relish. I hand-whipped the concoction with a wooden spoon and served it atop saltine crackers, or between two slices of white Sunbeam bread. I never officially recorded the outcome, but it seemed as if my hands would start burning uncontrollably about the same time that I could see again through the tears. Granted, my hangover remedy might be on the same level as a guy who bangs his thumb with a hammer so he forgets about his gout, but what the hell. By the time I knew what was going on, my headache had disappeared.

I should also add to any animal lovers out there that my Poor Man's Pâté Surprise, *minus* the peppers, has cured more than a few of my dogs when they scrawnied away during hot summer months and wouldn't eat regular chow.

I discovered another hangover cure that might work best for upwardly mobile people living in nice neighborhoods without a Vienna sausage aisle in their grocery store.

Take two catfish fillets and place them in a shallow, buttered, borosilicate glass pan, better known as Pyrex cookware. Sprinkle grated cheese on the fish. Cover the cheese with, again, diced jalapeños and habaneros. Cover the peppers with bread crumbs, then another layer of fillets.

Sometimes I grated more cheese—I preferred hoop cheese, but I'm sure some kind of high-priced and fancy Havarti, Gouda, or Edam might work—and added more bread crumbs. I baked the catfish at around 400 degrees for maybe fifteen minutes, depending on the thickness of the fillets. Then I pulled out the pan and carefully drained into a mixing bowl the fish water that had mysteriously accumulated.

It was important to keep the fish water, as I'll explain later.

Then I slid the pan back in the oven for about another five minutes. During this time, I made not-from-scratch hollandaise sauce, which I drizzled over the fish loaf after it cooled somewhat. Now, I'll admit, sometimes this particular hangover cure didn't quite work. For the most part—minus the butter, cheese, and hollandaise sauce—it seemed about as healthy as a shot of B_{12}. If my hangover didn't go away by the time I finished off about a four-by-four-inch square, there was one more step.

I went back to my pantry—or closet, file cabinet, Charles Chips canister, suitcase, roof gutter, dog-food bin, bookcase, etc.—pulled out a bottle of vodka or bourbon, poured about a jigger into the cooling fish water, and chugged it down. A little hair of the dog and scale of the cat pretty much relieved me of any discomfort. This little step works amazingly well for those who suffer from upset stomachs.

Let me reiterate that I only speak of what worked for me. I have no scientific evidence, but it seems to me that the blood vessels may actually constrict, despite the theories, and if so, there's nothing like a good, fatty Vienna sausage to ramrod those veins back into viable thoroughfares. The hot peppers, I'm certain, send out endorphins so fast that even a broken hip might feel like nothing more than a pulled groin.

Oddly, since the rehab stint, I've noticed how my knees, lower back, neck, and temples hurt pretty much continuously. I'm thinking that I might should go back to my old midmorning ways, pop those Vienna tops more often, and dice peppers like there's no tomorrow.

Dining Out

Crab Rangoon
and Bongo Bongo Soup

by Colman Andrews

from *Saveur*

Saveur editor Colman Andrews is well known for his sophisticated tastes, so when he says that his favorite restaurant was the late, not-generally-lamented kitsch eatery *Trader Vic's*, better sit and listen why.

When I think back on my many dinners at what was once, without question, my favorite restaurant, I recall first and maybe most of all the seductive aromas: the faint hint of smoldering wood from the Chinese ovens; the perfume of gardenias garnishing drinks; the sweet fragrance of the hot towels presented after the finger-food appetizers; the meaty scent of the rum-and-sugar-glazed barbecued pork and the roasted Indonesian lamb, with its hint of curry.

After the aromas, I remember the music: soft, slightly fuzzy, the sounds of slack-key guitar bands and Martin Denny–esque exotica, issuing from little speakers under palm-leaf ceiling panels above the replica tikis, giant conch shells, or amber glass fishnet floats. Then I remember the almost military orchestration of the service: the hostesses in their tailored hibiscus-print dresses, the captains in their jaunty crested blazers, the three (if not four) levels of waiters and busboys in uniforms of descending grandeur; the practiced presentations at the table of communal servings of stir-fried vegetables or crusty cottage-fried potatoes dished up with unobtrusive flair, and the deft carving of heroic slabs of glistening mahogany-hued meat.

And of course there was the way things tasted: simultaneously sweet and salty and moist and crisp and, hey, all right, maybe sort of silly sometimes, but good, really good. I *loved* Trader Vic's.

The piece of real estate that juts out, a spit of land into a sea of traffic, from the western side of the x-shaped intersection of Wilshire and Santa Monica boulevards in Beverly Hills was occupied by a gas station when I first noticed it as a very young boy—a Union 76, if I'm not mistaken. When I was eight or nine, the gas station disappeared and little by little became a handsome eight-story '50s-modern hotel called (I appreciated the punning elision even then) the Beverly Hilton. And in the prow of the hotel, on the very tip of the spit, was installed a restaurant known as—originally, when the hotel opened, in 1955—The Traders. Even just driving by in the car with my mom, I figured out pretty quickly that this was no ordinary restaurant. The windowless exterior walls were textured with stylized Polynesian (Maori?) patterns and guarded on one side by a quartet of 12- or 14-foot dark brown wood tikis set on pedestals (a fifth one stood by the entrance on the other side, off the parking lot); banana trees sprouted along the perimeter; and every time we passed, I was inevitably thrilled by the savory, smoky siren smell that wafted out from the place.

The Traders was in fact a Trader Vic's, of course—it was officially renamed that after a few years—and it wasn't long before my parents started taking me and my sister there for dinner. On my earliest visits, my favorite dish was a combination plate—I don't remember what it was called—that involved a hamburger patty, a toasted English muffin, a fried banana, and a heap of crisp shoestring potatoes. I subsequently learned to love the Cosmo tidbits—an appetizer assortment that included crab Rangoon (fried crabmeat-filled wontons), sweet barbecued spareribs, slices of lacquered pork loin, and deep-fried shrimp. I also developed an affection for the mahimahi, which was scattered with shards of almond, and, later, macadamia nuts—and certainly for the snowball: a big scoop of coconut ice cream topped with chocolate sauce and coated in shredded coconut.

But it wasn't just the food that attracted me. Trader Vic's introduced me to a whole new world. Stepping through the beautifully polished hardwood doors off the parking lot into this fragrant, romantic place—there was tapa cloth on some of the walls and an outrigger canoe, a real one, hanging from the ceiling!—meant more to me than just going out to dinner. It was an adventure in paradise—to borrow the name of what later became, perhaps not coincidentally, my favorite television show.

The South Seas were big in the 1950s. *The Kon-Tiki Expedition,* Thor Heyerdahl's account of his voyage by balsa-log raft from Peru to Polynesia, was much talked about in the early '50s, and the musical *South Pacific*—based on James Michener's 1947 collection of war-in-the-Pacific stories, *Tales of the South Pacific*—was running on Broadway (it was made into a movie in 1958). Michener's epic novel *Hawaii* came out in 1959, and at more or less the same time the Michener-inspired *Adventures in Paradise* debuted on TV, starring Gardner McKay as the dashing captain of the schooner *Tiki,* which sailed from one Pacific island and, well, adventure to another.

That was also the golden era of the tiki bar—a genre arguably invented back in 1933 by one Ernest Beaumont Gantt, a former bootlegger from New Orleans, when he opened a bamboo-and-palm-frond watering hole in Hollywood called Don the Beachcomber. Gantt, who later changed his name legally to Donn [*sic*] Beach, was an expert at concocting exotic cocktails, many of them combinations of rum and various fruit juices (he invented the zombie, so named because more than a couple were said to turn you into one). It is also quite possible that, after he expanded his establishment in 1937 to serve American-Cantonese food, he was the first to offer that assortment of snacks—dim sum as reimagined by a Hollywood art director and a fry cook—known as the pupu platter. Over the next two decades, Don the Beachcomber grew into a chain, and imitations and elaborations of the place opened all over the country.

None was to prove more successful, influential, and (in its extensions) resilient than Trader Vic's, which had its origins up in Oakland, also in 1934, when Victor J. Bergeron, a young entrepreneur with a wooden leg (he lost the real one to tuberculosis of the bone at the age of six) and a gregarious personality, opened a saloon called Hinky Dinks. Food became available, with a menu offering items like steak sandwiches and roast chicken; the only hint of things to come was a dish of ham and eggs with fried pineapple and bananas on the side, which Bergeron dubbed "ham and eggs Hawaiian." After a vacation that took him to Havana by way of New Orleans, though, Bergeron added daiquiris, planter's punch, and other "tropical" cocktails to the Hinky Dinks repertoire—and in 1937, inspired (he freely admitted) by a visit to Don the Beachcomber, he remade the place into a "Polynesian" restaurant, with an exotic-drinks menu and a Chinese-flavored bill of fare. Bergeron's wife suggested that he call it "Trader Vic's" because he loved bartering and making deals. He installed a barbecue pit behind the restaurant—the ancestor of the huge, tandoorlike cylindrical wood-burning ovens that Trader Vic (as he quickly started to call himself) later put in all his restaurants, claiming that their design dated to the Han dynasty.

Bergeron already had an East Bay following, but now, as San Francisco columnist Herb Caen noted in his introduction to Bergeron's "candid and informal autobiography," *Frankly Speaking: Trader Vic's Own Story* (Doubleday, 1973), "a few limousines were beginning to appear" outside the restaurant. By 1941, Caen added, he was able to write of it that "[t]he best restaurant in San Francisco is in Oakland." When Bergeron invented the mai tai "around 1944" and the drink became a sensation, the fame of the place redoubled.

Trader Vic's began evolving into a chain in 1949, when Bergeron opened his first outpost, at the Western (now the Westin) Hotel in Seattle. San Francisco followed, then Beverly Hills. Today the chain has some 22 restaurants around the world, mostly in Europe, Asia, and the Middle East. (The group also runs Mexican-themed Señor Pico eateries in Bangkok, Muscat, and Cairo and a Japanese restaurant in Giza.) There are only six Trader Vic's currently open in this country, however; among others, the restaurants in New York City and Washington, D.C., have closed. The Trader Vic's experience is different now from what it once was (hamachi tartare and crab cakes with wasabi rémoulade appear on the menu these days; the tikis are gone from the Beverly Hills dining room); *we*'re different now.

Much of the food at Trader Vic's is made up. It is highly doubtful that any Burmese cook ever wrapped crabmeat and cream cheese in a wonton skin and deep-fried it, or that any Chinese noodle shop ever tossed its lo mein with clarified butter, or that any denizen of Calcutta ever served curry with an array of condiments that included sunflower seeds and pickles in mustard sauce; but the results of so doing—which were Bergeron's crab Rangoon, pake noodles, and

Calcutta curries, respectively—were delicious. Maybe even more important, they were fun—food that was its own entertainment.

But Bergeron could boast of more serious gastronomic accomplishments, too. Through his travels and his network of friends, he was forever discovering new ingredients and new ways of preparing them. He was the first restaurateur to popularize kiwifruit (under the name Chinese gooseberries), limestone lettuce, morels, mahimahi, and green (or Malagasy, as he called them) peppercorns. He was one of the first, outside strictly ethnic restaurants, to use fresh cilantro, tofu, and Chinese (i.e., snow) peas. (You could make a pretty good case, if you wanted to, for Vic Bergeron as a pioneer of fusion cuisine.) He was also serving thin disks of fried parmigiano as an appetizer years before anybody outside Friuli had heard of frico— and until the late 1970s, his were almost certainly the only upscale restaurants in America that cooked much of their food on wood fires.

Trader Vic was also an early supporter of California wine, and wine occasioned my only personal contact with him: I wrote to him, in the early 1970s, complaining about the wine list at his Beverly Hills restaurant, meager compared with its San Francisco counterpart. He replied that the matter was out of his hands, that the Hilton management wrote the list—but he arranged for me to have access, whenever I dined at Trader Vic's, to the considerably larger list offered at the hotel's pricey French restaurant, L'Escoffier. This allowed me to enjoy more than one bottle of 1949 Clos des Lambrays with my Javanese sate. Of course, that was after I'd grown up and rediscovered Trader Vic's on my own terms.

It's 1970, more or less. I drive up to Trader Vic's in my dark blue Beetle, get out, mount the steps, and walk through the front door, maybe alone, maybe with my cinematographer friend and cotrencherman Allen Daviau, maybe even with a date. I have cascading long black hair and what my mother likes to call, with distaste, a Fu Manchu mustache but am wearing a coat and tie; and anyway, they're used to me here. Host Laurence Abbot, always tan and jaunty looking, greets me at the podium and hands me over to some vision of serenity in a flowered dress who leads me to my table. On the way, I stop to exchange pleasantries with Alex Kaluzny, the genial Russian-born manager of the place and a longtime Trader Vic's mainstay (he opened the San Francisco restaurant). As I sit down, my favorite captain, Jack Chew, appears, greeting me like some long-lost relative. Depending on my mood (or my date's mood, if that's an issue), I order a serious rum drink—a tortuga or a suffering bastard, probably—or ask for the wine list and choose something red and good. Then the food starts: Cosmo tidbits, possibly, or at least one or two of the assortment's constituent parts; maybe some cheese bings, little crêpe packets of ham and melted cheese. Or, if I'm feeling more like an adult, perhaps some bongo bongo soup (a silky if improbable purée of spinach and oysters) or just a limestone lettuce salad. Next, maybe messy, garlicky pake crab—one of those dishes whose flavorful residue lingers on your fingers for a day, hot towels or not—as an intermediate course. Then, almost certainly, meat: Indonesian lamb roast or Javanese sate or a triple-thick lamb chop, or possibly veal filets in tarragon sauce, a dish long vanished from the menu but still available to those who ask for it.

And on the side, pake noodles or cottage-fried potatoes, Chinese peas with water chestnuts, asparagus Chinese style . . . Alex comes by to ask how I like the wine. Jack wonders whether I'd like some more peanut sauce. The room is glowing. I'm glowing. I smell the meat, the wood, a gardenia. I'm in paradise.

⊶⊷

Crab Rangoon

This over-the-top elaboration of fried wontons has proven to be one of the most enduringly popular appetizers at Trader Vic's.

> 4 oz. snow crab meat or other crab meat, picked over
> 4 oz. cream cheese, at room temperature, cut into small pieces
> 1 clove garlic, peeled and minced
> ¾ tsp. A.1. Steak Sauce
> Salt and freshly ground white pepper
> Peanut oil
> 24 square wonton skins

1. Mix crabmeat, cream cheese, garlic, and steak sauce together in a mixing bowl with an electric mixer on low speed. Season filling to taste with salt and pepper and set aside.

2. Pour oil into a medium pot to a depth of 2" and heat over medium heat until temperature registers 325° on a candy thermometer. Meanwhile, put 1 of the wonton skins on a work surface with one of the corners pointing toward you. Put 1 tsp. of the filling in center of skin. Moisten both edges of skin farthest away from you with water, then fold skin over filling to form a triangle. Gently flatten filling and push out any air pockets, then press edges to seal. Moisten skin just above filling with a dab of water. Gather middle of flat edges on either side of filling toward moistened area of skin and pinch together, pressing sides to skin just above filling. Repeat with remaining skins and filling.

3. Deep-Fry wontons in batches until golden brown, 2–3 minutes. Drain on paper towels. Serve hot with tomato-based chile sauce and Chinese hot mustard, if you like.

MAKES 24

Bongo Bongo Soup

This unusual soup, a Bergeron invention, was perhaps inspired by the soup called boula boula, a purée of pea soup and turtle soup that was popularized by Jacqueline Kennedy in the early 1960s. Trader Vic's uses jarred Pacific coast oysters for this dish.

1 10-oz. package partially thawed frozen spinach
6 shucked oysters and their liquor
2 tbsp. bottled clam juice
1 small clove garlic, peeled and chopped
Freshly ground white pepper
4 cups half-and-half
1 tbsp. butter
2 tbsp. A.1. Steak Sauce
½ tsp. Tabasco
½ tsp. Worcestershire sauce
Salt

½ tsp. cornstarch

3 tbsp. heavy cream, chilled

1. Put spinach, oysters and their liquor, clam juice, garlic, and pepper to taste into a medium nonreactive pot over medium-high heat. Bring to a simmer, breaking up spinach with the back of a spoon, and simmer until heated through, about 5 minutes. Transfer to a blender and purée until very smooth. Set spinach–oyster mixture aside.

2. Preheat broiler. Bring half-and-half to a simmer in a medium pot over medium heat. Whisk in butter, then spinach–oyster purée, and return to a simmer. Add steak sauce, Tabasco, Worcestershire, and salt to taste. Dissolve cornstarch in l tbsp. water, then whisk into soup. Keep soup warm over lowest heat.

3. Whisk cream in a bowl until soft peaks form. Divide soup between 4 shallow heatproof soup bowls and put a big spoonful of the whipped cream on top of each. Place bowls of soup under broiler briefly to brown cream, then serve immediately.

SERVES 4

Sci-Fi Cooking Tries Dealing with Reality

by Frank Bruni

from the *New York Times*

With all the media buzz in the last few years about the fantastically inventive cooking of Spanish chef Ferran Adrià, it's long past time for a thoughtful survey of his American imitators. *Times* dining critic Bruni does so deftly.

O f the many ways restaurants have expressed their appreciation for bison, none is quite like Alinea's.

The dish might well be called Reefer Mammal. Or Stoned on the Range. Ribbons of bison meat filled egg-size indentations in the surface of a horizontal glass tube, the hollow interior of which contained burning sticks of cinnamon. Smoke seeped from the open ends of the tube, infusing the air and summoning associations well beyond the gustatory.

"This whole thing is like a bong," said a server.

The next of nearly 25 courses, a strip of partially dehydrated, butterscotch-coated bacon, arrived dangling like a Wallenda from a teensy trapeze. My friend and I were instructed to yank it from the wire with our fingers, a maneuver with a crumbly coda. She felt sure that a shard of hers had gone missing. She later found it—inside one of her pumps.

Alinea may sound like a restaurant off its rocker, like gastronomy gone round the bend. But it is much more: a multimillion-dollar wager—the most ambitious yet—that sophisticated American diners are ready to embrace a newfangled cuisine they have largely resisted. It boldly raises the stakes.

Its opening last week marks a milestone and invites an examination of how meaningfully this kind of cooking, born in Europe and pioneered in large part by the chef Ferran Adrià in Spain, has taken root in the United States. On this side of the Atlantic, its advance has been fitful. Its application has often been shallowly theatrical and its successes qualified, facts made clear during trips I took recently to some of the lonely outposts of this innovative style.

I went to Alinea and Moto in Chicago, which has emerged as an American center for this cuisine. I dined at Minibar at Café Atlantico in Washington, an experiment by José Andrés, who is closer to Mr. Adrià than any other American chef.

The efforts of these restaurants paled beside those of Mr. Adrià's El Bulli, where carnival flourishes more often had a payoff of pure pleasure. His American disciples are still struggling to integrate showmanship and artistry, an evanescent gee-whiz and an enduring wow.

But they are also providing transcendent moments, made possible by their willingness to toy with unusual textures, play with wildly unlikely flavor combinations and generally venture in directions that might turn out to be silly, but then again might not.

The movement or mindset to which they belong has been described as avant-garde. It has been labeled molecular gastronomy, because some practitioners deconstruct and reconstruct food with the tools and temperament of biochemists. It has been dubbed shock cuisine but could also be called mock cuisine, because much of it sets out to flout widely held values.

In this realm, centrifuges, dehydrators and chemical and technological transmogrification of food are not reviled methods of corporate kitchens but paths to discovery.

While many chefs extol the unsullied purity of their ingredients, Homaro Cantu commences an 18-course tasting menu at Moto with an ersatz maki roll that uses nori-flavored edible paper in the place of actual nori. This paper is imprinted with cartoonlike pictures of maki, a decorative motif that advertises the dish's artificiality.

Chicago is also home to the restaurant Avenues in the Peninsula hotel, where the chef, Graham Elliot Bowles, sprinkles a largely conventional menu with unconventional selections.

Mr. Bowles has been known to serve crushed Altoids instead of mint jelly with lamb and to present diners with lollipops of foie gras encrusted with Pop Rocks. His cooking typifies another facet of this cuisine: the way it recruits junk food into the service of fancier dishes or creates highbrow versions of lowbrow classics.

"Why *not* go to the store and get the curiously strong mint?" Mr. Bowles said in a telephone interview, going on to reject "that horribly boring quote, 'I love to use farm-fresh products and local ingredients and European technique.'"

On the opening night of Alinea, the name of which refers to a symbol for a fresh train of thought, the first course was a visually nifty riff on a peanut butter and jelly sandwich: a peeled, heated grape, still on a sprig, that had been dipped in a peanut puree and encased in a thin layer of brioche.

A later course paired slivers of rare beef with an undulating sheet of potato, which became a jagged landscape with discrete canyons and buttes of molasses, raisin purée, dried garlic, dried tomato and more: the flavors of A.1. steak sauce, candidly acknowledged on the menu.

In a telephone conversation shortly after, Alinea's chef, Grant Achatz, articulated part of his philosophy. He said that food should be not only delicious but also "exciting and theatrical and intriguing;" that it should take fuller advantage of the senses of touch, sight and smell as well as taste.

"We could take that bacon strip and lay it on a plate, but it would be lifeless," Mr. Achatz said. "It would be dead. You hang it on something that sways and it becomes alive. It becomes interactive. It becomes sculpture."

New Yorkers have not provided an especially receptive audience for this brand of culinary derring-do. From 2000 to 2003, the chef Paul Liebrandt tried it at Atlas and then at Papillon. Neither succeeded.

The only current showcase in Manhattan for consistently envelope-pushing cuisine is WD-50 on the Lower East Side, where the chef Wylie Dufresne uses enzymes and emulsifiers to create rarities like shrimp noodles without eggs or flour and cubes of mayonnaise that can be deep-fried without melting. The deep-fried mayonnaise is served beside pickled beef tongue in a deconstruction of a deli sandwich.

Mr. Dufresne is familiar with the charge that much of this is gimmickry, but he noted that potentially significant developments begin as potentially perishable novelties.

"The first person to put steak on a fire—that was novel, right?" Mr. Dufresne said in a telephone conversation. "Was that a gimmick because before that they were just throwing their spears at it and eating it?"

His comments reflected his awareness of restaurant industry titans' skepticism about what he and his peers are doing. When I called the chef Charlie Trotter to ask him about the importance of their work, he said, "If it's truly valid, I'll be delighted to have this conversation with you in two years."

Mr. Cantu, 28; Mr. Achatz, 31; and Mr. Bowles, 28, have all worked for Mr. Trotter in Chicago and all know one another, which is a principal reason for the city's emergence as a nursery for a new cuisine.

Mr. Trotter said that he applauded his students' ambition, but said creations intended to shock are "child's play."

He went on to invoke a derogatory phrase once used by the philosopher Jeremy Bentham. "I want to make sure our young colleagues are not literally producing something that is merely nonsense upon stilts."

They are and they aren't. In any case, Mr. Trotter is not their muse. They mostly look abroad for inspiration, to Heston Blumenthal in England and above all to Mr. Adrià.

Mr. Adrià is the mad culinary scientist who delights at better techniques for pulverizing, puréeing or aerating food. He more or less invented foam, the prevalence of which underscores the contributions this fringe cuisine makes to the mainstream. He devotes six months of each year to laboratory research in Barcelona, meaning that his restaurant on the Costa Brava, El Bulli, is open only from mid-spring to mid-fall.

I ate there in late April. At the start of dinner, when servers wheeled out a liquid nitrogen bath seething with a witch's cauldron's worth of smoke, I rolled my eyes. But that liquid nitrogen enabled the freezing of alcohol and the mixing of a caipirinha in which lime juice and cachaça were truly and utterly integrated—a seamless and impossibly creamy slush.

More often than not, the oddball shapes, textures and temperatures of Mr. Adrià's food represented methods for delivering more consistent or concentrated flavors. He has devised ways to encase purées, oils and other liquids in translucent membranes, which do not compete with the taste of what's inside them but let them explode in a heady rush across a diner's tongue.

I experienced this flavor epiphany with a ball of pumpkin seed oil, a liquefied olive and pouches of softened butter that floated in a potato skin consommé. By remaining intact and independent, these pouches provided spikes of richness that would not have been possible if the butter had merely melted into the soup.

Mr. Adrià had told me earlier that what he was always after was "the pure taste of things" and that his manipulations were paradoxically in the service of that. Most of the meal lived up to his motto.

His American acolytes more frequently lose sight of the line between purposeful improvisations and pointless flamboyance.

There was some harmless fun at Moto, where a dish called McSweetbreads presented three pieces of sweetbreads impaled on plastic pipettes that squirted versions of dipping sauces for Chicken McNuggets.

But why was he bothering with edible paper, not just in the faux maki but also in a dispiriting cheese course with a printed warning, which could be eaten, about a nearby hunk of smoldering ash, which could not? In both cases, the paper stuck unpleasantly to the roof of my mouth.

I was willing to play along with hard cold pellets of what Moto calls Kentucky fried ice cream, which tasted uncannily like the skin of Kentucky Fried Chicken. But my good will was gone by the time I was served hard cold pellets of what Moto calls green curry ice cream, a blast of frigid heat without any virtue beyond that oxymoronic effect. This was food as props in a theater of the absurd.

Minibar at Café Atlantico has absurdist touches but was more amusing, for several reasons. Mr. Andrés avoided obnoxious challenges to the palate. The minibar itself, a six-seat counter facing a team of cooks, had an informal feel and a theatrical aspect that complemented the performance art of the meal. And the meal was confined to two and a half hours, beyond which the spectacle would have grown wearying.

There was a deconstructed Caesar salad, a deconstructed guacamole and a "deconstructed glass of white wine," which was a translucent rectangle of grape jelly with pinpricks of herbs, nuts and fruits often evoked by wine. I was instructed to taste each and guess its identity.

Later on, servers distributed sheets that asked, "Can You Eat Light?" Then the counter was plunged into darkness, and in front of me appeared a translucent globe of spun sugar with a flickering filament inside: an edible light bulb, more or less.

Alinea keeps such playfulness somewhat in check. Its desire to be taken seriously is evident in the muted palette of its elegant dining rooms, the hushed demeanor of its servers and Mr. Achatz's words.

"We're not on the edge," he said.

But they are not far from it. A fillet of turbot was served with water chestnuts, eggless custard, Jerusalem artichoke purée and geoduck and razor clams—an elaborate enough dish if it ended right there.

It did not. The small bowl was set in a bowl of purple and pink hyacinths, the fragrance of which was released when a server poured hot water over them. My companion said it made her feel as if she were "in a flower garden at the bottom of the sea."

A few dishes were Dali-esque dioramas. A spiral of dehydrated prosciutto sat like a red wheel on a verdant lawn of spiky greens. Sautéed frogs' legs came in a miniature swamp of lettuces, leaves and morels; an epicurean everglade. A heart of palm salad arrived as five hollowed cylinders on five white pedestals lined up like vertebrae in a skeleton, lending a new definition to the phrase bone china. Each cylinder was filled with a different purée and topped with a different accent. The arresting combinations included prune with coffee vinaigrette and pumpernickel with black truffle.

Four and a half hours of this—a truncated version of Mr. Achatz's longest, 28-course tasting menu—exhausted me. This cuisine, so reliant on surprise and rapidly shifting sensations, can have that effect.

It can be pointlessly weird, like the cinnamon smoke or the dehydrated prosciutto, which put me in mind of a doggie treat. It can be so concerned with tickling the brain that it forgets the palate. Food should be artful but has responsibilities art does not. Unlike a Pollock painting or Botero sculpture, it goes into your mouth. Its worth depends on how happy a home it makes there.

But at its best, Alinea was spectacular, sometimes in utterly traditional ways. What made those frogs' legs memorable was not their moody habitat but their succulence.

And sometimes Alinea was spectacular precisely because it dared to be so different. Mr. Achatz puréed foie gras and molded it into a thin, hollow cylinder, which he then filled with a sweetened rhubarb foam and served cool. The temperature, texture and architecture of the dish turned the emphatic wallop of the liver into an ethereal whisper.

By taking chances and breaking rules, each of these chefs has hatched a few remarkable creations and crazily good ideas.

I see an imminent vogue in corn nuts. They appeared in dishes at Minibar and at Avenues, where much of what Mr. Bowles did—a pea soup enveloping a lavender-infused marshmallow, foie gras on a Rice Krispies Treat—elated me.

Mr. Bowles used the crushed nuts as a crust for braised bison on a bed of grits. Sandwiching the buffalo between iterations of corn was like a cunning culinary ode to the Great Plains.

"The idea that I have is that everything is an open playing field," Mr. Bowles said.

Why not encourage him and his compatriots to range across it?

See Food

By Jason Sheehan
from *Westword*

Sheehan's restaurant reviews in this Denver
weekly magazine may seem to wander way
off the point, but that *is* the point: They recreate the experience of dining out, which
inevitably also depends on who is eating,
when, where, and why.

*"I saw successively imprinted on every face the glow of desire, the
ecstasy of enjoyment, and the perfect calm of utter bliss."*
—JEAN ANTHELME BRILLAT-SAVARIN, *THE PHYSIOLOGY OF TASTE*

I t was the strangest sort of party, uncomfortably intimate and
cheerful for no reason at all. This was 1994, maybe 1995, the year
fixed loosely in my mind (like all other years) by what I was doing
at the time, where I was cooking and for whom. I still wasn't sure if
this was the career for me (in fact, it was early enough that calling
it a career at all was something of a joke), uncertain if food was
where I ultimately wanted to fix my gaze. The party was with the
family of my girlfriend at the time—the one destined to someday
become The Ex, like a proper name—and it was being held because
her grandmother had just died.

After she'd passed away at home, peacefully, her children had
found a hundred-dollar bill in her pocketbook and decided to use
it to throw a party. The day found me sitting at a long table at an
Indian restaurant in Rochester, New York, called the Raj Mahal,
drinking mango lassi and eating *channa chat* on the dime of a dead
woman.

Back in 1994 or 1995, I didn't know much about Indian food. It was as foreign to me, as thrilling and mysterious, as Chinese food had been when I was twelve, as sushi when I was sixteen, as French when I was twenty. I remember stupidly affecting some kind of accent when I ordered (a stupid thing I still do today), not wanting to botch the words on the menu that I thought were so beautiful, hoping to sound like I ate *mughlai* soup and *dal makhani* all the time. Besides, since I didn't know what to say, how to react or who to talk to, I was desperately trying to seek refuge in food—which, unlike death, I at least marginally understood.

There were lots of tears at the table, and a fair share of laughter, too. Half of The Ex's family were (and still are, I assume) psychologists of one breed or another, so all manner of coping mechanisms and grief strategies were on display. But as the food started arriving, that slowed, dried up, finally stopped altogether. And, as Brillat-Savarin wrote, "I saw successfully imprinted on every face the glow of desire, the ecstasy of enjoyment, and the perfect calm of utter bliss."

I was not exempt from this awesome, subtle power. Indian cooking, which I knew only barely and understood not at all, had moved a room full of mourners if not to bliss, then certainly to calm. The transformation was amazing and, frankly, a relief.

This unusual meal wasn't a turning point for me or my career in the kitchen. That kind of one-shot revelation only comes in the movies or under the influence of cheap hallucinogens. But it was a step. The incredible power of food had been laid out plain in that one moment when I was prepared to see it, and whatever magic it was that those cooks had, I wanted some for myself.

Flash forward ten years. Although I understand Indian food now, it's still only from the perspective of a diner. I don't know what an Indian kitchen is like because I've never worked in one, and while I'm not sure when something is done *right*, I do know when it is done *well*. I may not be clear on what spice goes where and how they all work together, but I know what I like and what moves other people. And I know a kitchen with the power when I see it in action.

At the table across from mine at Little India (the six-year-old original on Sixth Avenue, not the second outlet downtown), a couple is fighting. They're doing so quietly, faces pinched, voices hissing like cats. I, as eavesdropper, can't hear the specifics, but I can watch the body language—the back-and-forth volley, each one pitching and catching in turn. Balled fists. Clenched jaws. It's like spying on a highly personal game of Battleship, as one player crumples, as if punched, when the other scores a direct hit. Honestly, I'm waiting to see which one will sink first.

On the other side of the plainly decorated dining room is a family—mother, father, young kid, older kid—that's less exciting to watch but still provides a study in well-rehearsed parental routine. The adults manage to conduct a conversation while simultaneously taking the fork away from the baby, picking up dropped napkins, keeping the older child from upsetting his water glass—and all without really looking at the kids.

Most people come to restaurants for the food—to be thrilled and moved and transported, however briefly, by the daring, complicated, beautiful work done by the cooks. They come to be coddled, taken care of. At the very least, to get out of their own kitchens. I love watching the magic happen for other people, seeing Savarin's bliss and desire in action. I know the effect good food can have on me, and I thrill to see the trick work on somebody else.

There are no funerary moments in Little India's dining room tonight—at least, none that I know of—but I am nonetheless reminded of that terrible, wonderful party ten years ago. This food is just as powerful. At their table tucked up against the exposed-brick wall, the family has settled into a groove, conversation on hold, the smiling parents eating tandoori with one hand, trying with the other to keep unimpressed children from putting their fists in the lassi. *Saag paneer* and *alu paratha* inspire a truce between the warring couple. On its own, food may not fix anything (again, that only happens in the movies), but it temporarily stops the bloodshed, at least long enough for them to tear into their *naan* bread and scoop up pinches of delicately spiced creamed spinach and long-grain basmati rice. Her eyes flutter closed briefly, the corners of her mouth twitching up in what I figure is the closest thing to a smile her fella's seen in a long time. His brows furrow in concentration, like he's chasing the tail of some spice he can't identify.

I can sympathize: Little India's particular take on Indian food is an odd mix of regional specialties, all cooked in the tradition of northern Indian cuisine by a Punjabi chef hired by the restaurant's Punjabi owners, the Malhotra and Baidwan families. The menu is long and dignified, showcasing the curries and masalas that even casual eaters of Indian food would recognize, as well as seven kinds of saag, specialties of Madras, Danshak, Bombay and Punjab, and even colonial dishes like the vindaloos from Goa—their brutal heat and strange balance of spices a record of Portuguese occupation, British colonialism and unbroken Indian culinary tradition. Because I've become accustomed to the homogenization of varied ethnic traditions in Indian kitchens cooking for an American audience, Little India's food can be a surprise—savory where I expect spicy, hot where I expect sweet—but everything from the complicated vindaloo to the simplest chutney has the potential to transport a diner to utter bliss.

At another table, a woman dining alone eats with her eyes shut, the book in her hand (*The Da Vinci Code*, of all things) forgotten. In thrall to her *navratan korma*, she's oblivious to a dot of beaten curried cream sauce on her chin. Across the room, sitting near the dark wood bar with its foreign-label bottles and a cricket trophy (runner-up, 1998) standing between framed awards and pictures of family and friends, a table of three is sharing plates, forking cubes of *boti* masala and curried chicken in a thick ginger-and-tomato brown sauce into each other's mouths. Nearby, a plate of *alu mutter* (big chunks of potatoes and peas in a hot, red-brown gravy with hints of every spice in the rack) and warm Indian *puri* (deep-fried whole-wheat bread) has reduced two stick-skinny girls with the wasted look of terminal compassionate vegetarianism to a starved, brooding silence.

I sit beneath art taken from the pages of the *Bhagavad-Gita*, at a table near where, mid-day, the people will line up for Little India's lunch buffet. In front of me is an order of *channa chat*—cold chickpeas and potatoes in a simple, tart sauce heavy on the cilantro, which I pick up with triangles of warm, chewy *roti*—that tastes very close to what I remember from that day in Rochester. A little milder, maybe, and not so acidic or citrine. It's gentle in its use of intense spice, rather than the nine-volt surge of sour yogurt or vinegar. I've also ordered tandoori shrimp—huge and spiced red around the edges, but poorly veined—and a beautiful plate of heavy lamb masala that's so good, so overwhelmingly earthy and deep with spice that I have to eat it in small, delicate bites, afraid that if I shove big fistfuls of it into my mouth the way I want to, I will miss the point of the carefully balanced flavors.

Indian food—in particular, Little India's Indian food—uses spice like a painter uses his oils. Nothing is ever one color, but many, all mixed together, one giant wheel of shades and color. So the language of description falls strangely flat when tasked to explain the interplay of cold, thick cream and hot curry on the tongue; the swirl of yogurt, ginger, onion and tomato in a saag; the way the tandoor oven infuses smoke and mesquite sweetness into everything stuffed into its blazing maw, and how a simple squeeze of lemon can tame all the spice rubbed into the skin. It's much easier, perhaps even more accurate, to watch the food in action, to see how it makes other people feel.

I eat at Little India three times in two weeks, twice in three days, and each time, I keep my eyes on the crowds (which are never small), watching as they're overtaken by the wonder. Never once do I see anyone send something back, make a sour face, hide a bite in a napkin, seem unmoved by what's been set before them. In the faces of those around me, I see it all: the desire, ecstasy and bliss, the power of food to obliterate, to transport, to offer refuge from all things external. No one walks out the door without being touched, at least a little.

Least of all me.

Osso Buco Me?
Osso Buco You!

by Robb Walsh
from the *Houston Press*

What does a local dining critic do when a well-regarded hometown restaurant falls fall short of expectations? Leave it to Robb Walsh, author of *Are You Really Going to Eat That?* and *The Legends of Texas Barbecue Cookbook*, to pull no punches.

"**I**f you don't like it, there's the door. Pay your bill and go. And don't come back," says Alex Salmassi, the owner of Portofino Ristorante Italiano, pointing to the exit. I seem to have a knack for getting myself thrown out of restaurants.

This time, the fracas is over a plate of osso buco. Instead of the usual marrow bone enveloped by tender veal, I was served two small rounds of meat surrounding four skinny bones. So I asked the waiter if this was osso buco, or if he had brought me another dish by mistake. And I also asked him what kind of rice they used in the risotto, because it looked weird.

My impertinence earned me an audience with the owner who, as it turned out, was eating dinner a few tables away.

"You have a problem with the osso buco?" the slender, dark-haired young man began. I explained that I was used to a single large shank in my osso buco, not a collection of bones, but he quickly cut me off.

"Let me ask you something: What is osso buco?" Salmassi said, as if he were dealing with a small child.

"Veal shank," I replied.

"And how is it cooked?" he asked, his head moving backward and forward like a rooster's.

"It's braised," I said.

"And what's in the sauce?" he continued with his little quiz.

"It can be cooked in all kinds of sauces," I told him.

"No," he said adamantly. Then he delivered his big punch line with a whispered rage reminiscent of early Al Pacino. "When you know *what* osso buco is, then you can talk to me about *my* osso buco."

"You trying to tell me I don't know what osso buco is?" I countered in disbelief.

"This is our signature dish; everybody loves it," he said.

"This pile of skinny little bones is your signature dish?" I asked, gesturing at my plate. That's when Salmassi pointed to the door. Oh, well, it was fun while it lasted.

I took Alex Salmassi's advice to heart. Not only did I pay the entire bill and leave (after tipping the waiter generously), I also took some time to learn exactly what osso buco is.

According to *Barron's Food Lover's Companion*, osso buco is an Italian dish made of veal shanks braised with olive oil, white wine, stock, onions, tomatoes, garlic, anchovies, carrots, celery and lemon peel, and it's traditionally served with risotto. There are lots of variations, such as white osso buco made without tomatoes. And countless other versions are served by modern Italian restaurants in the United States, which seldom follow the strict formula.

Portofino's risotto, made with long-grain rice instead of the traditional arborio, is awful. And their osso buco sauce has too many tomatoes in it. But regardless of the risotto or what's in the braising sauce, the osso buco I was served at Portofino was made from a poor cut of meat. Maybe Salmassi figured if he threw me out, his problems would go away.

But while I was waiting for the bill, I asked the busboy to pack up the plate of osso buco in a Styrofoam to-go container. A few days later, I took that container to the corporate headquarters of Martin Preferred Foods, one of the state's top veal suppliers. Without mentioning the name of the restaurant, I showed the meat and bones to sales and marketing manager John Walker and sales rep Mike Disney and asked them for their observations.

"If you ordered osso buco for $24.95, and this is what you were served, what would you do?" I asked the veal experts.

"I'd send it back," said Disney.

Opening a veal supplier's brochure, they showed me photos of veal shank and explained the grades. Top-end restaurants use only the tender, meaty hindshank for osso buco, Disney said, pointing to a picture of the thick marrow bone surrounded by veal I expect when I order osso buco. At Martin Preferred Foods, they get around $11 a pound for the good stuff.

"Cost-conscious restaurants" substitute the foreshank for the hindshank, the meat man continued, pointing to another picture. The foreshank is a tougher cut from the calf's front shin that can be identified by the pair of bones that run through it. It sells for around $7 a pound.

"So this must be foreshank," I said, pointing to the squarish bones in my Styrofoam container.

"Yes," Disney agreed. But the foreshanks in the catalog were nearly as big as the hindshanks. And the ones served to me at Portofino were much smaller. I asked how that could be.

"They probably aren't center-cut," he told me, referring to the meatier, thicker part of the shank. A restaurant that's really cutting corners also can buy the entire foreshank cut "end to end," he said. But when they do, they get smaller end scraps along with the pieces cut from the center.

So how much does end-to-end veal shank go for? "We don't even sell it," Walker told me. When pressed, he estimated it might cost somewhere around $5 a pound.

Odds are most of the customers who order osso buco at Portofino get a decent-sized veal foreshank. But I had the great fortune to get a portion made up from two smaller end pieces. And no one who knows osso buco is going to be happy with such scraps.

The osso buco and risotto at Portofino are a bad joke. And the owner's behavior is, how shall we say, a little *troppo*. But I highly recommend the restaurant for its incredible fresh seafood.

Portofino is located about a mile from the Kemah Boardwalk. On my first visit, I stopped off in old Kemah before dinner to check out the seafood stores. The shrimp and fresh fish fillets looked fantastic that day, and so did the live crabs. I wished I'd brought along a cooler.

As you can imagine, Portofino has its pick of this bounty. The red snapper Milano is a big slab of Gulf red snapper pan-fried until the edges are crispy but the middle is moist, and served with a topping of fresh shrimp and lump crabmeat cooked in butter.

Okay, it's not the most original dish I've ever eaten, but with fish this fresh, who cares? The crab finger appetizer, an oval dish crowded with more than a dozen little preshelled crab lollipops drowned in a white wine, lemon and garlic butter sauce, is the best starter on the menu. On my first visit, I got redfish topped with shrimp, crab and tomatoes as an entrée. It was also tasty, but not nearly as exciting as the red snapper.

I won't be going back to Portofino, but if you're looking for good eats down by the bay, I recommend giving it a try. A few words of caution: Think of going to Portofino for dinner like going to the movies or a play. In order to enjoy yourself, you need to be willing to suspend disbelief.

In the light of day, you'll notice that the restaurant resides in a rickety house shabbily decorated with fake palm trees and other plastic plants. But in the dim light of the evening, when they turn on the Christmas lights on the porch overlooking the marina, with a little imagination it can seem quite romantic.

Be sure to stick with the seafood. Even the innocuous-sounding green bean salad is awful. And forget about the bread. It looks like a crusty Italian loaf, but it crumbles when you take a bite.

If you get the spiky-haired young waiter who reads the specials off the blackboard with a phony Italian accent, resist the temptation to ask where he's from. (He was born in Galveston and reared in nearby Santa Fe.) If you play along, he'll do this goofy Italian accent all night long for your entertainment.

But if you really want to see a great dramatic performance, complain about the food to Alex Salmassi.

Portofino Ristorante
1002 Aspen Road, Clear Lake Shores, 281-538-9060

Where You'll Sing for Your Supper

By Emily Green

from the *Los Angeles Times*

Like Walsh in the preceding piece, LA critic
Emily Green finds an artful way to dispatch a
dismal restaurant. Her weapons? Humor,
common sense, and a fair-minded assessment of what different people may look for
when they eat out.

We don't always go to restaurants to eat. We might go for
the view, or to propose marriage, to suggest divorce, for
a job interview, to fire or be fired, or to fiddle with bread rolls
while we rest our feet and read a map. The Lincoln Steakhouse
Americana in Santa Monica is a perfect example of a not-about-
the-food restaurant. It's for people who can't sing. I recognize this
because I am one. It was first discovered by the Episcopal Church.
As a child, my rendition of "Kyrie eleison" was so bad that I was
pulled from the choir and made what may have been our congre-
gation's first female altar boy. Many years later, having accumulated
half a lifetime's unsung songs in my head, it's hard to describe the
euphoria at having wandered into a restaurant with an all-
enveloping din of music, televisions and people shouting. The
possibility dawned on me slowly: I could sing here. Nobody would
hear, or care.

The inspiration crystallized after what should have been a
Bombay martini with two olives came tasting of olive bottle juice.
"I thought you said, 'Dirty martini!'" the waiter yelled apologet-
ically. As a test, I trilled, "No problem!" Not so much as a wince.
"Do-re-mi-fa-so-la-ti-do!" Only a smile.

Even before a drinkable four fluid ounces of gin had arrived, I was singing. First, the national anthem (for the Dodgers). Then "La Marseillaise" (for Humphrey Bogart and John Kerry). Then "John Barleycorn Must Die" (for me).

I have waited since the 1970s to sing back to Stevie Winwood, Jim Capaldi and Chris Wood, those tousled boys from Traffic, but the acoustics in my shower were too cruel. Only thanks to Lincoln Steakhouse of Santa Monica, California, have I finally realized the dream—full throat. As a result, I love Lincoln—adore it, love, love, love it, will not hear a word against it, except about the food, which is not very good and indefensibly expensive, and the wine, which is just indefensibly expensive. There was no bread.

Which brings us to Lincoln's real specialty. It's a nightspot for the Atkins generation. If you're between 21 and 39, on a steak and vodka diet, looking for a mate—same sex or hetero, animal or mineral—and like it better when you can't hear what he, she or it has to say, this place was made for you.

It opened last April on Wilshire Boulevard at the inland edge of Santa Monica, which is only now giving up its crusty old bohemians for a new generation of wealthier, beach-loving young. John Baydale, one of the founders, describes the group that owns the restaurant by saying, "Basically we're all guys in our 30s, and we're all big meat eaters." They wanted a steakhouse for their generation and evidently had the capital and experience to do it. Elsewhere around town, Lads Inc. (Baydale's company's real name is Star Group Management) has opened an Asian fusion restaurant called Tengu, a Cuban "bistro" called Paladar and a nightclub called Nacional, and he says a bunch of new places, including 9 Thirty and Venice Cantina, are scheduled to open in the next two months.

Back at Lincoln, the look is three-martini Tudor, with some exceptionally camp touches, such as hooded chairs in case Henry VIII, or Beelzebub, wants to guzzle claret in relative anonymity. The place has such an artful gloom that it comes as no surprise to learn the design is the work of Kelly Werstler, the woman behind the retro bar and wall of plates at Whist in the Viceroy hotel.

There is nothing retro about the service. Rather, a very modern sense of expedience governs the greeting. You enter through a narrow bar and are made to stay there until your companions arrive.

Protest to the manager that you'd prefer to go straight to the table, and he'll explain to you that they're very sorry, but they'll believe you have friends when your friends show up.

If it's not noisy enough to sing when you arrive, be patient. As the place fills up at night, and diets shift from solids to liquids, people who have eaten at a long banquette in the bar are left sitting eye to midriff with deepening ranks of drinkers. By 9 p.m., it should easily be deafening. The dining room is almost, but not quite, as loud. The wall between the bar and dining room is really an optical illusion, created by two suspended paintings.

If by some freak accident you end up in this restaurant to eat instead of drink, be advised that the menu is pretty much surf and turf, with some pre-Framingham desserts, such as bananas Foster. The safest choice would be to stick to the simple items. The prawn cocktail is a safe starter, with horseradish-happy dipping sauce. The Caesar salad tasted more salad bar-issue than the authentic restaurant dish. Made right, preparation of this savory salad should be a restaurant happening, with the anchovy mashed into the garlic at table and whisked into raw egg yolk. Diners salivate as they watch and are then treated to an American delicacy. Making a dull one is a silly failing in a place that hasn't been fazed by health police when it comes to steak, sugar and spirits.

To indulge in a few more complaints, crab fritters are ruined by the addition of avocado, which makes them taste strangely greasy. Whatever you do, stay clear of the lobster salad, which has so much truffle oil it overwhelms everything within three tables.

As a futile flourish, the waiters give what the management hopes are enticing spiels about the specials. You catch every third word through the din. "Heirloom," "drizzled," "grass-fed." If the kitchen had a soupçon of common sense, they'd skip all this gastronomic drivel, especially the bit about "bone-in" fillet. By definition, fillets of beef should have no bone.

Grass-fed or not, the beef at Lincoln was disappointing. The porterhouse, which can only be ordered for two at a cost of $64, was only marginally less bland than the Delmonico. That said, compared to the sawdust-dry pork chops, bland is a recommendation.

The garlicky French fries, however, were terrific. The wine list was a shocker: overpriced California reds poured too warm. Sixty-four bucks for a Mount Veeder Cab was borderline larceny. My advice: Stick with the hard liquor. The bar makes respectable cocktails, especially the Bourbon-laced health drinks also known as Manhattans. Those who order dessert after the main course deserve what they get, which might be a big, stodgy brownie or an ice cream sandwich or, in my case, a double shot of Hirsch Reserve 16-year-old Bourbon. Ahhhh, whew. Strong. Could ruin a singing voice, this firewater. So, before it's too late, ladies and gentlemen:

> *There were three men came out of the West,*
> *their fortunes, er, to find,*
> *Na-na-na-na-na,*
> *na-na-na-na,*
> *John Barleycorn must die.*

★

Lincoln Steakhouse Americana *Rating*: Satisfactory *Location*: 2460 Wilshire Blvd., Santa Monica; (310) 828-3304 *Ambience*: Noisy. Bring an opera singer to project your orders to the waiters. A flashlight wouldn't be amiss. The decorator is a believer in artful gloom. This is a steakhouse for the "Buffy the Vampire Slayer" generation. *Best dishes*: are liquid, including the Manhattan, Old-Fashioned and Lincoln Lemonade. Of solids, garlic fries and the shrimp cocktail. *Wine list*: Heavy on jammy-tasting big California reds such as Mount Veeder Cabernet Sauvignon, with big prices to match. Stick with cocktails.

Grabbing a Bite

Back to the Bayou

by Rick Bragg

from *Bon Appétit*

The regional restaurant round-up is often a deadly article to read, but in Rick Bragg's hands, his eating tour of Louisiana's bayou country becomes like a mini-novel, exploring the witchcraft of crawfish, cracklin's, and a zydeco breakfast.

I loved a Cajun woman once. It was her eyes, I believe. When I was a little boy, just because it is the kind of thing boys do, I would look at the hot sun through a green, sweating bottle of 7UP. The sunlight seemed to freeze in the middle of the bottle, and glow.

She had eyes like that.

I was afraid that coming back here, to her Louisiana, would make me think of Her. And sure enough, every mile, every road sign, tapped me deeper into that green bottle.

The Bayou Teche, seeming more mud than water, did not flow or even crawl, but just lay. Morgan City still existed on a bubble of oil, its conjugal beds left half empty by men who worked rigs out in the deep blue. Along the Atchafalaya River, blue herons, their beaks like stilettos, stabbed into the dark water and came back out with wriggling silver victims. Alligators and rumors of alligators haunted Lake Henderson, where gray trees raised stumps of arms into the haze.

All of it gritty, lovely, like Her.

My heart hurt, a little.

And my stomach growled.

The air on the side streets and outside the wood-framed restaurants smelled of crab boil and crawfish and hot lemons. In the roadside stores, big countertop Crock-Pots simmered with boudin, the sausage made from pork, liver, onions, rice, and spices. Iron pots in open-air cookshacks rendered tiny cubes of fatback into golden cracklin's, and old men and little children stood in gravel parking lots and ate them like M&M's. In the evenings, in dives and fine-dining establishments, chefs took the ingredients of their liquid country— the rice, crawfish, shrimp, oysters, okra, duck, trout, crab, catfish, turtle, and drum—and turned them into dishes that tasted better than the mere ingredients should have allowed.

With every bite I felt a little better, as if there were a tonic in the turtle soup—as if, since I had been hexed in the swamp, it was the swamp itself and its people that had to heal me.

They did their best. Descendants of French Canadian exiles who drifted south to these swamps and prairies in southern Louisiana more than two centuries ago, they have long been accused of fusing magic with their food. I ate it in oil towns and shrimp shacks and interstate gas stations, in themed restaurants with stuffed alligators swinging from the ceilings, and in late-night bars where there was more swinging than I care to remember.

I ate to forget.

Le Traiteur

The smell swirled from underneath the roof of the cooking shed and permeated the air over the parking lot, the smell of a million skillets of bacon all sizzling at once.

But it was a witch's cauldron of fatback, roiling, the cracklin's bopping up, the size of postage stamps, all crunchy skin on one side and thin layers of crisp-fried fat on the other.

Some people argue that Eddie Goulas makes the best cracklin's in Acadiana in his cook shed in Ruth, not far from Breaux Bridge. "I never did like cracklin's," Goulas said, as he and a few helpers trimmed the lean from big slabs of fatback, diced it, and fed it into the pots.

"I guess I thought if I can make them where I would eat them, they must be pretty good," he said. His face intent, he watched the trimming process, kept an eye on the heat. "It's not hard to do something," he said, "when you ain't guessing."

In the parking lot, I ate cracklin's from a paper sack. I listened to people speak to each other in French and smiled like an imbecile.

"The food, the music, it's the joy of life," explained 68-year-old Claude Simon Jr., as he handed me his business card—"Custom Woodwork, Antique Repair, Cowhide Furniture." At the bottom of the card, he has written in a single word: *Traiteur.*

Like his papa before him, he is a treater, a healer, someone the Cajuns—the ones who still believe—would ask to heal bellyaches, arthritis, or general malaise with herbs, roots, and prayers. His papa was a grand *traiteur.* Even when he was very old and in a nursing home, people came to be treated.

Sometimes evil spirits invade us, Simon explained, and make us forget to enjoy life. I nodded, my mouth full of cracklin's.

Before he left, Simon mentioned that he also does exorcisms.

"I don't charge. It's the Lord's work," he said. "I do accept donations."

LENA AND PAUL

I was healed a good bit more in Carencro, about a block from City Hall. Here, in a place called Paul's Pirogue, a spirit helped stir the pot.

It was a poor man's dish called catfish court bouillon, just a few catfish pieces smothered in stewed tomatoes, onions, and other good things. Paul's served it with some of the best potato salad, with Cajun spices in the mayonnaise.

I asked the man at the cash register: "Who cooked the catfish?" He told me he had, mostly, but his grandma, who has gone on, might as well have.

"It comes from her—I learned from her," said 43-year-old Terry Soignier, who manages Paul's Pirogue. "She lost her first husband in the yellow fever, I believe, of '46. Her name was Lena. My oldest brother had epilepsy, and she would sing to him in French. When she cooked, he was always on her hip."

He spoke about them both, the food and his grandmama, with such love that I expected to see her standing there. "A black cast-iron pot," he said, thinking back. "Fresh onions. Catfish, pulled from the bayou.

"Not a bad memory at all," he said.

I ordered a shrimp po'boy because I had seen one go by, and I lusted after it. It was deep-fryer hot, the shrimp spiced and peppery and served on the best French bread that I have ever tasted. It did not crumble into dust, like delicate, airy French bread, but was chewy, buttery, comforting.

I am sure someone's long-dead grandpapa kneaded that bread.

I walked out feeling loved.

T-SUE'S BREAD

I met the hands that had kneaded that bread, and I was half-right. Phillip "T-Sue" Roberts owns the bakery in Henderson that furnishes Paul's Pirogue—and much of the Atchafalaya Basin—with bread. The recipes go back to his grandparents, Pete and Delia Patin, who ran a family bakery in Cecilia from 1934 until 1975. It is not designed to be French bread at all, but just good bread.

Roberta's grandparents gave him his skill, and even his name.

"What does T-Sue mean, anyway?" I asked.

"Little drunk," he said.

"Oh," I said.

It involved a bottle of Crown Royal. "I was 13," he said, "and it was the first time they let me out of the house. It was an adventure."

I told him I reckoned so.

"I danced all night at the American Legion," he said, "whether the music was playing or not."

Someone told on him. His grandfather started calling him, in French, *tee soux,* or "little drunk."

That became T-Sue, and that is what he named his bakery.

I ate a piece of bread stuffed with boudin from Charlie-T's Specialty Meats in Breaux Bridge. I can't write well enough to tell you how good it was.

LIKE CHICKEN

The waitress was pushing the alligator at Prejean's, the big Cajun restaurant in Lafayette, but I don't like to eat things that are said to taste like chicken—snake, alligator, iguana—when what they really taste like is snake and lizard. Instead, I ate delicious corn-and-crab bisque, and asked about dessert.

How about the *gâteau sirop,* the syrup cake?

"I don't like it," she said.

It was dense and dark and tasted of molasses.

"Did you like it?" the waitress asked.

"Yes," I said.

"A lot of the older people do," she said.

The bakery chef's name is Roe Zenon, a smiling but no-nonsense woman who eyed a single fly in her bakeshop like it was a flying gopher. She told me she learned from her mom, Bulia Zenon, who called it spice cake.

Her mom would call to her from the porch, "and the kids in the neighborhood would smell that cooking and all come with me. 'Your momma cooking?' they'd ask me. She always was. Momma would say, 'We always got something burning.' "

The children ate their spice cake with Kool-Aid.

I ate mine with gratitude.

Before I left, the folks at Prejean's made me try the alligator. "We just use the tail meat, not the lung meat, and never from a gator over six feet," said Dean Dugas, the general manager. I didn't know what that meant, but it was good.

FOOD OF LOVE

Dickie Breaux and Cynthia Breaux, once married but still partners in Café Des Amis, the restaurant they founded more than a decade ago, are still bound. Their love of the Breaux Bridge restaurant, and its food, survived their breakup.

"I believe you and I were brought together to create this thing," Cynthia said to Dickie one night at dinner.

If that is true, then maybe I was left standing in a driveway in Miami, watching taillights fade, just so I could be healed by barbecued shrimp and a slab of white-chocolate bread pudding. All I know is, it is hard to be heartsick when you are eating crawfish étouffée served on hot cornbread.

"You have to be raised in the atmosphere of the food," said Dickie Breaux. "We just cook better than anybody else. A Cajun knows he's got it right when, after it's done, you can throw away the meat and just eat the gravy."

The gravy, then. The gravy is the antidote.

That night, I ate the best turtle soup I have ever had. I listened to people who love food talk about how it can hold something fine together that might otherwise have come apart. I knew I couldn't face my bed-and-breakfast on the Teche.

I knew I wouldn't sleep.

So I asked the question millions of men like me have asked.

"Know a good beer joint?"

SQUEEZE BOX

The dance floor at Pat's Atchafalaya Club was packed with a hundred, more. Geno Delafose wore his squeeze box low, like a gunslinger, singing in French and English as white people and black people and old people and young people danced like it was their last night on this earth. Crawfish corpses littered the tables. The band never took a break. The dancing never stopped. A big woman in a pantsuit looked at me a little too long, and I got scared.

The next morning, a Saturday, Café Des Amis opened for breakfast, but a breakfast like I had never seen. A zydeco band tore up the small stage at the front of the restaurant and people danced between tables loaded with bacon and eggs.

A lot of the people dancing were the same ones I had seen the night before. One of them, Ted Couvillion, said hello.

"My wife died of cancer two years ago," he said. He vanished into his grief, until his friends dragged him out dancing. Now, every week, he dances and dances his way out of heartache.

I can't dance a lick. But I have two bags of cracklin's in the trunk of my car.

Street Food: Jamaica

by Barry Estabrook
from *Gourmet*

On a Jamaican seacoast, Estabrook's evocative article stirs an appetite for true street food: open-air roadside stands where traditional island food is cheap and enormously satisfying.

Women surrounded my car before it had rolled to a complete stop, pressing their torsos against the doors and jostling for the best position to display their wares: bottles of Red Stripe nestled in washbasins of crushed ice; stacks of bammy, a flavorful flatbread made from the starchy tuber cassava; and whole snappers no bigger than my hand, fired to a beautiful golden hue and lying between fat slices of yellow, red, and green hot peppers.

I had just rounded a hairpin bend where the road skirted tiny, opalescent Scott's Cove on Jamaica's south coast. Scott's Cove lies on the border of St. Elizabeth, a lush agricultural parish and a mother lode of spontaneous roadside meals, all sold and prepared within arm's reach of the automobile window and available for a few crumpled bills. In Jamaica, it is on the streets, not in deluxe resorts, that the country's unique culinary culture comes alive. It was going to take more than the zealous sale tactics of the fry-fish ladies to deter me from my quest. Besides, it had been six hours since lunch. I was damn hungry.

I cracked open the car door and was assailed by a cacophony of island voices as the women crowded around, blocking my exit. "You see me first." "Buy from me." "Hot, mon. Jus' cooked." "Beer well cold." "You remember me." "I the oldest." "I the youngest." "Hey, Mister White Mon." "I the youngest." "Hey, Mister White Mon."

Feigning deafness, I managed to squeeze out and made my way toward several women who were tending large metal pots over open fires near the seashore. The boisterous entourage followed. One of the cooks snatched up a gutted whole snapper and tied it deftly with a few strands of tough dried grass to keep it from falling apart. She tossed it into the hot oil, where it bubbled vigorously. "You want fry fish?" she said. I nodded. "Bammy, too?" she asked and, not waiting for a response, gestured to one of the women. A second was summoned to provide a bottle of beer.

Introducing herself as Michelle, the cook pointed to a few drift-wood planks covered with a faded red-checked plastic tablecloth. Now that she had established an exclusive franchise on my business, the hectoring crowd dissolved as suddenly as it had appeared.

The fish arrived on a piece of foil, accompanied by four pancake-size rounds of warm bammy in a plastic bag. Seeing me hesitate, Michelle seized a piece of the bammy and, with a fork, flaked off chunks of the snapper, topping them with big slices of onions and peppers that had been marinating in salt and vinegar. She left me to eat in silence. The fish, moist beneath its crackling skin, was as sweet as only fish consumed a matter of yards from the sea can be; the perfect acid bite of the onions and peppers was quickly neutralized by the dense bammy. It was Jamaica's answer to the fish taco. I wanted to thank Michelle, but a minibus crammed with Jamaicans had pulled in. She had disappeared into the scrum that was pushing against its doors.

I rose early the next morning and nibbled a light breakfast. At a general store, I equipped myself with a roll of paper towels to deal with spills and dribbles and two liters of spring water, my weapon against the fierce heat that can lurk in even the most innocuous-seeming Jamaican dish.

I headed toward Middle Quarters, a village in the heart of St. Eliz-abeth that sits beside the Great Morass, a vast mangrove-choked estuary that is home to exotic birds and endangered crocodiles. But I couldn't resist stopping at a fruit and vegetable stand, where a young man was roasting several dozen ears of corn directly on the coals of a wood fire. He handed me an ear balanced on a corn husk napkin. It was substantial and chewy, with the flavor of a roasted corn tortilla.

Twenty or so minutes later, I stood beneath a vast archway of bamboo that framed a lone woman sitting beside a plastic picnic cooler and a pile of unripe (green) coconuts. She was young, slight, and soft-spoken, but she knew how to handle a machete. Holding a coconut outstretched in one hand she neatly decapitated it with three quick whacks and handed me the nut and a drinking straw. The cold, sweetish coconut water slipped down smoothly. But the best part was yet to come. She reclaimed the drained nut, chopped it in half, and hacked a rounded chip off the side. I used my biodegradable spoon to scoop out the gelatinous meat.

I didn't need a sign to know I'd arrived in Middle Quarters. At every narrow bend, knots of women hoisted plastic bags full of Day-Glo-orange crustaceans and lunged halfway out onto the pavement, shrieking, "Swimps! Swimps!"

On the theory that age begets culinary prowess, I stopped for an old woman hovering over a soot-blackened pot that sent up tendrils of fragrant steam. For about two dollars, I procured a bag of a dozen large freshwater shrimp. She showed me how to twist the tails off and pinch them to break them in half, liberating a morsel of flesh. They were like Louisiana crayfish, juicy and hot, yes, but not painfully so, their edginess rounded by a fulsome saltiness, along with hints that I couldn't identify. "Just island spices," she said coyly. "Stuff I find in the forest."

At every intersection, in every open-air market, beside every ramshackle rum shop, and sometimes from seemingly nowhere at all, the irresistible smells of jerk—whiffs of smoldering pimento, or allspicewood, coals; charring chicken and pork fat; and tingling fumes of Scotch bonnet chiles—escape from cut-in-half steel drums, often overseen by guys nursing spliffs in the deep shade of almond trees. I was determined to visit the source: Boston Bay, supposedly where jerk was invented, a contention as impossible to prove and as hotly disputed as the question of who invented barbecue in America. I'd heard, though, that "Shaggy" (Dudley) Taylor made some of the most authentic jerk pork on the island at his pit in Boston Bay.

Driving there would take an entire day, so I left my hotel before breakfast. At journey's end, a herd of spotted piglets wallowed in a mud hole just a few yards from where whole sides of their kin cooked. Shaggy was not manning the pit, though. The legendary jerk man had been forced to retire because of ill health, but, luckily, his son Kenford and daughter Sophia have taken over, and things are still done the traditional way. The pork rests on a grate of long, slender poles of mahoe wood placed across the sides of the pit 18 inches above smoldering pimento coals. Kenford hacked me up a pound. The meat was smoky, fall-apart tender, and almost buttery, like the finest barbecue. It tasted like American pork used to taste: Full of fat and flavor, it stood up to the smoke and spice. Scallions, allspice, and thyme played supporting roles, and the Scotch bonnet dope-slapped my taste buds.

The next day on my way to the airport, the yeasty aroma of baking bread at a roundabout in the bustling market town of Falmouth caused me to brake sharply. The scent emanated from a storefront operation called Spicy Nice Pastries, where I bought something called a callaloo loaf and a beef patty, as prevalent in Jamaica as the Big Mac is in the United States. (An island-wide chain called Juicy Patties is as hard to escape as the Golden Arches.) As I maneuvered the car through the crowded streets, clutching the crescent-shaped pastry packet in one hand, shards of annatto-hued piecrust showered onto my lap. When I bit in, a gravylike gush of highly spiced beef shot into my mouth.

The callaloo loaf turned out to be a bread-dough turnover filled with callaloo—a green, leafy vegetable that tastes like spinach—mixed with chopped onion and minuscule orange flakes of Scotch bonnet. I tucked it into my carry-on in anticipation of the long trip ahead. When the flight attendants began to push their carts down the aisle, I treated myself to one last jolt of Jamaica. After my savory odyssey, no way could I face a little bag of pretzels.

Jamaican Hot Pepper Shrimp

ACTIVE TIME: 10 Min   START TO FINISH: 1½ Hr (Includes Cooling)

Peel these fiery shrimp as you eat them.

4 cups water
½ cup chopped scallion
4 garlic cloves, crushed

3 fresh thyme sprigs
3 fresh Scotch bonnet or habanero chiles, halved and seeded
2 tablespoons salt
½ teaspoon black pepper
10 whole allspice
1 lb large shrimp in shell (21 to 25 per lb)

Combine all ingredients except shrimp in a 4-quart heavy pot and bring to a boil, then reduce heat and simmer, covered, 20 minutes.

Stir in shrimp, making sure they are just covered by liquid, and remove pot from heat. Cool shrimp in liquid to room temperature, uncovered, about 1 hour. Transfer shrimp with a slotted spoon to a plate or bowl and drizzle some of cooking liquid on top.

SERVES 4

A Sonnet in Two Birds

by John T. Edge

from *Fried Chicken: An American Story*

> First in a delicious quartet of books about iconic American foods, *Fried Chicken* traces Edge's cross-country pilgrimage to find the "authentic" version of this beloved dish, from home kitchens to roadside stands to top restaurants.

S cott Peacock, chef of Watershed, a hip, celadon-hued restaurant and wine bar in Decatur, Georgia, fries chicken on Tuesdays. And only on Tuesdays. John Fleer, chef of the Inn at Blackberry Farm, a luxe resort in the Great Smoky Mountains of northeastern Tennessee, fries chicken on Saturdays. And only on Saturdays.

In the modern South—where fried chicken is oftentimes a dish of immediate resort, a fast-food commodity purchased by the box and on the go—once-a-week restaurant chicken feeds are both romantic and practical. Romantic in that they bespeak a time when fried chicken was known among many rural folk as a farm-raised, Sunday indulgence, a gospel bird. Practical in that the two-plus days of prep work now employed by these chefs is onerous.

Prevailing wisdom—as communicated by Southern cookbooks of the past century, especially by those books geared toward home cooks—leads you to believe that fried chicken is among the most elemental of dishes. Many contemporary recipes dictate such simplicity that, if the fried chicken actually tastes as good as promised, I'm inclined to look to sorcery as the reason.

Cut and wash the chicken, dredge in flour, season with salt, and fry. That's what Mary Randolph, author of the 1824 masterwork *The Virginia Housewife,* would have you do. And if you talk to a Southerner with puritanical culinary inclinations, they are likely to subscribe to the Randolphian school. These cooks believe in paying homage to great ingredients by allowing their integrity to shine through.

But chicken ain't what it used to be. Big-breasted, spindly-legged birds, raised in close confinement and shot through with all manner of growth-promoting hormones and antibiotics, are now the rule. Yard birds raised *en plein air,* scratching about for scraps and grain while developing stronger muscles and, by extension, darker and more flavorful meat, are the exception. And so it follows that, if chicken ain't what it used to be, then neither is fried chicken.

One of the abiding themes of my pilgrimage has proven to be that, throughout the country, the most intriguing fried chicken dishes seem to be served by restaurants where the cooks monkey the most with the birds. In the South, this trend rings truest. At Gus's, chicken marinates in a viscous, pepper-laced solution that resembles crimson yogurt and gives the chicken a lip-tingling heat; Austin Leslie swears by topping his deep-fried chicken with a confetti of garlic and parsley as well as a spot of pickle juice; and at Greenwood's the chicken emerges a bit dry from the fryer, but is redeemed by dipping the breasts in pepper vinegar and then drizzling them with honey.

And yet, these folks have nothing on Peacock and Fleer, the aforementioned weekly fryers. I am not inclined to posit that either cooks the best fried chicken in the South—or even that such a such a designation has merit—but I am convinced that both gentlemen have achieved a modern mastery, balancing age-old ways and new imperatives of flavor.

Scott Peacock's chicken *looks* simple. The presentation is straightforward. Breast, leg, and thigh, each piled one atop the other on a white plate, each burnished a coppery brown. Accompaniments are whipped potatoes and garlicky green beans. Fat and fluffy biscuits too.

I bite into the breast. The crust has fused with the skin, and it crackles upon contact with my teeth. You can actually *hear* the crunch. And while most white meat is dry, woody even, this bird squirts juice. Not grease, but juice, rivulets of pork-scented chicken broth. After spending a few hours at Watershed, talking chicken with Peacock, scribbling notes as he advanced various theories of cookery that both met and confounded my expectations, I was prepared to be disappointed.

No taste could be worth brining the bird for twenty-four hours in a saltwater solution, soaking it for an additional day in buttermilk, and then, after rolling the salted and peppered pieces in a mix of flour and a smidgen of cornstarch, frying them in a fifty-fifty mix of butter and lard infused with country ham. But there it is, on the plate, for all to admire: the perfect fried chicken breast.

It did not surprise me to hear Peacock say that he prefers to fry his chicken in a skillet. "Skillet cooking works from the bottom to the bone," he told me. "It's slower, more seductive than deep frying, like taking a warm bath instead of a scalding dip." And yet, although he dearly loved his grandmother, Peacock is not the kind of cook who wields her old skillet.

Instead, he fries his chicken in an oversized Italian-made stainless-steel pan that will accommodate twenty pieces. And then there's the matter of frying medium. Though he grew up in southern Alabama where the soil is a sandy loam, perfect for growing peanuts, he came to see that the peanut oil with which he was accustomed to cooking couldn't match the flavor punch of the aforementioned lard and butter admixture favored by his eighty-something-year-old mentor, Edna Lewis of Freetown, Virginia.

If forced to categorize his ethic, I would label Peacock a neo-traditionalist. His career has taken him from cooking quail at a hunt camp in southern Georgia, to serving broiled lobsters alongside a nasturtium salad at the Georgia governor's mansion. Along the way, Peacock has honed a very personal cuisine. Granted, he'd be the first to pay his due to his longtime friend and present housemate, Lewis, revered as a grande dame of the South. But by the sheer act of frying chicken this well, Peacock lays claim to his own place in the pantheon.

• • •

John Fleer's sweet-tea-marinated fried chicken will be cold by the time you taste it. Well, maybe it won't actually be cold—room temperature might be the best way to describe it. No matter, it won't be fresh from the fryer, for it was cooked about seven in the morning. More than likely, you will bite into your first drumstick on one of the switchback trails that went around Hurricane Mountain, eventually leading back to the Inn at Blackberry Farm. That's where, since 1992, Fleer has been cooking in a style that he's dubbed Foothills Cuisine.

Fleer came up with the idea of tea-brining while conferring with his sous-chef: "We were talking about how brines incorporate salt and liquid and acid, discussing how a little red wine never hurt. And then it hit me: sweet tea, the house wine of the South. . . . It's always seemed like the hardest part of my job has been packing five-star expectations into the green boxes we hand out for picnic lunches. I had been searching for something that was definitively Southern and distinctly ours. That was it."

On Wednesday, Fleer and his crew make tea. Sweet tea with lemon, the same brew served in hundreds of lunchrooms across the South. After stirring salt in to make a brine, the cooks submerge the chicken—they use legs and thighs only—in the marinade. Two days in the refrigerator follow, during which the salt carries the musky sweetness of the tea throughout the chicken. Early each Saturday the morning crew drain the birds before soaking them in a buttermilk and egg solution and then, finally, rolling the chicken twice in a mixture of cornflour and wheat flour spiked with salt and pepper and Old Bay seasoning.

I am present one recent Saturday morning when the first batch emerges from the fryer. The crust boasts a kind of pleasantly gritty exterior. But while Peacock's fused with the skin, Fleer's crust announces autonomy. As for the meat itself, the brine gives the legs and thighs a muted herbaceous quality that, if I were not aware of its source, I might attribute to unlikely origins, say bourbon or bitters or prune juice.

But Fleer's chicken, served hot from the fryer, is disappointing. Thanks to the heavy jacket developed during the double battering, that autonomous crust proves not to be an asset but a liability. It's tough. Truth be told, I don't realize the genius of what Fleer and his crew are up to until later that same day. I am an hour down the highway, when I start digging through the box that, upon checking out, I found waiting on my passenger seat.

Most guests get their first taste of Fleer's chicken the way he intends them to—after forging a stream or ascending a mountain. I, on the other hand, have merely set the cruise control and pushed aside a cob of basil-marinated corn, a tub of creamy pineapple coleslaw, a sesame cheddar biscuit, a deviled egg, and a marshmallow-smeared oatmeal cookie sandwich, before finding my prize: a cardboard box-within-a-box of the type that Chinese takeout restaurants favor.

Within are a leg and a thigh. In the six hours out of the fryer, they've mellowed. What's more, the sweet tea flavor has come to the fore. The crust that was unyielding at seven in the morning has softened to a point still shy of collapse. Now pliable, now a kind of cornmeal-cracklin' appetizer wrapped around a drumstick, it proves to be the ideal vessel for the odd but delicious consommé of chicken and Lipton's that dribbles down my chin.

Even after eating my fill of the fried chicken cooked by Peacock and Fleer, I remain unsure about what conclusions I should draw from their approaches. Both are ardent students of Southern cookery. Both are committed to working with fresh, local ingredients. Both have a predilection for buttermilk and a resolve that chicken—and for that matter, most any domesticated pork or poultry—tastes best when brined. But are these guys technocrats, intent upon reinventing fried chicken? Or are they fellow travelers in the tradition, bent upon wresting the most flavor and succulence from a bird that can be, at times, uncooperative?

Beats me, but their chicken eats great. And neither chef is secretive about sharing recipes. If you want to try to replicate Peacock's, just pick up a copy of his book *The Gift of Southern Cooking,* coauthored with Lewis. It's right there on page 104. As for Fleer, he's also at work on a book. And you can bet that when he hits the cooking school circuit, sweet-tea-brined fried chicken—served cold—will send his students into a collective swoon. Until that fine day, an adaptation of his recipe follows.

———∞∞∞———

Sweet-Tea Fried Chicken

| WALLAND, TENNESSEE |

John Fleer is a thinking man's chef, a onetime doctoral candidate in religion who chucked it all for a career in the kitchen. One of the best ideas to spring from his mind is this brined chicken, which manages to pay tribute to the traditional South of days past and the multicultural South still on the horizon.

8 chicken leg quarters, cut into thighs and drumsticks
1 quart brewed tea, double strength
1 lemon, quartered
1 cup sugar
½ cup kosher salt
1 quart ice water
3 cups all-purpose flour
2 cups cornflour (or fish fry)
2 tablespoons Old Bay seasoning
1 tablespoon chili powder
1 teaspoon salt
1 teaspoon pepper
8 eggs
1 cup buttermilk
Peanut oil

Combine tea, lemon, sugar, and kosher salt, and simmer for 5 minutes or until salt and sugar are completely dissolved. Pour in ice water and cool brine completely. Submerge thighs and drumsticks in brine for 48 hours.

Remove to a wire rack and allow chicken to drain. Combine 2 cups of the flour and the cornflour, Old Bay, chili powder, salt, and pepper in a large bowl. Place remaining 1 cup flour in a medium bowl, and in a third bowl beat eggs with buttermilk. Line up bowls of flour, egg-buttermilk mixture, and flour-cornflour mixture, in that order. Coat the chicken in the flour, then the egg-buttermilk mixture, and then the flour–cornflour mixture, applying pressure to ensure even adherence. Let the chicken sit in the refrigerator for ½ hour before frying.

Pour oil into a heavy pot at a depth of at least 3 inches. Heat oil to 300°. Fry chicken, submerged in oil, for 15 minutes, or until an internal thermometer registers 170° for dark meat, 160° for white meat. Drain on a rack. Cool to room temperature, and then place in refrigerator for at least 4 hours and no more than 24. Serve cool from a picnic basket or cold, straight from the fridge.

SERVES 8

Some Like It Extra Hot

by David Ramsey

from *The Oxford American*

Nashville's culinary specialty, hot chicken, is not just a meal, it's an experience. Ramsey—editor of Little Rock, Arkansas's *Localist* magazine—captures not only the flavors but the culinary psychopathology of hot-chicken addicts.

My friend, on his first visit to Nashville, is trying to make his way through a breast of our fair city's strange specialty, hot chicken. On my suggestion, he ordered the Hot, and I am feeling guilty. He is crying. Sweating heavily. His face has turned the color of watermelon fruit and the hue is growing redder and spreading down the neck. His eyes are bloodshot and his lips are puffed out to about twice their size. "Don't try to talk," I say.

And he dives back in, droplets of his own sweat and tears landing on each bite of chicken before it reaches his mouth. The thought that he might pass out crosses my mind, but slowly, gruntingly, he manages to finish off the breast.

To my surprise, around midnight, he insists that we make a return visit to Prince's Hot Chicken Shack, and there is no talking him out of it. He is smiling, but his tone is firm and serious: "I gotta get some more of that chicken."

Though hot chicken is not peculiar to Nashville, the city is uniquely obsessed with the dish (which gets its own category in the weekly paper's dining listings). Prince's is Nashville's oldest hot chicken joint still in business, and the best. Despite the moniker, it's not actually a shack; the small restaurant is located alongside several hair and nail salons in a small shopping center just off Dickerson Pike in north Nashville, near a stretch infamous as an active pickup spot for the city's prostitutes.

Prince's serves its bird piping hot, fresh out of enormous cast-iron skillets, over slices of white bread: crispy-fried breast, leg, or wings, thoroughly marinated in the most savage combination of spices I've ever encountered (recipes are closely guarded, of course, but there's no doubt that copious doses of cayenne are involved). The result is a truculent re-thinking of the very possibilities of fried chicken.

Prince's chicken is offered in degrees of heat, and you can tell them apart by the color of the crust. The Mild is orange and plenty spicy, what most restaurants would label "hot." The Medium is dark red and even more sizzling, what most folks would label "unreasonable." Ordering anything above that will earn you a stern warning from the staff if you're a newcomer: The Hot is a deep, peppery maroon, hotter than the spiciest Indian or Thai food. Cayenne, much of which has caked into little bunches, has been applied so generously that the entire outer layer, though moist, is also dusty in texture.

The first bite is like taking a punch, the muscles stiffening and the heart beating fast. You feel like every organ in your body is saying, "What the hell was *that*?" It's otherworldly, so fierce you're ready to make up brand-new cuss words because no existing exclamation is sufficient.

And that's the easy part—thereafter, the heat steadily amplifies. The tingle on the lips and the tongue slowly turns to outright pain. Sinuses explode open and everything from the neck up swelters.

Among those eating at the restaurant's five tables (still with the original benches from sixty-odd years ago), there's never much talking. This isn't a meal, but rather an experience, and getting through it takes a healthy measure of sheer will, endurance, and guts. Once finished, folks wear a different brand of satisfaction on their faces: Not simple fullness or the light afterglow of a pleasant meal, but a sense of *accomplishment*. Wiping the orange-red coating off their lips, eyes wide and watery, sighing and smiling and sighing again. They look like mountain climbers who have just planted the flag.

Maybe to eat at Prince's, you have to be a little crazy. To order the Hot certainly requires a basic neglect for personal safety. But for true culinary psychopaths, there is one other option, a fearful choice that sits off to the side on the menu, beckoning the loony.

Extra Hot.

I have a pretty high tolerance for hot food (I have won bets by putting away substantial lumps of wasabi in one swallow). But this is something altogether different. I already order my chicken Hot and the very notion of a meaner, nastier cousin is almost unfathomable.

But if you eat chicken at Prince's long enough, if you work your way up to the Hot and start to get used to it (and hooked), the temptation to take that final step becomes overwhelming. For more than a year, in fact, I have pondered taking the plunge. And now, I have decided, the time has come to try the Extra Hot. I pray that I am ready.

I am taking on this mission against the wisdom of anyone with sense. My mother briefly concerns herself with the possibility of an ulcer. Customers in the store guffaw at the very idea. "Make sure you bring plenty of toilet paper," one counsels me. "There's no polite way to put it."

And then there are the dire warnings from those who've tried before me.

About a year ago, I was in a parking lot in downtown Nashville, about to hit the honky-tonks and eating some Hot chicken I'd picked up from Prince's. A homeless guy wandered up to me. "I knew it," he said. "I could see by the look on your face that you just came from Prince's." I shared a few bites with him and we agreed that Prince's served up some life-changing poultry.

"You know," I told him. "I've been thinking about trying the Extra Hot."

The man stopped eating, took a step back, and looked at me like I was a ghost.

"Well, I've been eating the Hot for a while," I said. "I think I'm ready to take the next step."

He just shook his head. "Hot is all right," he said. "I love Hot. But Extra Hot. . . ." His eyes squinted. "I tried it once. I want you to look at me. Now you can see that I can't afford to be wasting no food. Well, I tried that Extra Hot, took two or three bites, and had to throw away a whole bird. That there was *too much.*"

• • •

Andre Prince Jeffries has been running Prince's for twenty-five years. The business opened in 1945 as the Bar-B-Que Chicken Shack, and Jeffries changed it to the family name when she took over in 1980.

The restaurant's founder was Thornton Prince, Jeffries's great-uncle. According to legend, it was a girlfriend of Thornton Prince who got this whole thing started. Prince was a notorious woman-izer, and on one occasion when he stayed out all night long, his girlfriend—an adroit cook—decided to get back at him. If the way to a man's heart is through his stomach, she must have figured, it's not a bad pathway for revenge. She spiked his fried chicken with a vicious bevy of hot peppers. She wasn't trying to kill him, exactly, but it wouldn't be too far off to say that she meant to poison the man.

She served it to him, and the strangest thing happened. He loved it. Couldn't get enough. And so, the story goes, hot chicken was born.

"She was mad, but her madness turned into something good," explains Jeffries. She smiles, adding, "She did it for punishment, but he liked it."

And that remains just about the perfect way to describe eating chicken at Prince's—like you're being punished, but you like it.

"You hear all kinds of things," says Jeffries. "One man said it took the hair right off his chest, another one said it put the hair *on* his chest."

"We'll have pregnant women come in. I advise against it, of course. But they want it. Some of them come when they're overdue. They eat this chicken and the baby pops right out."

If customers don't call in the order ahead of time, a wait of an hour or even more is not unusual, even in the wee hours (Prince's is open until four in the morning on Friday and Saturday nights). "This is definitely not fast food," says Jeffries. "We're known as the mature chicken. This is adult chicken."

The long wait doesn't slow down the demand a bit; customers aren't just devoted regulars, they're addicts. "I don't know what it is," says Jeffries. "It has something to do with the chemistry of the body. It ignites something—have mercy!"

• • •

Jeffries is right, it does have something to do with chemistry. The chemical in question is capsaicin, the active component of chili peppers. While such spices as pepper, cinnamon, ginger, cloves, and tumeric have been popular in Europe, Africa, and the East for thousands of years, food as diabolically hot as Prince's was exclusive to the Americas until Columbus's landing.

The ante for Old World spice was considerably upped with what Columbus found: scalding New World peppers like cayenne, habanero, and jalapeño. *"Mejor que pimienta nuestra,"* he wrote—better than our own peppers. Just as it's hard to imagine Italians without tomatoes or Russians without potatoes to make vodka, it's hard to imagine, say, Thai cuisine without chilies. But all of that came after sixteenth-century fusion using New World crops.

Capsaicin is what gives these peppers their kick. The chemical is fat-soluble rather than water-soluble, which is why fatty foods or milk ease the residue's burn and water doesn't. It's also the active ingredient in pepper spray (if you eat at Prince's, wash your hands before wiping your eyes). It would take a whole lot of chili peppers, but a capsaicin overdose is theoretically possible. If you could manage to drink, say, a gallon of Tabasco sauce, you would probably turn from red to blue, pass out, and die from respiratory paralysis.

Capsaicin has also been used as an animal and insect deterrent (birds are not affected, so it's a good way to keep squirrels away from feeders). Indeed, biologists theorize that the very reason that plants came to produce it in the first place is to keep away mammalian predators. Human beings are the only mammals nutty enough to actually *enjoy* the painful reaction.

No one knows exactly why this is. One popular theory is that sufficient quantities of capsaicin release endorphins. Endorphins are natural painkillers produced by the pituitary gland. They act like morphine (the name itself is a shortening of "endogenous morphine"). In addition to an analgesic effect, they produce a feeling of elation and euphoria. "Runners' high" is thought to come from endorphin-release, and riding on a roller coaster is another way to get a dose. Or, if you can handle them, chili peppers. A need for the endorphin buzz might help explain why so many Nashvillians can't go long without a fix of Prince's.

There's another addictive effect of capsaicin, which may or may not be separate from endorphins: It reconfigures the experience of flavor. *"Sin chile, no creen que están comiendo!"* remarked Bartolome de las Casas, a sixteenth-century Spanish explorer, of the Native Americans. ("Without chili, they don't think they are eating!")

When I'm recommending Prince's, I usually say, "It will change the way you think about chicken." Imagine someone whose only exposure to dairy had been skim milk suddenly trying a pungent cheese. That's the kind of new possibility represented by hot chicken. It is flavor mutated, and fresh nuances emerge. (Some folks, of course, think this is a bunch of hooey—and argue that severe heat represents the negation of flavor. This argument is usually expressed thusly, often by a wimp: "It's so hot I can't taste a thing!")

Finally, there's the simple thrill of grappling with the extremity, the rush of powering ahead despite the danger signals screaming inside the body. "There is no more lively sensation than that of pain," wrote the Marquis de Sade, on a slightly different subject. "[I]ts impressions are certain and dependable, they never deceive. . . ."

The most intense varieties of pleasure and pain might feel close to the same. It's not that big a jump, in other words, from "this is so good it hurts" to "this hurts so good." A little bit of torture, within reason, can be a lot of fun. Of course, the idea of what's reasonable varies dramatically from person to person, which is why Prince's offers different degrees of heat.

Maybe it's the endorphins or maybe it's just damn good. Either way, hot chicken takes me somewhere I like to go.

With this kind of heat, strategy becomes important. Ordering with fries is a must, and one must be careful to conserve them, as well as the two slices of bread and four slices of pickle. The pickle is a surprising coolant and the carbohydrates are your lifeline.

Though sodas are offered, they're a bad idea; the carbonation prickles too harshly on the way down. I always go with lemonade. Technically, nothing water-based can provide relief, but I find that holding the drink and swishing it around is a comfort, however fleeting.

The other key is to not pause in the eating for too long. The scorching inside the mouth only gets worse. Like a drug, when eating hot chicken, the only cure for the pain is more of that which causes the pain.

Then there are more creative approaches. "We have one man who always gets the Extra Hot to go," says Jeffries. "He takes it home, runs a tub full of cold water, and eats his chicken in the bath."

Once consumed, hot chicken affects different people different ways.

"There's a prostitute who picks up men at the truckstop and brings them here every Saturday night," Jeffries tells me. "She makes them buy her this chicken before they get involved. She always gets the Hot. It turns her on. One time she just couldn't wait. She got out there and did the final act right on the hood of the car. That chicken—it does something to her."

New Jersey indie rockers Yo La Tengo came upon Prince's while recording in Nashville and were so smitten that they have named several songs in honor of the restaurant—including "Flying Lesson (Hot Chicken #1)" and "Return to Hot Chicken." Nashville mayor Bill Purcell, a longtime regular, had Prince's officially designated the best restaurant in the state of Tennessee in 1996, when he was the majority leader in the state House of Representatives. "It was my last act, using all the powers of the office, which were unlimited—at least that's what I decided on that day," says the mayor, who always has the Hot and conducts business meetings at Prince's with anyone willing. "Hot chicken is Nashville's one unique food. It's unlike anything you've had before. It's an immediate connection. I find myself renewed for all purposes. Eating it immediately reinforces whatever is best about you."

Jeffries herself has never gone past Mild. She's a solid and sensible woman, one gathers, who just happens to be in the business of feeding maniacs.

When I tell her I'm planning to give the Extra Hot a go she pulls back and sighs. She looks half like she wants to scold me and half like she wants to give me a hug. "Just make sure you get an Alka-Seltzer," she says, patting my arm. "And don't travel any long distances."

It's a good twenty-five-minute drive from Prince's to my house, which I decide I'd better keep to myself.

"When you get done, lay down a little while, rest yourself," she says. "Get comfortable. This is what I call twenty-four-hour chicken. Be near a restroom. This is a cleansing. This is a filter. Allow it to just filter on through."

. . .

My day of reckoning comes on Friday, January 28. The whole day is spent on prep work. In the morning I do some stretches, some jumping jacks to get loose. For lunch: two toasted bagels. This seems solid. I mix some aloe vera juice with my orange juice. I try to visualize success. I have read about basketball players picturing the ball leaving their hand and falling through the net before a game; I try to imagine picking up the final bite with a corner of bread and wiping my mouth upon completion, but other more disturbing images come to mind: the collapse of several internal organs, taste buds swollen beyond function, a breast of chicken personified as a fanged, marinated devil, etc.

I arrive at Prince's around 7:00 PM. Though I called ahead, my order's not quite ready. I pace around the restaurant, trying without much success to appear calm and collected. I rub my belly.

Someone finally calls my name and casually repeats my order: Extra Hot breast, fries, and a lemonade. At the mention of "extra," a couple of heads turn. "Oh boy," says one guy, and his friend just stands there trying not to laugh. The chicken is several shades darker than blood. It's almost brown; almost black, in fact.

A customer has just left, so I'm lucky enough to have a table to myself. The bread beneath the chicken has been entirely soaked through with red. I break off a small piece and use it to pick up some chicken. I take it in. The crust crunches softly under the bread. There's the jolt, but at first it's more or less the same as the Hot. Okay, I think, I can do this. Then comes the afterburn: It's as if a chute of lava enters at my throat and runs down the length of my body and right back up. I can feel the prickling all the way to my fingertips. I try to calm things down with a french fry, but it's no use. I have to keep going. With each bite, the crust singes every nerve in my mouth. Only the tender white meat inside briefly eases the burn.

About halfway through, sweaty and a bit dizzy, I start to wonder whether I'll be able to finish. Every breath hurts. I feel a bit faint. My vision seems to be going.

An ambulance happens to pull up. For a moment, I honestly think that it has come for me. I am fairly certain that I might be dying.

I stop and breathe slowly. I eat a small piece, and another. Then it happens: The fire starts to feel good. I feel the surge of what distance runners call a second wind. I may be a little woozy, but I am in the home stretch. I'm a cartoon character with steam coming out my ears; I can't wait to take another agonizing chomp. I can no longer feel my lips. It no longer matters.

"How was it?" someone asks me as I scoop up the final morsels of fiery skin with my remaining dabs of bread. "Are you all right?"

But I can't answer him. I can't even speak. I am gone, on some other planet, loving it, burning away.

It's to Die For

by Brett Anderson
from the *New Orleans Times-Picayune*

> Brett Anderson is one of those local writers
> who does it all—reporting on the city's food
> scene, reviewing restaurants along the full
> range of the gourmet spectrum, and putting
> into words how we as diners relate to our
> food.

Earlier this year, I went to the doctor for the first time since
moving to New Orleans almost four years ago. The visit was
prompted by a cough that wouldn't quit, although the cough,
which was rather quickly attributed to asthma, did not dominate the
patient-physician dialogue. Instead we talked about my job.

Which led to a discussion about my diet.

Which led to my doctor scheduling me for a stress test.

Which led to an appointment with a clinical dietitian.

The turn of events was not surprising. While health-consciousness
is not a prerequisite for vocational dining, people commonly respond
to the revelation that I eat out for a living with a shiver of disbelief
("You get paid to do that?"), quickly followed by what I like to think
is concern for my well-being. The inquiries are so similar and recur-
ring that I've developed stock answers:

"Yes, I'll eat basically anything, although I've never really understood why people enjoy kidneys."

"I'm not skinny. I wear baggy clothes."

"Sometimes, er, sort of. I mean not so much. But I do belong to
a gym!"

That last response was not the one my nutritionist wanted to hear when she asked about my exercise habits. As expected, she was somewhat flummoxed by how fully my profession and temperament restricted me from acting on her diet advice. But I sensed her enjoying the challenge, and her dissertations on cholesterol, high-mercury seafood and assorted flavors of fat (saturated, omega 3, etc.) did not fall on deaf ears.

I have not strayed from my long-held conviction that the body is, in fact, a plaything (brain included). But I also don't need a doctor to tell me I'm not getting any younger.

I'd consider going easy on the foie gras.

My only worry was that I'd have to shelve my plans to visit Tuckers Tavern.

As its sign and menu advertises, Tuckers is "Home of the Stuffed Deep Fried Burger." Its existence was brought to my attention a few years ago by a friend who assumed that I'd feel a professional duty to investigate the restaurant's distinctive specialty. He assumed correctly. The public would want to know about these hamburgers.

Then I discovered that there was more: Jabba Jaws Bar & Bites, a Metairie saloon, offers a long list of deep-fried stuffed burgers as well. Having decided that I'd sat on the scoop for too long, I actually made it a New Year's resolution to get to the bottom of the story.

But the doctor/nutritionist trips complicated matters. As a populist who gets paid to lionize food that most people can't afford, I'm no stranger to hypocrisy. But the manner in which my job is at odds with my health has never really given me pause. Or at least that's what I thought before the folks at Ochsner made me realize that I'd developed what might be called a health subconsciousness.

I'd avoided those deep fried burgers for a reason: I suspected them to be profoundly unhealthy. The realization made me feel like a pro football linebacker who'd just discovered that his affection for tearing apart running backs could lead to injury.

Lucky for me, I didn't need to look far for the gumption to tackle the fried burger challenge. Just as I had started to subconsciously count calories, I began to notice a cultural shift in people's attitudes toward dining and its perils.

In February, just a few weeks after my meeting with the dietitian, the paperback of a book by someone called Starbuck O'Dwyer appeared at a bookstore not far from Jabba Jaws. The title, *Red Meat*

Cures Cancer, caught my eye, as did its tale of an oily fast food tycoon trying to market his (yes) deep-fried, mayonnaise-slathered hamburgers to a health-conscious public. It's a crudely unsubtle piece of writing strung with laugh lines. (Such as: "Phrases like 'belt-tightening' are frightening when spoken by a man with a 66-inch waist.")

Not long afterward I was reading "Debarking," the latest short story by Lorrie Moore, one of my new favorite writers. It starred Zora, a fiercely eccentric, steak-loving pediatrician whose car's bumper sticker distilled the spirit of O'Dwyer's book down to two sentences: "Red meat is not bad for you. Fuzzy, greenish blue meat is bad for you."

Red Meat and "Debarking" both struck me as highly original, not to mention very different. (Aside from Zora's steak fixation, "Debarking" isn't about food at all.) But the stick-out-the-tongue worldview recalls a whimsical attitude that has long flavored choice works of serious food-related non-fiction. You can see it in books as disparate as Calvin Trillin's sublime "American Fried" or "The Pleasure Police: How Bluenose Busybodies and Lily-Livered Alarmists Are Taking All the Fun Out of Life" by the Pulitzer-winner David Shaw.

And it's there in *Supersize Me*, the hit documentary that follows filmmaker Morgan Spurlock over a month in which he eats nothing but McDonald's. Spurlock set out to implicate McDonald's in the nation's obesity epidemic with a fit of daring culinary exhibitionism, and the film contains plenty of chilling sequences. The moment of truth comes when one of Spurlock's doctors notifies him that his liver, which he said "is now like pâté," is leaking dangerous enzymes into his blood.

But, still, levity pervades the film. Spurlock comes off as a slimmer, less dominating version of Michael Moore. He's self-effacing enough to let his girlfriend talk about how the diet is affecting his sexual performance. When he describes his physical discomfort—the "McStomachaches" and the way it sometimes "feels like somebody's yanking on the tendons behind my eyes"—it tends to garner laughs, not groans.

There's nothing funny about eating years off your life, but Spurlock did remind me how much easier hard kernels of truth go down with a chaser of comic relief. This is always useful around the table, particularly in New Orleans, where diners are experts at weighing risk against pleasure. Everyone should know about the dangers of the assorted fat flavors. But that knowledge doesn't have to impinge on the joy of consuming them.

In fact—as I h°ad apparently forgotten in the months surrounding my Ochsner visits—a little danger can be titillating. The deep-fried stuffed burger at Jabba Jaws certainly was.

I ordered the least intimidating burger on the list: The Big Jabba Jack, the one stuffed with sautéed mushrooms and pepper jack cheese. Since only the patty is deep-fried, it looked perfectly normal at first, just a burger between buns. Then I noticed that the meat had a blond, battered shell. Then I took a bite. The burger was juicy as an orange, with cheese spread throughout the patty's interior, as if it were binding the ground meat together.

I put two bucks in the chef's tip jar.

When I called her, Ochsner clinical dietitian Eve Dansereau reacted with astonishment that a deep-fried cheeseburger existed, and I didn't even tell her about the one that's stuffed with bacon, hot sausage and two kinds of cheese. Having had no experience with such a specimen, she couldn't tell me exactly how hazardous my meal was. Dansereau did say that a piece of flounder jumps from 35 calories per-ounce broiled to 75 calories per-ounce fried; she figured a deep-fried cheeseburger would probably be similarly more caloric than its grilled brethren. A doctor I consulted was less scientific. A week after eating a fried cheeseburger at Tuckers Tavern, he reported, "I still feel pregnant."

I cannot say that eating at Jabba Jaws put me in the mood to swim laps. But it did reawaken the culinary daredevil within.

I was undaunted by the selection of stuffed, deep-fried burgers at Tuckers Tavern, which is conspicuously similar to what's offered at Jabba Jaws. The Big Al—according to my waitress, Tuckers' signature fried burger—was identical to the Big Jabba Jack: battered shell, molten pepper jack cheese, fresh sautéed mushrooms. It was just as delicious, too. I ordered it with sweet potato instead of regular fries, figuring that if they're good enough for dieters they might help push back the date my liver turns to pâté.

"Is everything as it should be?" my waitress asked. I struggled to answer. Tuckers is within walking distance of the LSU Health Sciences Center.

As I looked up, I noticed a doctor walking in.

The Last Burger Stand

by Jonathan Gold

from *LA Weekly*

In his Counter Intelligence column, Jonathan Gold exudes a wonderful, infectious enthusiasm for the street food of Los Angeles—the entire multiethnic kaleidoscope range of it, from tamales to pad thai to Spam sushi.

Across the street from Hamburger Mary's and cater-cornered from the ultramodern City Hall, Irv's Burgers is a patch of unreconstructed California in the epicenter of sleek West Holly-wood—a bright Coca-Cola sign, faded groovadelic lettering dating back to the Bicentennial, and locals lining up for shots of purest cholesterol on a block dominated by organics-conscious emporia and vegan health-food joints. Seared ahi may have its place on a menu and decaf chai may too, but since 1950 Irv's has been a redoubt of hand-cut French fries and double cheeseburgers, pastrami sand-wiches and Denver omelets, onion rings and tuna melts, root beer and egg salad, and its fans seem almost to live at the place, reading the trades, meeting with groups of friends, stapling up posters advertising readings at A Different Light and Fatboy Slim CDs.

Jimi Hendrix and Janis Joplin ate at Irv's. Linda Ronstadt shot an album cover there. The dancers playing Jets and Sharks in *West Side Story* reputedly hung out there during crew breaks in the '60s.

Irv's current proprietor, Sonia Hong, is nice—just totally, mani-cally nice—greeting two-thirds of her customers by name, asking after absent boyfriends, seemingly aware of just who in her clientele has been away on vacation or traveling with a road-show production of *The Producers*. (Her brother and her mother work behind the counter too.) She personalizes almost every paper plate and to-go bag with a scrawled "Just for Larry" or "For You Guys!," usually adding a happy face or a drawing of a baby sticking out its tongue. The hamburgers are totally, infinitely customizable, and if you've been going there a while, you probably have a variation or a private sandwich configuration named after you, a sandwich that is irrevocably yours.

I'm just a newbie to Hong (I was a semi-regular at Irv's years ago), but I'm fond of something called a Simon: a pastrami-topped cheeseburger on a French roll, and I have no doubt that after a half-dozen or so more visits, my particular take on that sandwich, with extra-crisp fried pastrami, a shot of Sriracha hot sauce and double pickles, would have my name on it too. But I might not get the chance.

There used to be hundreds of places like Irv's in every part of Los Angeles, tiny walkup hamburger stands: six stools and a rack of chips, coffee by the barrel, brightly lit urban refuges perfuming entire blocks with cigarette smoke, grilled onions and the funk of frying meat. You went to a stand for a burger and a Coke, maybe a pickled egg, but mostly because you could bolt down a meal in the 30 minutes you had for lunch and get change back from a five-dollar bill. You could get a Danish and coffee in the morning, a hot dog for a midafternoon snack, probably a pack of Luckys. Some of the stands may have been better than others, and some of them actually became famous, but you went to one stand or another because it was close to the place you worked or lived. Nobody sane would have driven across town just for a shot at a hot dog at the original Eddie Blake's or the chili size at Pete's Grandburger when they could just walk to the stand on their block.

Over the years most of the stands disappeared, their customers lured away by the big hamburger chains, their street corners developed into mini-malls or leveled for office complexes. To the utter horror of local West Hollywood residents, Irv's Burgers is set to be bulldozed out of existence too—Irv Gendis, the owner of the property (and the original Irv) is set to develop the site into a branch of Peet's Coffee & Tea. The Hong family, who have been running Irv's for the last five-odd years, would be put out of business. More than 1,400 neighbors signed a petition of protest (1 in 40 citizens of West

Hollywood, as one petitioner puts it) and a group calling itself the Burger Brigade has been holding rallies in front of the restaurant—rallies, it goes without saying, fueled by some pretty good hamburgers. I haven't seen this level of community support for a doomed restaurant since developers threatened to raze the Formosa a decade or so back—and the Formosa still stands today.

To be fair, it is easy to see both sides of this issue. Gendis spent his time behind the counter of the hamburger stand, and if he wants to develop his land, he is well within his rights, karmically as well as legally, to do so. Peet's makes decent coffee and is generally a good neighbor—it's not like the place is being bulldozed for a Republican Party headquarters or a Domino's. And it would be unfair to penalize Gendis for being practically the last person in the neighborhood to redevelop, the last hamburger stand of worth left standing. But Irv's is an awfully nice place, and it would be a shame to see it go.

Irv's Burgers, 8289 Santa Monica Blvd., West Hollywood, (323) 650-2456. Open Monday–Saturday, 7:30 a.m.–8 p.m. Cash only. No alcohol. Difficult street parking only. Lunch for two, $8–$12.

Eat It While It's Hot

by Diana Abu-Jaber

from *The Language of Baklava*

Like many immigrant families, Abu-Jabar's Jordanian clan preserved ties to their homeland through the foods they ate—but acclimatizing to life in America can divide the generations, throwing new tastes into the pot.

I love to be in the kitchen and watch my strong father at work in his undershirt, baggy shorts, and sandals. He's singing along with the radio and not getting a single word right. But what he lacks in accuracy he makes up for in gusto and verve. He slides a whole side of lamb out of the refrigerator, hoists it up for me and my friend Merilee to admire, and says, "Here he is! Here's Marvin." Bud likes to name all big cuts of meat—usually Tom, Dick, Harry, or Marvin. I stand close beside him, four feet high in flip-flops, bony shoulders poking through the crossed straps of my sundress, plastic heart-shaped sunglasses propped on my head, and watch as he centers the meat on his chopping block and *whomps* his cleaver down. My friend Merilee, with her freckles and straw yellow pigtails, shrieks and clatters out the back door. I happily tote the bloody kabobs from the block to the marinade of garlic, rosemary, vinegar, and olive oil. Bud tells me that someday I will make a fantastic butcher.

Next, Bud pushes the big, glistening chunks of beef and onion and tomato onto skewers. The skewers are iron, with round hoops at one end and cruel, three-sided points on the other, so heavy that once they're threaded with meat, I can carry only one at a time to the refrigerator.

Shish kabob means that there will be coolers and ice chests, blankets and salads, pita bread, iced tea, salty braided cheese, hummus,
maybe a visit to Rudy's stand, where they dip the scoops of ice
cream into a kind of chocolate that hardens into a shell. Maybe our
mother will bring frozen pound cake, because who wants to bake
anything in this heat?

There will also be sisters and cousins and aunties and uncles and
even more cousins, because there's no telling who's just "comeover,"
meaning come over from the old country. You never know when
suddenly a second cousin you haven't seen in years will be standing
in the living room, asking for a little cup of coffee. They'll be hungry because everyone who "comesover" is hungry: for home, for
family, for the old smells and touches and tastes. If we're not at the
park, sometimes these cousins and noncousins and friends and
strangers will drop by the house. Coincidentally, they always come
at dinnertime. Always at the moment we turn on the stove.

Bud says that today we children need to be extra pleasant, polite,
and cute. Today Cousin Sami (Samir) will be with us. He is newly
arrived, twenty years old, sensitive, and willowy as a deer. He walks
tentatively in this new country, looking around himself as if about
to break into flight; his eyes glisten, eternally on the verge of tears.
I overhear Bud telling Mom that he doesn't know if Sami will
"make it." Mom blows a filament of hair out of her face; she's
twenty-six years old and tall, but she doesn't have much more meat
on her than I do. Her reading glasses are smart and serious. I can tell
that she's thinking, *What is it with these sensitive, crazy men?*

We pack up the family and drive the road to the north, over tiny
wooden bridges, past taverns with names like Three Rivers Inn and
gurgling minute creeks, up to Fair Haven Beach on Lake Ontario,
thirty miles from Syracuse. After we arrive and roll along behind
people walking to their car in order to secure the best parking spot,
it will take an even longer time to unpack the trunk and find the
exact picnic tables and get out the bags and coolers and cousins and
sisters. We cover several tables with red-checked tablecloths, paper
plates, plastic containers full of everything. Bud piles briquettes
into three different grills, and Uncle Hal adds more and more
lighter fluid—usually while it's burning—so the flame roars right up
at him in a fabulous arc. I draw in the rich chemical aroma: Barbe-

cues are the smell of lighter fluid, dark and delicious as the aroma of gasoline.

Another car pulls up and there is Cousin Sami unfolding from Uncle Danny's Volkswagen. Sami holds out his hands as if testing the gravity on this new planet. He looks as if he might topple over at any moment. I adore him. Big, hearty Businessman-Uncle Danny, who's looking after him because his full-time father, Rich-Uncle Jimmy, lives in Jordan, laughs and calls him "a poet." I know immediately that's what I want to be, too, and I say this to my father as he's carrying a platter full of shish kabob. He looks unhappy at this news, but then Uncle Hal shouts, "Oh yes, there's a lot of money in that," and the adults laugh for inexplicable reasons and then forget about me.

The cousins—except for Sami—and sisters and I run in the frothy surf along Fair Haven's pebble beach. The water is electrically cold, threaded with mysteriously warm currents. We go in up to our necks and the waves lift us off our feet. We can do just this, standing in ice water and bobbing, for hours. A game for lunatics. We don't ever want to come in, even when our mother and one of the aunties wade out and says, "Your lips are purple, time to come in." First we make Mom demonstrate her ability to float in the water so that her shoulders submerge and her pink toes bob up and she looks as if she's sitting in a recliner. This, I assume, is a talent innate to all Americans. We all try, and our chicken-bone bodies just sink. Dad and his too many brothers don't even own bathing suits.

There's a commotion on shore. My father and the uncles are shouting and waving their arms: Shish kabob is ready! Uncle Hal is ferrying the sizzling skewers—we call them sheeshes—to a big platter on the table. Bud is turning more of them on the fire.

The shish kabob comes like an emergency. It sizzles at the table, and Uncle Hal pushes the chunks of meat off the skewers with a piece of pita bread. They all go to one central plate. He says, "This piece is for you and this one for you." It's best to wait for the second sheesh because for some reason the meat on the first always looks scrawny and shriveled and smells of uncooked lighter fluid. But there's no time to wait! You have to eat the lamb when it's hot enough to burn your fingers and scald your tongue.

"Eat it *now*," Uncle Hal says. "It's good right this second."

This is one of the secrets of shish kabob: how quickly it dries and hardens on the skewer. Not like a roast leg of lamb or breasts of chicken that fall off the bone when you cook them long and ruthlessly enough. Shish kabob is fierce. It comes charred and crusty outside and pink, almost wet red inside, richly redolent, in its special way, of marrow and pepper. It sizzles in your mouth and tastes faintly of the earth.

In the midst of all this drama and pageantry, however, I notice that Sami hasn't left his perch on the far end of the most distant picnic bench. His eyes are glowing as he watches us with both curiosity and aloofness. I pluck a morsel from the plate and run to him while it burns my fingertips. To my mind, this is the best way to show love—to offer food from your own hand. But he only closes his eyes and shakes his head dolefully.

Because I am six, I am typically the one being fed—I've never tried to feed anyone from my own hand like this before. But I've never had a cousin like this before. Usually my older Jordanian cousins arrive resplendent in polyester bell-bottom slacks—this being the late sixties—tall and strapping and hungry for America. With big mustaches, huge laughs, wild eyes, and big—very big— plans. Not Sami, though. Earlier that morning, Bud talked about it on the phone with one of his brothers. Sami didn't even want to come to America. In our family, we assume that everyone is simply dying to come here. It's like a law of nature: Grow up, go to America. I learn from sitting at the kitchen table, helping Bud poke kabobs onto skewers while he talks on the phone, that Uncle Jimmy sent Sami to America to "cure him" of something or other. When I ask Bud later what Uncle Jimmy wants to cure him of, he thinks about his answer for a while before he decides to say, "Of being a poet."

I stand before Sami, watching and admiring him, the lamb cooling in my hand. Finally I say, "What's a poet?"

He turns that vivid, astonished look back on me again and says, "I'm not a poet." He rubs the back of his neck and sighs. Then he murmurs, "I embroider shawls. Would you like me to make you one?"

I nod vehemently.

Uncle Hal overhears us. He laughs and shouts, "He's not a poet! *I'm* a poet—listen: 'If white is the color of mourning in Andalusia / It is a most fitting color. . . .' "

"You didn't write that," Uncle Danny says, and a new fight percolates among the brothers.

For some reason, then, Sami changes his mind and takes the piece of meat from my hand. It is cool now, and it won't be as good, but he eats it anyway, his luminous eyes fixed on me. His features undergo an alteration, as if a transparent veil has lifted from his face. It is the first time I've seen him smile. He says quietly, "It's good."

At the end of the day at the beach, about to drive home, we might stop at Ontario Orchards, a big farm produce stand, and buy a bag of fresh cherries, black with sugar. We pass them around during the ride and spit the pits out the windows. Then my sisters and I fall asleep. I'm so deeply asleep when we get home that I hope I'll get carried in. But lately I've grown arms and legs that hang and dangle and might knock over just about anything.

One day, the shish kabob goes a little differently.

Professor-Uncle Hal and his wife, Writer-Auntie Rachel, and my favorite American-born cousins, rangy, roustabout Jess and Ed, live in a big country house right down the road from Ontario Orchards. Uncle Hal lives in a library filled with leathery historical books, selected for their carved covers and the heft and density of their language: He prefers lengthy books written in very small type. His library is filled with the Ottoman Empire, Boswell, Australian Aboriginals, Oliver Goldsmith, Southeast Asia, and James Fenimore Cooper. Though he teaches international politics, he has a broad, eclectic scope, and his dinnertime stories are as likely to include the details of the Oneida Indians as the intricacies of the medieval Arabs or the war in Vietnam.

They have chickens and a goat and a water-gray barn that my professor-uncle has filled with things like oil paintings in immense gilt frames, junked toys, battered pots, ancient clothes, unidentifiable tools and broken farming implements, Persian rugs, sacks of grain, silver coins and jewelry, rusted watering cans, abandoned birds' nests, and so on. It is a place stuffed with all the history in the world, the stories of ten thousand strangers, all living together here with all their separate textures and dusts and smells, along with the musty grain of the hayloft. I am obsessed with the barn and plan to live there someday.

My cousins are jumping up and down in the driveway as our car pulls up. "There's something so great," Ed gasps. "It's in the barn, come on!" We run to the barn, and as we get close my breath snags in my throat. There, in the open doorway of the barn, stands an ivory-colored lamb with dense fur, a piercing, plangent bleat, flipping ears, and rolling black eyes. I am stricken, paralyzed with love. I want to name him Harry, but Jess says no, this is Lambie, even though Mom and all the aunties are saying don't do that, that this kind of lamb doesn't like names. We surround Lambie, admiring him. Cousin Sami arrives and I want to introduce him to Lambie. They remind me of each other because of their gentle eyes and the way they turn away from things, their entrancing skittishness. But Sami pulls his fish-soft hand out of my grip and says no, he doesn't want to look at the lamb, and neither should I, for that matter. I find this notion so perverse as to be hilarious, and I run away from him, laughing.

The children cozy right up to Lambie, hug his hot neck, feed him handfuls of grass that we tear out of the lawn. He breathes his sweet, grassy breath on our faces; there are long canopies of lashes around his eyes. Ed comes running out of the kitchen with some string cheese and leftover spaghetti and meatballs he found in the refrigerator, and we try to feed it to him. Uncle Danny keeps jingling his change and looking around; Uncle Danny doesn't like a lot of monkey business. He clears his throat and says, "You know what, kids, it's going to be a while until dinner's ready. Why doesn't Auntie Yusra drive you to the ice cream stand?"

Fantastic! Let's go! We pile into the Beetles—Auntie Yusra will drive one, Auntie Jasmine will drive the other. Too many children climb in; we spill over one another's laps. Before we leave, Auntie Jasmine tries to coax Sami into joining us. "It'll be fun," she says. "You can help distract the children—teach them some of your poetry."

His delicate features contract. "I don't know any poetry," he says.

Auntie Jasmine folds down the Beetle's canvas convertible top, and we children are astonished to discover that three of us can fit into the pouched pleats of the folded-back top, which bends and sways under our weight. "I'm not positive that's safe," Auntie Jasmine says to Auntie Yusra. But they shrug and we set off, the canvas top thumping us wildly.

On the way there, I have a thought, and the thought is this: We are never. Under any circumstances. Ever. Allowed to have ice cream before dinner.

I start to formulate this curious and very interesting thought out loud, but right in the middle of my sentence, Auntie Yusra says energetically, "Hey, kids, why don't I teach you some Arabic drinking songs?" Fantastic! We learn the words to "*Ah Ya Zain*" ("Oh, You Beauty!") and "*Ridi Ha*" ("I Want Her") and even "*Gameel Gamal*" ("Beautiful Beauty"), which we belt out, lifting our voices over the rush of wind.

Rudy's is a tar-paper shack perched on the gravel lip of Lake Ontario. It leans a bit to the east, and the sticky black roof sits at a drunken angle on top. There's just a window with an apple-cheeked blond girl waiting in it with her pad of paper and a chewed stub of pencil. This lumpy little place with its ice-crusted freezers produces a lovely, buttery-satin ice cream. And even though we already know what we want, we still all study the lists of flavors, toppings, and novelties chalked onto the blackboard. I agonize over chocolate malts, root beer floats, and tin roof sundaes, but in the end I always get the scoop of vanilla dipped in the chocolate shell. The ice cream softens and slips, and the chocolate shellac stays semi-rigid and glossy, a minor miracle.

By the time we get back, a curious lethargy hangs over the house. The men are all asleep in the backyard or on the living room floor, and my mother and the aunties are murmuring at the kitchen table. There's been a change of plans, my mother tells us, we're not having shish kabob after all, we're having chicken and stuffed squash for dinner. The kitchen stove is covered with burbling, lid-ticking pans; the air is towel damp and heavy with mystery.

None of us is really hungry anymore, anyway. We're dozy and full from the ice cream and the sunshine and the hearty, full-lunged singing. My sisters settle down to nap, and my cousins and I play game after game of Parcheesi on the wool Persian carpet in my uncle's library. The walls of old brown books seem to mutter and sit up, staring. Somewhere in the middle of the seventh or eighth game, my cousin Jess, who at nine is the oldest and shrewdest of any of us, Jess of the Cleopatra eyes and shining black hair like patent leather—suddenly looks up and says, "Let's go see Lambie!"

We clatter down the back steps, calling for the lamb, and we accidentally wake Uncle Jack, who sits up in the grass outside the barn. "Ah . . . oh . . . well, Lambie had to go visit his grandmother," Uncle Jack says.

Among our black-eyed, black-haired uncles and father, Diplomat-Uncle Jack was rumored to have somehow had ineffable red hair as a boy. Whenever he acted up, my Palestinian grandmother would put her hands on her hips and say, "That's the Irish devil in you!" Even though he is the oldest of the brothers in America, he acts like the youngest. He is the clever *mishkeljee*—the "troublemaker," with a fondness for stirring things up, spreading rumors, sprouting arguments, then disappearing.

"Lambie has a grandmother?" my cousin Ed asks skeptically. "Where?"

"Ah, yes, okay, um . . . she lives in Wisconsin. On a lovely lake filled with swans, in a house with glass doorknobs on every door."

"I doubt it," Ed says, though somewhat less incredulous now. It happens that Jess and Ed have glass doorknobs in their house. And I myself have heard of Wisconsin. I glance at the barn and think I see, moving quick and lithe as a lizard, the long slim arm and leg of Sami disappearing around the corner.

Dinnertime comes and we eat our chicken and stuffed squash, though the ice cream has dampened our appetites. Everyone does his or her usual. The grown-ups pile our plates with too much food. And there's the customary struggle with Uncle Hal, who likes to feed the children gaping mouthfuls of food from his own hand. He even tries to feed our mother and our aunties, who roll their eyes and bat his hand away, preferring to eat their own dainty American portions on forks. Uncle Jack offers me some important life advice, which is, he says, to never start drinking before noon or I'll grow up to be a bum. Auntie Rachel eats all the toasted pine nuts off the rice. Cousin Sami sits trembling with his hands on either side of his plate, eyes closed, not leaving the table. None of the adults seem to be comfortable with looking at him, and no one tries to coax him into eating. Their eyes roam toward him, then veer away; the mere sight of him is like an accusation. Even I can feel it, and I feel terribly guilty, though I don't know what I'm guilty of. Uncle Hal spears a few stuffed squashes and puts them on my plate. And then something very strange happens: Bud reaches over and plucks the squashes from my plate. I blink and look at him. This is such an oddity, so counter to all I know of my father, that I don't even have the words to comment on it.

That evening, after the frozen pound cake has been produced, the coffee brewed with cardamom, the dishes washed; after Auntie Rachel teaches us something in Russian that she says means "Require the children to work"; after the evening news has been watched and discussed, and the children have been quizzed on world geography and political history—I am sitting alone on the slanting back steps with my cousin Jess. We sit listening to the high, white chiming of crickets in the fields when she suddenly says, "We ate Lambie today."

I, however, at age six, am already showing a real aptitude for not believing inconvenient truths. "That's not scientifically possible," I say, using a phrase I have picked up from *Monster Movie Matinee.* "Lambie was a lamb," I state. "We had chicken and squash."

Jess stares at me with the direct, remorseless gaze that will carry over into her adulthood and eventually strike fear into the hearts of men. "Squash stuffed with ground lamb," she says. I gaze at the darkened barn, crammed with its boxes and piles of junk. Never before has it struck me as being quite so empty. I don't dare to venture any closer.

When we leave that evening, Bud, as usual, is the first out the door, waiting behind the wheel, the car engine murmuring in the lavender night. The women linger over their farewells. There is no sign of Sami, although as we walk down the long gravel driveway past the barn, I think I hear someone weeping behind the wall of the hayloft.

This story had to wait twenty years or so for its ending. I was already done with graduate school, already moved away from home, teaching and living on my own in another state. But one day I came home for a visit and something reminded me of that lamb, and I said to my father, "Remember Lambie, the little lamb at Uncle Hal's house? What really happened to him?"

Bud shook his head and said exactly what he has so often said over the years, which was, "Ya Ba, where on earth did you ever get this memory of yours from? You know, most men won't like having a wife with such a big memory."

Then he fell back into his bottomless recliner—his favorite and most auspicious place for storytelling and philosophizing, and began at the beginning before the beginning:

On that day, the day of the lamb, Bud and his brothers were all still young men, in their late twenties and early thirties, none of them all that far away from their childhood in Jordan. When they were children, their parents had owned orchards of olive trees, figs, and lemons and fields of corn, thyme, and jasmine, watering holes and greenhouses, herds of horses, goats, and lambs. They drew their silvery drinking water from a well, baked bread in a stone oven, and in the desert nights my father and his eight brothers had liked to sleep under a sky scrawled with stars or inside the billowing goat-hair tents that the Bedouins used.

Half my father's brothers stayed in Jordan, but the other half came to America, for education or money or some sense of promise that was the opposite of homesickness. They thought, even after ten or fifteen years away, that they were still the same wiry, tough-skinned wild boys running barefoot through briars and hardscrabble land. When Uncle Hal saw the runty lamb in his neighbor's fields, he thought of the feather-light springtime in Jordan when the countryside was filled with new lambs and of the scent of freshly grilled meat and the way he and his brothers stood between these two events, birth and food, though they were only boys; so much responsibility for a miraculous, sacred transformation. How could he help himself? Even though he knew better, even though he told himself not to, Uncle Hal bought the runty lamb from the farmer. Then he called his brothers. Together, they decided they would butcher the lamb the way they used to when they were children and their parents were still alive and nobody knew anything about the bright grocery stores of America or the way meat appeared, bloodless, gleaming with cellophane, stacked in cold rows.

This was the way it was supposed to happen: Four of the brothers would hold the lamb still, and with one powerful, swift stroke, Crazy-Uncle Frankie would cut its throat. Uncle Frankie was nominated for this unpleasant task by virtue of being the youngest brother in America as well as having the least exciting job (washing school buses) and because none of the brothers wanted to slaughter the lamb after seeing the children cozying up to it. Uncle Jack, it seems, had a change of heart and wanted to return it to the farmer, but Uncle Danny, who didn't have any children yet, said that was ridiculous and wimpy. And my father, the pragmatic chef, said they were all turning soft and silly. At the time he told me the story, he still wasn't sure why he had said this: He hadn't wanted to kill the lamb, either.

But then they were all saying things they didn't really want to say as they converged on the knock-kneed lamb. Hal held the lamb on one side, Jack held the other. Danny held the legs. Bud held the head. Frankie unsheathed the big, sharpened knife and held it up with trembling hands. Bud had owned this knife a long time and cut many things with it, but never before a living thing. In that moment, he had no memory of ever having killed a living thing. Was it true? Had they done the slaughtering back in Jordan, or had it been done for them? He started to ask, but then his brother's eyes bulged, the knife rose, Bud turned away, and Frankie slashed. He made a terrible, ineffective cut, deep enough to make the lamb scream and buck, for blood to course freely, but not deep enough to kill it.

The lamb was wild. Its head rolled back, and its neck gaped like a bloody smile. The brothers panicked and lost their grip. The lamb kicked in a frenzy; its back hoof cut right through the fabric of Uncle Danny's pants and gashed his knee. Hal grabbed the knife from Frankie and tried to make a better cut, but he missed and made another shallow cut in its face. The animal bawled and writhed. Jack picked up a rock, wildly attempting to knock it unconscious, but it again lurched out of their grip. Finally, Bud gripped the knife with both fists and, as the lamb stumbled to one side, plunged it straight into its neck.

Then everything went still. They could hear a bird trill three fragile notes from a nearby tree. The barn walls were covered with blood; the floor was covered with blood; their faces were covered with blood; their arms were covered with blood. And then my father realized that what he'd thought was a bird was the sound of weeping. For a dreadful, unreal moment, he thought it was the lamb. Then he heard Cousin Sami's voice rise from the hayloft: "I want to go home!"

Telling the story twenty or so years after the fact, Bud looked a bit gray, his face filmed with distantly recalled panic. He closed his eyes, remembering the way the lamb's neck strained, its soft, wide-open mouth, its babylike cry. The meat was spoiled, shot through with blood and adrenaline. But Uncle Hal insisted on salvaging a few pieces and ground it up to make stuffing for the squashes. None of them touched any of it.

"We thought we could still do it," Bud said. "But we couldn't."

Making shish kabob always reminds the brothers of who they used to be—the heat, the spices, the preparation for cooking, and the rituals for eating were all the same as when they were children, eating at their parents' big table. But trying to kill the lamb showed them: They were no longer who they thought they were.

"Eat It Now" Shish Kabob

4 tablespoons olive oil

1\2 cup red wine

2 tablespoons red vinegar

4 cloves garlic, crushed

2 teaspoons dried oregano

2 teaspoons dried rosemary

Salt and freshly ground pepper

2 pounds boneless leg of lamb, cut into small cubes

1 large onion, cut into chunks

1 large tomato, cut into chunks

Whisk together the oil, wine, vinegar, garlic, and spices in a large bowl. Add the meat and stir to coat it thoroughly. Cover and refrigerate overnight; turn occasionally.

Thread the cubes of lamb on skewers, occasionally adding a piece of onion or tomato. Grill over hot coals, turning once. Cook to medium rare and eat while still sizzling.

SERVES 6

Food That Makes You Happy

by Ruth Reichl

from *Garlic and Sapphires*

The third of Reichl's memoirs about her life as a restaurant reviewer digs deep dish about her times at the *New York Times*. Late in the book comes this wonderful chapter about how a jaded critic can rediscover her love of food.

Every kitchen is filled with flames and shards, fire and glass, boiling liquids and sharp objects eager to attack you. Cooking is too dangerous to permit distraction. If you step into that arena without the proper respect, you will certainly get hurt.

"Blood!" screamed a sign over the stove in my first professional kitchen. Beneath, spelled out in large letters, were the appropriate steps to be taken in case of severed appendages, injured limbs, or major burns. Peril pounces on the careless cook, and for me this lurking menace is part of the attraction. I have found that meditation at the edge of the knife makes everything seem better.

But while cooking demands your entire attention, it also rewards you with endlessly sensual pleasures. The sound of water skittering across 5 leaves of lettuce. The thump of the knife against watermelon, and the cool summer scent the fruit releases as it falls open to reveal its deep red heart. The seductive softness of chocolate beginning to melt from solid to liquid. The tug of sauce against the spoon when it thickens in the pan, and the lovely lightness of Parmesan drifting from the grater in gossamer flakes. Time slows down in the kitchen, offering up an entire universe of small satisfactions.

That fall, worried about Carol and wondering about my work, I spent weeks standing at the counter, chopping onions, peeling apples, and rolling dough. I made complicated soups and stews, and I began baking bread every day, as I had done when Michael and I first lived together.

In the end I came to realize that a restaurant critic's job is more about eating than writing, and every time I cancelled a reservation I grew more seriously behind. I was having a secret affair with cooking, and I knew it could not continue. But every morning, after walking Nicky to school, I'd go home and sit in the kitchen, sifting through my recipes. A jumble of handwritten pages, they were gathered into an ancient, torn manila folder filled with memories. Tomorrow, I'd think, tomorrow I'll go out to eat, tomorrow I'll go back to the restaurants. And then I'd turn over another page and a long-gone meal would come tumbling out, more evocative than any photograph could ever be.

Here was apricot upside-down cake, written in my mother-in-law's neat, careful script. Here was Aunt Birdie's potato salad, scratched in her feathery penmanship and signed with her funny little bird. My own recipes for six different pie crusts were carefully printed for the students at my cooking classes. Serafina's scrawled instructions for coconut cake were almost illegible, as if she had not quite wanted to part with the recipe. My mother's thick, bold writing danced exuberantly across a page torn from the *New York Times* in the mid-sixties. "Sounds like you!" she'd written across a recipe called "Minetry's Miracle." I looked it over; it required a pound of butter, a dozen eggs, a pint of cream, and a cup of bourbon (not to mention chocolate, pecans, ladyfingers, and macaroons). Indeed.

Then a recipe written on blue-lined paper leapt into my hand. The writing was not familiar. "Aushak," I whispered, and suddenly it came to me. An Afghan exchange student had given it to me when I was an undergraduate with a reputation as a cook. At the time these scallion dumplings had seemed too strange, too exotic, too time-consuming, and I had never attempted them. Now, studying the ingredients, I was curious. The dumplings sounded delicious. Yes, I thought, writing out a grocery list, this is my recipe for today.

I walked to the market, strolling past Citarella, where the man who decorates the windows with fish was contemplating his latest creation. He added a few oysters to the design, stood back to observe the effect, and waved at me. Next door at Fairway the bins were filled with six kinds of local apples, the last of the deep-blue prune plums, the first of the pumpkins. There was some sad-looking corn and some fine-looking tomatoes. I grabbed a basket and walked in. People were sliding through the sawdust, pushing, tugging, shoving past the raucous dairy counter and the shiny dried fruits, eager to get to the deli counter and jockey for position in the smoked salmon line.

I gathered mint, scallions, and fresh garlic into my cart and went off to find the wonton wrappers. As I passed the bread a baguette called to me, and as I reached for it a voice said, "Not that one."

Looking up, I found a man with a boyish face staring at me. His warm brown eyes and mischievous grin seemed surprised to find themselves attached to such an oversized and awkward body. With one hand the man dangled a baguette before me; with the other he stopped my reaching arm. "Take this," he said. "It's baked later and delivered earlier."

"Hi Ed," I said.

I barely knew Ed Levine, but he had a reputation as the ultimate connoisseur of New York food. For years well-intentioned friends had been telling me that I should cultivate his friendship. Nobody, they assured me, knew more about the city's edible landscape. There was apparently not a pizzeria in the city that Ed hadn't sampled. If I wanted to meet the jerk chicken king of Brooklyn or the tofu man of Flushing, Ed could introduce me, and he was one of the few people who knew where to find the last women in the city still stretching strudel dough by hand. The best fried chicken in Harlem? Ed could lead me to it. SoHo's finest sandwiches? Ed was on to that as well. But although we had been introduced any number of times, neither of us had pursued the acquaintance.

"Have you tried the donuts they've been getting from Georgie's?" Ed asked now, drawing me over to the bakery counter. "Well, you should."

Ed was full of opinions: I should be buying this olive oil instead of that, my coffee should come from next door, and he did not approve my choice of smoked salmon. But his enthusiasm was so infectious that I couldn't be annoyed. When he said that my Afghan dumplings would surely be better with yogurt from the Middle Eastern store in Bay Ridge, I suspected he was right.

"I could take you there," he offered. He stopped himself, eyes gleaming. "In fact, why don't you let me take you on a food tour of Brooklyn?" He ran his fingers through his short red-blond hair and added, "You'll meet some amazing people. Bakers and butchers are undervalued in our culture, and they're so happy when you recognize what they do. We'll have a great time. Please come." How could I possibly refuse?

"You were right," I said a few days later as I climbed into his car. "Those dumplings were great, but they would be better with home-made yogurt."

"The Middle Eastern place is going to be one of our last stops," he said. "I want to take you to Carroll Gardens first. But we're going to make an unscheduled stop before we go to Brooklyn. I want you to meet Jim Leahy at the Sullivan Street Bakery. Okay?" Ed was looking straight at me as he talked. "He's an amazing guy," he continued, still looking my way. "When Jim talks about bread it's like he's speaking in tongues. Besides, we might as well pick up a little snack to tide us over."

"Okay," I said, thinking that if I didn't argue he might look back at the road.

But Ed, it soon became clear, was a trusting driver who relied on his car to take care of itself when he was otherwise occupied. For long stretches he looked at me, at the itinerary, at the passing scenery. "I haven't seen that bakery before!" he'd cry, swerving across three lanes to get a closer look, convinced that any cars foolish enough to be in our path would move before we reached them.

I was relieved when we got to Sullivan Street and Ed maneuvered the car into a conveniently vacant loading zone and turned off the engine.

It was warm inside the bakery, and hushed. Flour swirled through the air, so much like snow that when a woman came to throw her arms around Ed the two looked exactly like figures in one of those little paperweights you shake. "Ed!" she said. "Jim's going to be so disappointed that he missed you!" The air smelled of yeast and heat, and if you listened carefully you could hear, above the whirr of the ovens, the faint burble of rising dough.

Great mounds of crusty loaves surrounded us like soft mountains, and Ed stroked one fondly, saying, "Jim is obsessed with getting the right textures." As he moved through this soft white world, flour settled on his jacket and frosted his hair. He stretched a hand to a long swath of *pizza bianca* stretching across the counter like a languid cat and broke off a corner. "Have some," he said, handing me a piece. The flatbread was crisp and slightly oily, dotted with rosemary, and so delicious that each bite enticed you into another.

"This is perfect!" said Ed, sounding surprised. He took another bite and shook his head. "When Jim first made pizzas they were cardboardy. Then they got soggy. But now he's really nailed it. What happened?"

The woman pointed an affectionately accusing finger at Ed. "This guy," she said, "can really drive you crazy. He won't accept just any old thing. He keeps nagging at you, nagging at you, nagging at you until you make it better." She smiled at Ed and added, "Your complaints were heard."

Ed nodded his head. "I wish everyone was so obedient." As far as I could tell, there was not a whiff of irony in the statement. "Tell Jim I approve."

We left and went from one small shop to another, gathering food as we traveled. By the time we walked back to the car we were laden with warm little pear tarts, turnovers, jars of jam, loaves of bread, goat cheese, and zucchini wrapped in flaky dough.

"You see why I love these people?" Ed asked. He looked longingly at the shops we were passing, loath to leave any off the tour. Suddenly he ducked; ahead of us a large man loomed in a doorway and he was pointing a finger at Ed. "You!" he commanded, coming towards us. "You! Come in here right now!"

Ed speeded up. "Sorry," he whispered out of the side of his mouth, almost running now, "but we have to get away." To the man he said, "Tomorrow, I'll come back tomorrow." And then, in another whisper, "Keep moving. If we stop and go into the store he'll start feeding us and he won't stop. He'll never let us go; we'll be here all day."

The shopkeeper was now trotting at Ed's side, trying to stay with us. "You promise?" he asked.

"Yes, yes, I promise," said Ed.

"I'll be waiting." The shopkeeper, reluctantly, gave up the race. "I have some new eggplant dishes you *need* to taste."

"See you tomorrow," said Ed, diving into the car.

Winded by the race, neither of us said anything for a few minutes. But when we were safely in the tunnel, halfway to Brooklyn, I asked, "Will you really go back?"

Ed stared at me incredulously. "Of course," he said. "I promised." He raised his hands to the sky. "I love all these people; they have so much passion. They're a little bit crazy, but they use their craziness for their business. They live right."

"Uh, sure," I said, wishing he would reconnect with the steering wheel. "You're right. Yes. Passion. Watch that car!"

"Oh, don't worry," he said, patting my leg as if I were a fussy old lady, "I've never had an accident. Really."

We came out of the tunnel and nosed deep into Carroll Gardens. Ed gestured around and said happily, "Isn't this neighborhood wonderful?" He parked, setting off a couple of car alarms in the process. They were howling as we walked into Esposito's Pork Store, but Ed paid them no mind.

It was comfortable in there, rich with spice and personality, a throw-back to a vanishing New York. Housewives with loud nasal voices demanded this piece of veal breast, that slice of *bracciole,* and a little salami, not too thick, are you listening to me? They examined the heap of softly steaming stuffed peppers, asking when they were made, and wanted to know if this was yesterday's sausage and where the hell was today's? Firemen from around the corner stood shouldering their axes and arguing over their order, scooping up mountains of chopped meats and cold cuts.

"Isn't this great?" asked Ed, as if he had personally conjured the scene. "Isn't this amazing? Doesn't it make you happy that places like this exist?" His enthusiasm was irresistible. "Meet George," he said, offering up a handsome man with tattooed arms and a thick gold chain around his neck as if he were Exhibit A. "His grandfather started this place. And you know, they still make all their own dried sausage, even their own pancetta."

"Dad's in back now," said George, "making sausage."

"See?" said Ed, as if I had doubted him.

In the darkened kitchen an old man stood quietly tying sausages with string. The air was deliriously funky, filled with the scent of pepper seeds and the fine aroma of aging meat. The man pressed a dried sausage with a weathered thumb, rejected it, tried another. He nodded to himself, sliced off a few hunks, and handed them over. The sausage was sharp, spicy, and very fine. "That's my *sopressata*," said Dad, emphasizing the possessive. "It's good."

Ed's next gift was a tiny shop filled with bakers mixing dough, melting chocolate, pulling pastries from industrial ovens. When Ed stepped through the door they all stopped to welcome him, and there was something in the gesture that made me think of those sweet moving figures department stores put in their windows at Christmas. If the bakers had broken into song, I would not have been surprised. "What they make here," said Ed, grabbing a small pastry from one of the pans, "is the most amazing rugellach I've ever found."

He popped one buttery little morsel into his mouth, and then another. By his eighth he was shaking his head sadly and saying, "It makes you realize how much bad rugellach there is in the world. Oh, okay, I'll have just one more."

The car alarms had finally subsided when we climbed back into the car, but as Ed pulled out of the parking space they started up again, sending us off with a flourish we could hear for blocks. The sound faded into the distance as the car plowed through the Brooklyn traffic, heading for Bay Ridge.

"Look," said Ed, suddenly slowing to a crawl. He pointed out the window, simultaneously lifting his foot from the gas. "Look at that collision of cultures!" As Ed indicated a Mexican grocery store, an Asian emporium, a Scandinavian shop, the car slowly drifted to a standstill. He gazed beatifically out the window as a cacophony of angry honking started up. "Don't you just love New York?" asked Ed, setting the car back in motion.

The Family Store greeted us with a virtual onslaught of sensations. A riotous mixture of caraway, cumin, cardamom, and sumac perfumed the air while bins of seeds and spices spilled onto the wooden floors. Behind them a rainbow of olives and pickles created a colorful backdrop. The refrigerated cases were filled with vivid jewels of food: pale spheres of stuffed cabbage, billowing mounds of beige hummus, bright pink muhammara, and deep emerald zucchini fritters.

"We've come for your yogurt," Ed told the smiling man behind the counter.

"Ah, my friend," he replied, running out to greet Ed, "first you must taste this." In an instant he was spooning up soft white curds with the consistency of double cream and plopping it into our mouths. It was smooth and tangy, incredibly good. He looked delightedly at our faces. "This," he cried, "is no ordinary yogurt. This is *goat milk* yogurt. I have to go to the Amish to get the milk. It is very good for you. So much calcium." He was a large man, but light on his feet as he danced through the store, insisting we try his homemade cheese ("One customer comes all the way from England in his private jet just to get this"), his pomegranate molasses, his baba gannouj. As he spoke he was taking foods from the cases and feeding us with his fingers. "Wonderful, wonderful" he crooned as we ate.

"Save your appetite if you can," whispered Ed.

We left, the yogurt cradled in my arms, and I held my breath as Ed banged the car out of the parking space and headed toward Coney Island. We nosed down streets with names like Neptune and Surf toward the looming Cyclone, a great construction of white boards and twisted metal. "There's Totonno's," said Ed in a mournful and reverent voice and the car began to slow of its own volition. "Their pizza is really great." He stared longingly out the window and then said, "Stop! Oh my God, Gerace's is gone." His foot stomped on the brake and he came to a complete halt in the middle of traffic. The honking started up. Ed, filled with lamentation, paid it no mind.

"Oh my God. The sign said 'For rent,' did you see that? This drives me crazy. They taught me how to make prosciutto bread. That place had been there forever. Oh my God, this is a tragedy." He took his foot off the brake and started forward, keeping up a keening wail for Gerace's as we drove.

Near the crumbling roller-coaster we pulled up at the original Nathan's hot dog stand, which presided over the litter-strewn sidewalk with the proud air of an ancient relic. We got out, and as we approached Phillip's, a battered candy shop, a toothless man began begging for money. With the instinctive gesture of the easy touch, Ed reached into his pocket and handed him a dollar.

He was not even aware that he had done it, for he was standing, rapt, in front of the candy shop window. "Look at that!" he said reverently. "Charlotte Russe, a classic Brooklyn confection! You can't get these anywhere else anymore." He dug another dollar out of his pocket, plunked it onto the outside counter, and burrowed his face into one of the little white cups. When he looked up his chin was covered with whipped cream and he looked like an overgrown ten-year-old.

"Hey, big guy!" A gray-haired leprechaun of a man emerged from a side door. His face ablaze with a grin, he stared up at Ed as if the sun had just come out and swung the door wide, inviting us in. In the tiny shop lollipops dangled from the ceiling, a wild swirl of colors, their sizes ranging from a few inches to a few feet in diameter. Candy apples marched along the counters, and bags of cotton candy hung from the walls like a soft rainbow. In one corner a huge, battered copper candy kettle filled with bright red sugar syrup balanced precariously atop a hot plate. Next to it apples, sticks raised like so many exuberant tails, waited to be dipped. "John makes everything you see," said Ed. And then, shaking his head as if this fact were both incredible and undeniable, he reiterated, "I swear he does!"

I reached for the largest lollipop. "How much do you charge for the big ones?" I asked, staggering as the candy fell onto my shoulder. It was as tall as I am and stunningly heavy.

"Ten bucks," he said.

"That's all?" I asked, reaching into my pocket for a bill. "I've wanted one of these since I was a little kid," I admitted, slinging the giant confection over my shoulder, "but I thought they cost a fortune."

"Other places," said Ed, heading for the door, "they do. John's the last of the old-time candy men."

"I don't know for how long," said John. "This is a dying way of life. Nobody wants to do this anymore." And then, as if talking to himself, he added, "Who can blame them? The kettle alone weighs thirty-five pounds, you get burned all the time, and you should see me when I'm finished." Then, as if shaking off the gloomy burden of his thoughts, he hugged Ed and opened the door, and as we navigated the broken sidewalk, he called out, "Don't be a stranger!"

"Isn't he amazing?" asked Ed, unlocking the car door. "People like that just make me glad I'm alive." As I settled the lollipop in the car I realized that for the first time in months I was feeling the same way.

We drove past the sign in Gerace's window, which caused Ed to retreat once again into the keening wail of loss, heading for Flatbush and what he assured me was the best jerk chicken on the planet.

It was late afternoon as we drove back to Manhattan, accompanied by the ever-present music of the cars. My yogurt was nestled into a bag, waiting to turn into aushak, and all around us were sausages and pastry, lollipops and spices, chicken and cheese. Any world that contained all this, I thought surveying our loot, was a very fine place. I felt reinvigorated, alive, optimistic. The thought of getting back to work suddenly seemed like fun.

"Oh Mommy," said Nicky when he saw the lollipop, "this must be the most beautiful thing on earth." He gazed at it, dazzled by the gorgeous object that had just entered his life. "Can I really eat it?"

"Yes," I said, "but it might take a couple of years."

He stood back and examined it. "I don't think I will," he decided, petting the giant candy. "This isn't one of those foods that you eat. It's one of the ones that's only supposed to make you happy."

Aushak

MEAT SAUCE

> 3 tablespoons vegetable oil
>
> 1 medium onion, finely chopped
>
> ½ pound ground beef
>
> 1 clove garlic, minced
>
> 1 teaspoon ground coriander
>
> ½ teaspoon diced or grated fresh ginger
>
> ½ cup water
>
> 2 tablespoons tomato paste
>
> ½ teaspoon salt
>
> ¼ teaspoon pepper

YOGURT SAUCE

> 1 cup full-fat yogurt
>
> 1 tablespoon minced garlic
>
> ½ teaspoon salt

DUMPLINGS

> 2 bunches scallions, white part discarded, green tops finely
> chopped (about 2 cups)

½ teaspoon salt

½ teaspoon pepper

1 teaspoon red pepper flakes

1 teaspoon minced garlic

25 to 30 wonton or Gyoza wrappers, preferably round

GARNISH

2 teaspoons chopped fresh mint

Make the meat sauce: Heat the oil in a small skillet. Add the onion and cook for 5 minutes, until golden. Add the beef, garlic, coriander, and ginger, and cook, stirring, until the meat is no longer red, about 3 minutes.

Add the water and cook, stirring often, until it is reduced by half, about 5 minutes. Add the tomato paste and cook, stirring, for about 5 minutes. Season with the salt and pepper, and set aside.

Make the yogurt sauce: Blend the yogurt, garlic, and salt in a bowl, and set it aside.

Make the dumplings: Combine the chopped scallion tops, salt, pepper, red pepper flakes, and garlic in a bowl. Toss to mix.

Lay a wonton wrapper on a flat surface and brush the edges with water. Spoon 1 teaspoon of the scallion mixture onto the center, fold the wrapper in half, and press the edges to make a semicircle. Repeat with the remaining wrappers. (If you do not have round wrappers, fold them into triangles.)

Heat 3 quarts salted water in a 6- or 8-quart pot. When it is boiling, add the filled dumplings and cook for 5 minutes. Drain in a colander.

Assemble the dish: Spoon ¼ cup yogurt sauce into a serving dish, and cover it with the dumplings. Spoon the remaining yogurt sauce on top, and sprinkle with the mint. Spoon the meat sauce all around, and serve at once.

SERVES 4

Someone's In the Kitchen

Mr. Clean

by Patrick Kuh

from *Gourmet*

Himself a trained chef, Patrick Kuh—who regularly reviews restaurants for *Los Angeles* magazine—knows well what goes on inside a restaurant kitchen. This profile reveals how an almost obsessive attention to detail sets apart acclaimed chef Gray Kunz.

Cooks are not like other people. They have their own code of conduct, which demands they never let a waiter see them crack. They have their own hierarchy, which places a trusted dishwasher above any newly arrived sous-chef. Working skewed hours in often-windowless kitchens, they even have their own sense of time. A cook's day does not progress from light to dark or morning to night. A cook's day goes from clean to clean.

Gray Kunz likes things clean. Very clean. Color-coded cutting boards, biodegradable cleaning products, chamois cloths to polish stainless-steel surfaces, motorized sanders to remove carbon deposits from the range—the entire kitchen at Café Gray, on the third floor of New York City's Time Warner Center, represents a completely new vision of the way kitchens should be cleaned and cared for. Visiting it requires a visual adjustment. You won't find knife bags, those symbols of the profession that can be as battered as a fifth grade lunchbox and as pungent as old sneakers. Instead, you'll see custom-made wooden slots to hold knives that each cook is issued. And instead of the usual floor mats found in most restaurants, which are stacked like beached stingrays each time the floor is mopped, there is an upright dark blue cleaner. Kunz first spotted it skating across an airport corridor. With the purr of a luxury hotel vacuum, the power of an L.A. car wash, and the lines of the latest Vespa, it has pride of place in Kunz's kitchen. It is one of the reasons why working here requires a rethinking of what it means to be a chef.

Kunz is considered a chef's chef. He made his reputation at Lespinasse, in The St. Regis hotel, a restaurant that, despite the ancien régime connotations of its name (Mademoiselle de Lespinasse having been one of the great *salonnières* of the mid-18th century), was known as a kitchen where a brilliant talent was at work. Today, after years without his own restaurant, the 49-year-old chef is repositioning himself, not in another grand hotel, but in a retail center where he will be cooking for 200 or so people at a time. This may seem like a big change, but Kunz has a brain that thinks of a kitchen as a theater of operations. When asked how the food served at Café Gray will differ from the food he made at Lespinasse, he answers with the direct efficiency of someone who has thought everything out. "Each dish," he says, "requires two steps less than it did at Lespinasse."

But ask what cleaning means to him and he stalls, smiling as if bemused by his own foibles, and eventually answers: "You really haven't finished cooking until you've finished cleaning."

To understand this, you need to see the entire process, to follow a Styrofoam crate full of sole as it hits the loading dock beneath the Time Warner Center. Yes, these are fish, but there's an E.R. pacing to what happens next. First, the crate is wheeled down two floors and along bare institutional corridors to a receiving room where the fish are transferred to clean plastic containers. Kunz doesn't want the boxes that have been sitting in grubby trucks in his clean kitchen. A steward takes them via tunnels and freight elevators to the kitchen.

A fish chef is waiting at a spotless stainless-steel sink with a custom-made cutting board running across it so that trimmings drop down below the work surface. Kunz doesn't want fish being cleaned amid trimmings. The process involves nipping fins, cleaning insides, scaling, and skinning, the gestures punctuated only by the occasional use of a hand-activated hose. Of all the cleaning actions the sole undergoes, the most telling is when the cook takes a pair of sharp poultry shears to the tiny bones that run all around the fish. The French have a word for this procedure, they call it *ébarber*, to debeard—but even they don't actually do it anymore. It's a classic technique that adds a degree of delicacy to the dish when the sole is served whole, but almost everywhere, this has been allowed to slide. Not, however, chez Kunz. If his desk in the corner of the kitchen weren't already crowded, there might be room for a sign reading "The Slide Stops Here."

For Kunz, cleaning his ingredients is a way to extract them from all the bustle of a professional kitchen and return them to a pristine state. That is where his cooking starts. And it's absolutely crucial. Kunz takes control of the end result from the very beginning, maintaining an iron grip on the way each ingredient is treated and cleaned.

It is only when that almost-sterile quality has been established that he can lead each ingredient back to the sedge-lined field, forest undergrowth, or cold waters it came from. Somehow, the act of cleaning releases the great earthiness that Kunz himself responds to and that his cooking displays. Yes, he is the chef who might *ébarbe*; but he is also busy pickling cattail shoots and putting up for-aged mushrooms like a homesteading grandmother. Yes, he is the chef who insists that no carrot can touch his color-coded cutting boards until it has been topped, tailed, and peeled; but he is also the chef who, when talking of those very same carrots, supplied by a farm in upstate New York, can run his hands over their loamy lengths and, moved by the connection to the land that they represent, say, "I love dirt."

"Maybe it's a Swiss thing," Kunz says about the paradoxes of his approach. In Switzerland, first thing in the morning, the citizens fling open their windows and leave their eiderdowns to hang in the alpine air. A public gesture, a private moment, symbolic and functional at the same time.

So yes, maybe it is a Swiss thing—but only in that Switzerland represents just one side of who he is. For Gray Kunz was born in Singapore, and Asia is where he feels most deeply at home. Asia, sensual, alive, teeming; the Asia where, as Conrad would have it, the night descends like "a benediction." The tension is resolved in his cooking, where the Jungfrau and the floating market coexist, where the gleam of an alpine stream is captured in Shantung silk. In Kunz's cooking, Switzerland and Asia beat like the systole and diastole of a single heart.

On a recent morning, Kunz was on the third floor of the Time Warner Center. Outside the window, Central Park opened up like a pie wedge behind the monument to the *Maine*. Serried along the park's southern flank were the grandes dames of Central Park South; in the middle distance, the slender tower of The Pierre. Kunz was taking none of it in. He was at the controls of his dark blue floor cleaner and he was looking straight down at the floor. It would be nice to be able to report that his face carried the expression that crosses Itzhak Perlman's face during a particularly sublime solo passage, but it didn't. Kunz simply wanted to make sure the machine hadn't left the slightest trace of water in its wake. He was essentially frowning at a floor that sparkled back at him.

To realize his goals, Kunz has surrounded himself with a band of workers who think the way he does. And when cooking and cleaning are one, the chef misses nothing. Take Akinbayo Alli, for instance. At night, when all that's lit in the kitchen are the pilot lights, he comes with the steam guns. Alli worked at Lespinasse; now he owns a cleaning company. He remembers the day Kunz took him aside. "'Today,' he said, 'you are cleaning floors, but one day I know you'll do something great,'" he recalls. "I didn't even know he was looking at me!"

The crew must teach every new arrival how Kunz wants things done. There is a system: a hand sink right beside the time clock, so cooks can wash their hands as soon as they get to work; spatulas to scrape down the sides of stockpots before they are left to simmer. First thing is to learn the system. Not recipes, not techniques, but how to bear down on a squeegee and make no concession to dirt.

By isolating the acts of cleaning and bringing his full intelligence to bear on a subject that would seem to be about surfaces, Gray Kunz has found a way to access the cooking profession's most resonant depths. It's not that cleaning is transformed into metaphor. Cooks don't do metaphor. It's that his single-minded pursuit of the luminously clean kitchen is a means of ensuring that this can happen to others, perhaps even the young cooks just finding out that they won't be needing their knife bags.

Quintessential Californian

by Thomas McNamee

from *Saveur*

McNamee's profile of Judy Rodgers, chef and co-owner of San Francisco's *Zuni Café*, not only defines what makes her restaurant special, but also explores what the essence of the dining experience is all about.

Zuni Café is not a perfect restaurant. Eating at a perfect restaurant, or one that aims for perfection, as do the great three-stars of France, is exhilarating, a peak experience—like seeing a masterly performance of a Shakespeare play. Part of the magic of the performance is the appearance of effortlessness onstage, and part is the audience's utterly absorbed attention. But how often do you really want to experience something like that? Wouldn't eating that way very often be, in fact, exhausting?

Zuni is not exhausting. Many San Franciscans will tell you that they could eat there every day and never get tired of the place. The restaurant celebrates its 25th anniversary this year, and Judy Rodgers, Zuni's tall, miniskirted chef and co-owner, has won a dazzling array of culinary awards, including the James Beard Foundation's Outstanding Chef award for 2004; but there's more to Zuni than its longevity and its superb food—something hard to put your finger on, something that is actually many somethings.

At 11 on an ordinary morning, nine of the famous Zuni hamburgers are already hissing on the grill. Rodgers dips a finger into a salad of farro and fava beans with arugula, radishes, scallions, and cilantro in a buttermilk vinaigrette. "Ah," she breathes, closing her eyes for a single beat. "Now, *that* is definitive." How many chefs, I wonder, use words like *definitive*?

Before every meal, the cooks at Zuni gather to present the dishes of the day. They watch Rodgers as a family of field mice would watch a circling hawk. She takes a bite of the fettuccine with English peas, pancetta, and black pepper: "I think you need to cut back on the pancetta. It's too much of a rustic note." The pizza with spicy tomato sauce, marinated fresh sardines, red onions, and capers: too spicy? No, good and spicy—Rodgers likes it that way, though the dough is a little tough. "Leave it out at room temperature for a while, and it'll soften up." The house-cured pork chop with rapini, flageolets, and toasted-bread-crumb salsa: "The flags [flageolets] are inedible. Way too salty." Emergency measures—a great dilution of broth, a dose of stock—and it's okay. Even the classic caesar salad, of which Zuni sells a good hundred day after day, is tasted and tuned.

The great glass wedge of the front room, 19 feet high, with sun pouring in through the liquor bottles above the polished copper bar, is the space that gives Zuni its visual identity—grand and odd-ball at once. Idiosyncrasy and diversity are Zuni's hallmarks, and San Francisco's. Some people doubtless would prefer the terms "eccentricity" and "chaos." Neither this town nor this restaurant is for them. Both are a little bit fanatical, priding themselves on surprising you. (I have yet to see a Zuni menu, for example, that didn't feature at least one ingredient I'd never heard of.) The restaurant is nevertheless deeply comfortable. There's always the soothing polenta with mascarpone, always the zephyr-light ricotta gnocchi, always the incomparable shellfish plateau. The waiters greet everyone with breezy grace, they know the food and wine up and down, and they quite clearly enjoy working here. The crowds that surge through Zuni day and night are a living exhibit of what San Francisco is all about: investment bankers and transvestites, bestudded bike messengers and bespectacled intellectuals, models and mooks, tourists gawking at the openly necking gays and soigné social swans, all cheek by jowl in Zuni's peculiar congeries of dining rooms—the high front room with its grand piano and splendiferous flowers and scattered few tables; the L-shaped back room, wrapped around an immense wood-burning oven and open to the adjacent kitchen; a mezzanine overlooking the bar; another, smaller mezzanine reached by a back staircase; a secretive little side room; and, my favorite, a sort of bridge over the kitchen, bearing only two tables for two and looking straight down to the mouth of the oven.

There's something wrong with every one of these rooms. This one's drafty, that one's too hot, this one's noisy; have too much wine in this one, and you may break your neck falling down the irregular, very hard stairs. Friends of mine complain about bathrooms too seldom cleaned and the winos and crackheads thronging the nearby streets. Zuni Café is not a perfect restaurant.

Judy Rodgers was evidently drawn by destiny to good eating. With no gastronomic ambitions whatever, she went to France for her high-school senior year, and destiny plunked her down in the household of Jean Troisgros, whose family's eponymous restaurant in Roanne is one of the finest in the world. She was in the restaurant kitchen after school every day, taking copious notes—hardly typical teenage behavior, but such was young Judy Rodgers. Stanford University doesn't usually train chefs, but even before her graduation with a degree in art history in 1978 and for some years thereafter, Rodgers was cooking at Chez Panisse, where distinguished degrees have never been rare.

Troisgros has all the luxurious trappings obligatory in a Michelin three-star restaurant and is stupendously expensive. There remains, nonetheless, a family resemblance between Zuni's food and that of Troisgros and Chez Panisse, owing mainly to their owners' shared commitment to freshness and seasonality. From both the Troisgros family and Chez Panisse's Alice Waters, Rodgers learned to value superlative ingredients and to disdain culinary showboating. One of her proudest creations is the Zuni hamburger—harder to get right, she says, than sautéed foie gras: "There are 50 ways to screw up a good hamburger."

In the basement prep kitchen, Quang Nguyen, an émigré from Vietnam who has been at Zuni for 22 years, deftly slices rabbits into forelegs, hind legs, bellies, and loins. "This guy is a genius," says Rodgers. "He can bone anything, even if he's never seen it before." These rabbits, in classic Zuni/Panisse fashion, were raised as the

4-H project of a friend's daughter. Before they're roasted, the legs and loins will rest for a few hours in the cure that Rodgers developed in her first days of fame, as chef of the Union Hotel in Benicia, California, from 1981 to 1983—rock salt, thyme (pounded, so the oils are released), and roughly cracked black pepper." The presalting," says Rodgers, "lets the herbs sneak a ride into the flesh. You should never use oil in a marinade—or wine or vinegar. All they do is cook the surface." The bellies get a bacon cure of just salt and pepper. Tomorrow, the bunny bacon will be grilled and julienned, to be served with the kidneys and liver in a warm rabbit salad.

The restaurant creates an astonishing range of preserved products, which play off the rigorous seasonality of the fresh stuff. Here's a partial enumeration from Rodgers, "just off the top of my head": anchovies; jams; pickled cherries; brandied grapes, cherries, prune-plums, and mirabelles; dried figs in red wine; fresh figs in grappa; pancetta; soppressata; bresaola; coppa; mortadella; chorizo; goose breast ham; duck leg confit; preserved lemons and limequats; pickled herring; preserved grape leaves; salt cod; cèpes in olive oil; and oven-dried costoluto tomatoes. "We're always asking ourselves," she says, not quite half-joking, "what can we do to make this harder?"

Rodgers's frankness is emblematic of the larger enterprise. The wavy glass windows, some of which probably date from the building's rather slapdash construction in 1913; the unhidden structural steel added after the 1989 earthquake; the resolutely liberal politics of Rodgers and co-owner Vince Calcagno; the worn concrete floors and tabletops; the no-nonsense presentation of the food—everything at Zuni looks like what it is.

When it opened, in February 1979—in what is now one of the back dining rooms, with nine tables, a couple of hot plates in the minuscule kitchen, and a Weber grill outside in the alley—the restaurant was known as the Zuni Café and Gallery, and to this day the art on the walls, though not marked with prices, is for sale. Calcagno arrived in 1981 and did everything from tossing salads to scraping paint. Soon he and the original owner, Billy West, acquired a few adjacent small rooms in the building as well as the soaring glass triangle that is now the bar. The first room became the waiting room, complete with piano; the new upstairs area lacked electricity. "It was very dark," says Calcagno, "depending on what kind of candles we bought that weekend." The big space, which they couldn't afford to renovate, was simply filled with junk for the next four years.

In 1983, after leaving the Union Hotel, Rodgers was making salamis for Café Fanny (a casual offshoot of Chez Panisse). "Billy walked into my apartment, and all these salamis were dangling from the hallway. And he was just like, 'You're hired. You're weird enough.' But I wanted to do my own thing." In 1986, after cooking and traveling in Europe, then planning a restaurant of her own in Berkeley and consulting in New York when the restaurant didn't work out, Rodgers had another visit from West. Zuni's front room had finally opened. He begged her to take a look. "I walked through the door of this place at eight o'clock at night in January [1987], and it was bustling and beautiful and there were champagne and oysters everywhere, and I was like, 'I gotta work here.' "

The menus from Rodgers's early days are surprisingly similar to today's. Not that the dishes are the same—indeed, except for a few icons that her faithful will never allow her to relinquish, such as the perfect roast chicken with bread salad and the rich chocolate gâteau Victoire, her menus through the years are a narrative of continuous invention—but the style, the essence, remains remarkably stable.

Imaginative variation on classic themes is what makes Zuni's food familiar yet exciting. There is almost always a piccolo fritto (little fry), but the ingredients change constantly. The democratically appealing hamburger will be balanced by a connoisseur's dish of chicken and squab livers. If steak there must be, let it be a hanger steak, with one of a number of sauces. Pasta, always, often a variation on a classic, like spaghetti (rather than linguine) with clams. Salad, but with a twist: frisée with roasted fruit, say.

Touring her kitchen, Rodgers focuses on the many things that went wrong in its very expensive redesign two years ago. Her pride in its obvious capabilities is not what Rodgers would focus on; her mind lunges straight for the problems. "The place still leaks like crazy," she complains. "All the floors upstairs have to be redone. It's the kind of restaurant where people really relax and kind of bang around a lot, so a lot of damage is done, and it's hard to get a good cleanup crew because they think, 'Well, your esthetic is kind of rustic.' It's very hard to get someone to understand that raw steel doesn't equal dirty or dusty."

Judy Rodgers never stops thinking that Zuni can be better than it is. It is not a perfect restaurant. It's a great one.

———— ✺ ————

Roast Chicken with Bread Salad
Although Zuni's menus constantly change, this is one dish that's always on the menu—at the insistence of regular customers.

1¾–3½-lb. chicken, preferably a fryer, lump of fat inside
    chicken discarded
4 tender sprigs fresh thyme, marjoram, rosemary, or sage
Salt and freshly cracked black pepper
½ – ¾-lb. day-old chewy country-style bread (not sourdough),
    cut into large chunks, crusts removed
8 tbsp. mild olive oil
2 tbsp. white wine vinegar
1 tbsp. dried currants
1 tsp. red wine vinegar
2 tbsp. pine nuts
2–3 cloves garlic, peeled and thinly sliced
2 scallions, trimmed, white and pale green parts only, thinly
    sliced
2 tsp. lightly salted chicken stock or lightly salted water
4 handfuls (about 3 oz.) baby red mustard greens or arugula or
    frisée leaves

1. Rinse chicken, pat very dry inside and out, and put on a plate. Loosen skin from breast and thighs without tearing it and tuck an herb sprig into each pocket. Liberally season chicken all over with salt and pepper. Loosely cover and refrigerate for at least 24 hours and up to 3 days.

2. Put bread on a baking sheet and brush with 3 tbsp. of the oil. Broil until lightly colored on each side, 2–3 minutes per side. Trim off any badly charred tips, then tear bread into 2"–3" wads and put into a large bowl. Preheat oven to 475°.

Mix white wine vinegar, 4 tbsp. of the oil, and salt and pepper to taste in a small bowl. Toss ¼ cup of the vinaigrette with the bread. Soak currants in red wine vinegar and 1 tbsp. warm water in a small bowl.

3. Heat a 10" ovenproof skillet over medium heat for 5 minutes. Wipe chicken dry, put in skillet breast side up, and roast in oven for 30 minutes. Turn bird over and roast for 10–20 minutes more, then flip back over to recrisp breast skin, 5–10 minutes more.

4. Meanwhile, warm pine nuts in oven for 1–2 minutes, then add to bread. Sweat garlic and scallions in 1 tbsp. of the oil in a small skillet over medium-low heat for 5–6 minutes. Add to bread and toss well. Drain currants and add to bread, then add stock or water and toss again. Put bread salad into a small baking dish and tent with foil. Transfer to oven when chicken gets its last turn.

5. Remove chicken from oven and turn off heat, leaving bread salad in oven for 5 minutes more. Transfer chicken to a plate. Pour off fat from skillet, leaving pan drippings behind. Swirl 1 tbsp. water in skillet. Slash skin between thighs and breast of chicken, then tilt bird and plate over skillet, draining juices into drippings. Allow chicken to rest for 10 minutes, then carve into 8 pieces.

6. Simmer pan drippings over medium heat, scraping up browned bits, for 1 minute. Toss hot bread salad with a spoonful of pan drippings in a bowl, add greens and remaining vinaigrette, and toss well. Put bread salad on a platter and arrange chicken on top.

SERVES 2–4

Frisée Salad with Hazelnuts, Parmigiano-Reggiano, and Roasted Prune-Plums

Rodgers used a variety of fruits for this salad, among them cherries, little bunches of grapes, and ripe figs. She also uses a range of greens, sometimes substituting mesclun or arugula for frisée.

12–16 shelled hazelnuts
6 small ripe prune-plums, pitted and halved or quartered
1½–2½ tbsp. extra-virgin olive oil
Pinch sugar
Salt
3 oz. (6 cups) frisée leaves
1–2 tsp. red wine vinegar
¼ tsp. hazelnut liqueur, such as Frangelico (optional)
Small chunk parmigiano-reggiano

1. Preheat oven to 450°. Spread hazelnuts out on a small baking sheet and roast until skins darken, 4–8 minutes. Wrap nuts in a clean dish towel and rub off skins. Coarsely chop nuts and set aside.

2. Put plums into a small shallow baking dish, toss with 1–2 tsp. of the oil, sprinkle with sugar and salt to taste, and toss again. Roast plums until warmed through and their skins start to blister, 5–15 minutes.

3. Put frisée into a large bowl and toss with 1–2 tbsp. of the oil. Season to taste with salt, add vinegar, and toss well. Adjust seasonings. Add hazelnuts and liqueur (if using) and toss again. The salad should be heavily dressed and juicy. Add roasted fruit and gently toss again. Divide salad between 2 plates. Using a swivel-blade vegetable peeler, shave some cheese over each salad. Serve with a couple of pieces of grilled or toasted crusty country bread, if you like.

SERVES 2

Grilling with the Steak Whisperer

by David Leite

from *Ridgefield Magazine*

Leite, freelance food writer and founder of the website www.leitesculinaria.com, has an engaging way of playing kitchen apprentice, encouraging a master—in this case Waldy Malouf, of Manhattan's Beacon Restaurant—to reveal tricks of his trade.

When Waldy Malouf, owner of Beacon Restaurant in New York City, broke his ankle in several places, I couldn't have been happier. Nothing against Malouf. If anything, he's a friendly bear of a guy, unlike the pan-throwing heathens I had the bad luck to work with when I was a waiter. Nor was it thinly veiled sadomasochistic tendencies that warmed me inside when I got word of his misfortune. Rather it was something far more sinister: grilling season. It was fast approaching, and I couldn't present my claque of culinistas with yet another platter of incinerated chicken breasts. Because Malouf had to hang up his tongs temporarily, thanks to a cast that came up to his knee, I did what any desperate cook would do. I ambushed him at home, in Connecticut.

My arrival was announced by a sonic boom of barking from his four dogs—Xena (warrior-like and very much a princess), Rollo (a Corgi who as a puppy always lost footing when running down hills), Mr. Pink (from *Reservoir Dogs*), and Puddles (for obvious reasons). I assumed it was all this snuffling canine activity underfoot that caused Malouf's condition. But apparently it was a weekend stroll on the patio.

"He fell only two inches off the flagstone, and what does he get?"

asked Meg, Malouf's wife. "Nine pins, scaffolding, and a surprise six-week vacation," she added, shaking her head.

Malouf waved off the comment with his meaty hand. "Let's cook," he bellowed.

Clearly his medical house arrest gave him a severe bout of cabin fever, because laid out on the long wooden counter were four large trays filled with cups, bowls, and bundles of precisely measured ingredients for the dishes we were going to make. The menu: chicken breasts with balsamic marinade; New York strip steaks with black pepper, onions, and garlic; sea scallops on rosemary skewers with tomato-ginger chutney; and grilled swordfish steaks in a mustard-seed crust.

I was all set to head out back to learn a showy trick or two that would get me through the summer, but it was clear Malouf wasn't going to allow me anywhere near his grill without at least a lesson in the basics of open-fire cooking, which he outlines to great effect in his book *High Heat* (Broadway Books, 2003). "Marinades, dry rubs, and glazes impart flavor through ingredients," he said while chopping tomatoes for the chutney.

Not exactly headline news, Waldy, I said to myself.

"But searing and smoking impart taste through technique," he added, as he swung himself Fred Astaire-like on his crutches to the fridge. I suddenly understood the reason for my hook-and-ladder-company chicken: It never occurred to me there was such a thing as theory or technique when it came to open-fire cooking. Hell, wasn't the idea to get primal and throw a hunk of meat on the fire just as our prehistoric ancestors did—the only difference being we'd had the evolutionary good fortune to come along after the discovery of vodka and tonic?

Apparently not, according to Malouf. "People often confuse open-fire cooking with out-of-control high-heat cooking. They're not the same. You have to coax the fire, work with it." For example, he often starts things at high heat, but finishes them at a lower heat. "Your goal isn't to incinerate dinner," he added a bit too presciently.

For the next half hour, Malouf gave me what amounted to a cultural anthropology lesson on the use of open-fire cooking, which circled around the Mediterranean and hopscotched through South America. "Putting food on the fire is a basic and ancient human experience—all cultures share it," he said, gathering the ingredients. "But whether I'm inspired by the spit roasting of Greece or Spain or by the way the Argentines sear beef on skewers, I always try to add some American back yard to my cooking." He handed me a few trays, and we made our way outside.

On the patio, the scene of Malouf's misadventure, the Viking grill had been pre-heating for 30 minutes. This was not the tabletop hibachi of my youth. It was bigger and sexier-looking than some European cars. Inside was a special smoker box, where wet wood chips are scattered for a perfectly controlled smoky flavor. And there were enough knobs and dials to make a NASA engineer feel right at home.

"Okay, so now what?" I asked.

"We put the food on the grill," he said simply. What a minute! This didn't seem any different than what I did every disastrous Saturday night. Where was the theory, where was all this technique? I was about to balk when Malouf passed his hand over the grill, lingering in some spots, skimming over others. Then he plopped down the steaks, swordfish, and chicken in three discrete groups. *He's a human thermometer,* I thought.

"Then you leave them alone." I wondered if he said this because he could tell just by looking at me that I'm carker, someone utterly too codependent with his food to let it simple cook without anxiously fussing over it.

"For how long?" I asked.

"They'll tell you." Okay, this fell into the build-it-and-they-will-come category, but I decided to be a sport and let the food speak to me.

While we waited, Malouf continued the lesson. "This is where the grill turns into a smoker and an oven." By closing the lid, he explained, the smoke from the wood he had tossed in permeates the food, adding flavor. But at the same time, the heat circulates like in an oven, cooking the food more evenly. Flare-ups, the bane of most weekend warriors, are controlled, too; deprived of oxygen, they die out instantly. The subtle interplay of technique and science was making itself felt.

A while later, he opened the grill and gently lifted a steak. He motioned for me to get down and look at its underbelly. "See how it's not sticking and has real prominent grill marks?" he asked.

"*That's* how you know it's ready to turn." He slid the steak back and forth along the slats to completely loosen it and then flipped it. He did the same to the rest.

"How do you know when they're done?"

"Rely on an instant-read thermometer at first. If you get in the habit of using it, you'll get to the point where you don't need it—you'll go by how things feel."

He then had me poke the fleshy triangle of skin between my thumb and index finger. "That's what rare meat feels like," he said. Then he poked the inside of his muscular forearm. "And that's well done." I poked my arm; it didn't feel much different than my hand. I jabbed a few other parts of my body. There wasn't a place on me that was well-done.

"But most important," he said, transferring everything to platters, "make sure to take the food off the grill when it's still below temperature. It'll continue to cook."

We took the platters to the kitchen, and after letting the food rest so the juices could redistribute—another key technique point—Malouf put together a plate for me. Everything was beautifully crusted and juicy, and the bold tang of the marinades and the deep muskiness of the rubs mixed with the smokiness, making for excellent eating. Meg offered me some food to take home, but I demurred. I knew that as soon as I got there I'd be lighting up my grill and committing to memory everything this patron saint of open-fire cooking had told me.

After lunch, I took the train home. The woman sitting next to me began sniffing in my direction. I smelled my shirt and it reeked of the satisfying, manly scent of fat and smoke. "It's me," I assented. "I was playing with fire." A wave of fear rippled across her face, and she got up and moved across the aisle.

Hickory House Memories
Oklahoma City Barbecue

by Rick Bayless
from *Saveur*

From his vantage point as a successful cookbook author and restaurateur (Chicago's Frontera Grill and Topolobampo), Rick Bayless reassesses his childhood, growing up in his family's Oklahoma City barbecue restaurant.

Not until I was in the seventh grade did I realize that my clothes smelled different from everyone else's—that my smoke-saturated shirts were an aromatic advertisement for the family barbecue restaurant in Oklahoma City, Oklahoma, in whose dining room I'd literally grown up (first paying job: refilling cups of iced tea and lemonade at a catering gig at the age of seven). By that time, the blood coursing through my veins must have been replaced at least partly by barbecue sauce. My family has a long and proud history in the food business. It all started with my great-grandparents, who came from Kansas and Tennessee to this former Indian territory, thought to be a wasteland until oil was discovered here in the late 1800s, and opened Oklahoma's first grocery store, shortly after statehood was won, in 1907. My grandfather started out with a bread delivery route, a career he abandoned in order to open a drive-in restaurant in the 1950s. He had three children. One went into the grocery store business, one did the drive-in thing, but my father, John, somehow saw barbecue as his niche. I have no idea why: before he married my mother, he sold black-and-white TVs, and no one else in the family knew anything at all about barbecue. He always said that it was a "calculated choice," but I've never been sure what he calculated, or how.

What I do believe is that most people don't think of Oklahoma barbecue as unique—in contrast to the kind found in Texas or Kansas City or Memphis or North Carolina. In fact, this barbecue is usually described in terms of what it's not: it's not as saucy as barbecue from Kansas City, though both places commonly use hickory wood, and what sauce it has can be similar to K.C.'s, with ketchup as a main ingredient. It's not as tangy as Memphis barbecue and not as vinegary as what they serve in North Carolina. It's not as dry as most classic Texas barbecue, and it's not inclusive of just one kind of meat: both pork ribs and large cuts of beef (like brisket) play a major role. What it has in common with the other well-known barbecue styles of this country is that its tradition has existed for almost as long as theirs and was likely created by the same combination of European immigrants and black workers who came to the area and looked for good, cheap food when they arrived.

My parents opened their place in a small redbrick building at 25th and South Western streets, in the then promising neighborhood of Capitol Hill, in 1949. They named it Hickory House for the wood they burned, and they lined the walls and ceiling with aroma-absorbing pine planks and built a massive indoor brick pit. The dramatic presence of the pit in the restaurant's one room gave the impression that it had somehow been discovered there and the building constructed around it.

By the time my memory became active, the brick pit had been abandoned (it cooked too unevenly) in favor of an old-fashioned trough-type pit behind the restaurant. That in turn was replaced by a series of old "refrigerator pits"—discarded commercial reach-in units, to which a welder friend of my father's attached gas–wood fireboxes to help keep the temperature inside the pits a smoky 275°. Still not completely satisfied, my father equipped his last refrigerator pit with fans to circulate heat and smoke, lending more moisture to the cooking environment and providing additional flavor for the barbecue sauce, and placed a wide pan at the bottom to collect the drippings.

Over the years the place itself changed, from a one-room joint with carhop service and a take-out window into a legitimate three-dining-room complex. And the Hickory House menu kept expanding. It was more ambitious than that of many barbecue restaurants.

Everything was made from scratch: seven meats (pork ribs were the big draw, though the thought of the earthy hot links instantly makes my mouth water); seven hot side dishes (folks drove across town for the twice-baked potatoes); seven cold side dishes (sour coleslaw was the most popular, but the sweet slaw had its devotees). We also offered "French" and rye bread, hot and mild barbecue sauces, olives, peppers, dill pickles, and spicy chowchow (pickled vegetable relish). This is the brawny, spice-happy, deep-rooted food that molded my spirit. When I fell in love with Mexico at the age of 14, the bold flavor and artless simplicity of Hickory House barbecue were all I knew. Mexico's regional cooking, with which I am now closely associated, felt like a long-lost relative.

For the 37 years our family ran Hickory House, smoking dry-rubbed meats, making straightforward ketchup-based sauces, and stuffing deviled eggs, the place persevered through my dad's fruitless investments in Sonic Drive-ins and, once, a steak house. The solid brick building survived the legendary weather of Oklahoma's tornado alley (we ran to the restaurant's thick-walled walk-in refrigerator for shelter more times than I care to remember). Employees like Irene Hile (30 years), Harry Felter (25 years), Faye Spencer (19 years), and Chris Jentry (15 years) helped us keep going through bouts of alcoholism, quarrels, and other kinds of tragedy. During it all, we took our turns making salads and cooking ribs, catering, and bussing tables.

And then one day in 1986, the place was gone. The neighborhood hadn't been good for a while. My sister was happy teaching school. I'd moved to Mexico, then to Los Angeles, and then to Chicago to open my my own (Mexican) restaurant. My brother the sportswriter had never like the business. Since 1968, when my parents split up and my my mom, Levita, began running the place, she had been alone in supervising the daily cooking of 500 pounds of ribs. Tired, near retirement age, she sold the business to an inexperienced, undercaptialized fellow, who went broke after six months.

I didn't miss it right away. When I left home for graduate school in Michigan, the lure of the Midwest corn roasts and fresh-pressed cider quickly captivated me. The few times I invited friends for Oklahoma-styled barbeque, the ribs from my small kettle grill and the baked beans and the sour slaw didn't turn out like what I remembered. I'd made those dishes a hundred times, but I couldn't get them right in small quantities and without the familiar restaurant equipment. Besides, the flavor seemed strange in my new home.

But then one day my sister, LuAnn, happened to mention that she occasionally made Hickory House sweet slaw for her family, and not long afterward my mother told me that she sometimes took Hickory House twice-baked potatoes to potlucks. Then, coincidentally, around the same time, my now 13-year-old daughter Lanie asked me what kind of restaurant Grandma had had. It was then that I resolved to reconstruct the Hickory House recipes—for Lanie.

My first step was to go back to the brown photo album–cum–cookbook that I'd put together in high school. Its recipes called for tubs of this, #10 cans of that, and brands of spice mix that had long since ceased to exist. The recipes needed major modifications in the interest of practicality. Luckily, sometime in the 1970s I'd written down the components of the Cain's barbecue spice blend that we used as a dry rub. After several rounds of tests (which included the replacing of garlic powder with fresh garlic—a purely personal preference), I invited my family to Chicago for an attempted re-creation of the flavors of my youth.

Well, what I had imagined would be a perfect, harmonious, idyllic day of cooking together—with everyone purring over the perfection of my recipes—was a comedy of errors. To start, my mother, who's never been much for following recipes, was caught in a struggle between the force of habit and the intrusion of my written words. She ended up with a plate of inedibly salty deviled eggs. LuAnn, an excellent cook, was so flustered at having to follow a recipe for something she knew well that she staggered along like a novice. She turned out twice-baked potatoes so soupy that they ran onto our plates like sauce. Both Mom and LuAnn argued with me about whether we'd put parsley into the sour slaw, about whether it's celery seed or mustard seed in the potato salad, and about the consistency of the beans. I was so discombobulated by the fracas that I burned the ribs. It wasn't until later, when I thought about my sister's adamant defense of the way she had developed her own sweet slaw recipe, that I admitted to myself that there really is no Hickory House food anymore; there are only our personal memories of it. Flavors are evocative, but they can't bring back the past. I've come to think of traditional flavors—family flavors, regional flavors, cultural flavors—as both part of and apart from us; they thrive when they're revived by each cook, each generation, as the perfect expression of the present moment.

A few years after our disastrous first cook-out, I've come to terms with that fact of life. When my family visits, my wife, my daughter, and I make "Hickory House barbecue" for them. We do our versions of baked beans (I've changed to pintos from the original navys), the garlicky sour slaw flecked with flat-leaf parsley, and, of course, the deviled eggs and stuffed dill pickles. I use pickles smaller than the ones we served at Hickory House (they are only part of a huge spread), but everybody seems to like them. A recent discovery has helped a lot: the Hasty-Bake charcoal oven, a kind of backyard grill that has been produced in Oklahoma for more than 60 years (coming from a barbecue family with access to pits, I had never bothered to try one before), offers the simplicity of design, ample grill space, and adjustable firebox that I love. On it, I can cook my spareribs to a smoky tenderness that rivals what we achieved in the final Hickory House pit.

The last time my mother was here, she said, "You know, these are the closest things to Hickory House ribs I've tasted in the years since we closed." Ultimately, then, the spirit of Hickory House is alive and well.

Hickory House Deviled Eggs

Adding mashed potato to the filling of this traditional hors d'oeuvre helps bind it.

6 eggs
1 medium red-skin boiling potato, peeled and cut into 8 pieces
1 tbsp. salt
2 tbsp. sweet pickle relish
2 tbsp. mayonnaise
1 tbsp. prepared yellow mustard

1. Put eggs and potatoes into a medium pot and add enough cold water to cover them by 1". Add salt and simmer over medium-high heat for 10–15 minutes. Reduce heat to

medium to medium-low and gently simmer for 9 minutes more.

2. Pour off water from pot. Transfer potatoes with a slotted spoon to a medium bowl, then put pot of eggs under cold running water to let cool for 3 minutes. Meanwhile, add relish, mayonnaise, and mustard to potatoes, thoroughly mash together with a fork, and set aside.

3. Peel and cut eggs in half lengthwise. Using a fork or spoon, carefully scoop out yolks, add them to the potato mixture, and mash together with a fork. Spoon filling onto hard-cooked whites, mounding filling slightly and covering whole cut side of egg. Garnish with chopped chives and/or bachelor's buttons (which are edible), if you like.

MAKES 12

Hickory House Sour Slaw

Bayless recalls that this oil-and-vinegar-based tangy slaw, was the most popular of the seven cold side dishes served at Hickory House.

¼ cup vegetable oil
¼ cup white vinegar
1 tbsp. dry sherry
2 small doves garlic, peeled and coarsely chopped
1 tbsp. sugar
Heaping 1 tsp. salt
½ medium head green cabbage, cored and very thinly sliced
    (about 8 cups)
¼ cup chopped parsley leaves

Put oil, vinegar, sherry, 2 tbsp. water, garlic, sugar, and salt into a blender and purée until smooth. Put cabbage into a large bowl and sprinkle parsley on top. Pour dressing over slaw and toss well. Cover bowl and refrigerate for at lease 1 hour before serving.

SERVES 4–6

——∞∞∞——

Hickory House Sweet Slaw

LuAnn Tucker, the author's sister, prefers this mayonnaise-enhanced slaw, another Hickory House specialty, to the tangy "sour" version.

½ medium head green cabbage, cored and very thinly sliced
    (about 8 cups)
1 2-oz. bottle chopped pimentos, drained, or 1 small red bell
    pepper, roasted, peeled, seeded, and cut into ¼" pieces
3 ribs celery, cut into ¼" dice
¾ cups mayonnaise
1 tbsp. sugar
Salt

Put cabbage, pimentos, celery, mayonnaise, sugar, and 1 tsp. salt into a large bowl and toss well. Adjust seasonings with more salt, if you like. Cover bowl with plastic wrap and refrigerate until ready to serve. The flavor and texture are best when slaw is made an hour or two before serving.

SERVES 4–6

——∞∞∞——

Appetites

Norwegian Wood

by Margit Bisztray

from *Gourmet*

Bisztray writes lyrically of the foods she enjoyed during childhood summers in Norway—farm-fresh produce, foraged wild plants and mushrooms, and newly caught game and fish—and how she is introducing them to her children.

The sky, a tie-dye of pastels, glows although it's after 10 PM. My mother, my husband and I, and our two children, sit around the table at my mother's country house in southern Norway, 30 miles inland from Kristiansand. Beyond the lace curtains and eight-pane windows, birch leaves flip gently in the wind, and swallows chase insects around the gooseberry bushes. Down the hill, the river turns from copper to pewter, and the mountain ridges on its far side appear blotted. Earlier today, we hiked in those mountains, picking the blueberries that now stain our dessert plates. Except for seasonings, flour, and an ice cream cake, everything we've just eaten is wild or farm-fresh. At this table, sights and tastes are one.

When I was little, I believed Norway was edible. We lived in Chicago, where anything that grew might be polluted. But in my mother's homeland, where we summered, I ground clover between my teeth, and sucked wild chamomile, and bit the resin from pine needles. When we took walks between my grandparents' house and the community's thousand-year-old church, I plucked stalks of barley from the fields and chewed the raw grains. To buy produce—with a garden and a forest to provide for us—would have been as odd as buying water.

. . .

My grandfather cast fishnets on his strawberries to keep away crows, and underneath them I gorged myself. Norwegian strawberries mature slowly, simmering in sunlight around the clock from May through July, until they taste halfway to jam. With thin skins and a pulp unlike that of commercial varieties, they are at once weightless and juicy. The only thing better is wild strawberries, which dangle among triplets of leaves and have a flowery, intoxicating perfume. My grandmother's whole-grain bread was creamy, with a crackerlike crust. Lightly buttered and paved with mashed strawberries, it is the best food I've eaten in my life. I ate of it until my entire body ached.

I took for granted the heaps of crabs my mother's uncle pulled from his traps, the homemade *saft* (plum or currant syrup blended with water), the caramelized cheese from goats that romped freely in the mountains, and the unpasteurized honey from my great-aunt Sigrid's bees. I considered these trade-offs for the potato chips, corn on the cob, and Kentucky Fried Chicken that Norway didn't have.

Then, in my twenties, I met my husband, Markham, and became a food fanatic with him. We subscribed to food magazines, spent hours preparing recipes, and grew discerning. The more we learned, the more I began to realize not only how delicious but how world-class, gourmet, and extraordinary the wild foods of Norway are. I read about chefs parceling out wild strawberries and chanterelles and glacial char as though they were precious. Once we realized the relative scarcity of our foraged summer staples, our gathering of these wild foods became more ardent and uncompromising. We now want raw milk for our café au laits, and we buy it at a farm near my mother's house. We want the farm's pale yellow butter, weeping in its parchment wrap and resembling fresh cheese. We want the amber, sun-warmed plums that ooze syrup and plop onto the grass in my mother's yard.

Hunting for food takes time. On a typical August day, our family traipses into the forest with birch baskets, sharp knives, buckets, and berry pickers. My mother leads, wearing a Mr. Bubble T-shirt, a pair of stirrup pants, and running shoes so frayed they are like Velcro for twigs and moss. She drops to one knee, claws grass and leaves aside, and severs something quickly with her reindeer-horn knife. It is a chanterelle a luscious shade of apricot. The cap looks like a tutu on a single ballerina leg, and our two-year-old, Vivian, shouts *"Kantarell!"* We scramble for the rest of the circles, concentric as splash rings and ranging in size from a fist to the forest's full circumference. In the Middle Ages, people believed that chanterelle circles were evidence of witches, but even our six-year-old, Blue, knows they grow in gravelly soil, on old roads, and under heather bushes. A good patch might yield a dozen mushrooms, which we dust clean with a pastry brush and place in our basket.

We then climb up to the timberline for blueberries. Picking them reminds me of hunting for Easter eggs. My children sit on lichen-covered rocks and eat until they look like two blue-violet trolls. On the hike back down, we snip sorrel from a creek bed and snack on wild raspberries.

Driving home, we stop at a farm advertising eggs, new potatoes, and pull-your-own beets. Marta, the farmwife, fills our empty carton with caramel-colored eggs wisped with chicken down. As Blue plants his feet and tugs a wad of beet greens, Marta nods. "Beets—much work," she says. Blue looks astonished as roots pop from the soil, and as potatoes emerge between the tines of his pitchfork.

Back at my mother's house, Blue and I snip baby greens and herbs into a salad bowl. The Bibb and red-leaf lettuces, the spinach and the arugula, are barely petals, and look too fragile to have butted forth and clasped the sun's fingertips. Tossed with nasturtium, lovage, dill, chervil, and tarragon, then slicked with a simple vinaigrette, the leaves spiral and bounce as if still growing. Cubes of roasted beets add an edge of candy, mellowed with roasted small potatoes, whose skins are thin as membranes and whose flavor is as buttery as pine nuts. After the salad, we enjoy a soup of our wild sorrel (or wild nettles or garden lovage) puréed with cooked onions, homemade stock, and fresh cream. It is delicious, stinging with earth and sun and every layer between the two.

The farm eggs we purchased have made the pasta we eat next as bright as marigolds. On top, we spoon the mushrooms, sautéed with butter, fresh cream, and Cognac. Blue says the mushrooms smell of dirt, and they do—and of rain, moss, pinecones, tree bones, and minerals I can't even name.

We've had some luck catching small trout in the river, but mostly we rely on our relatives, who have more experience and better fishing gear. The pink flesh is light and pure, and the taste is as subtle and stunning as the taste of spring water compared to tap. My cousin often dives, off the coast, for scallops, padded with orange roe, sweet as the ocean is salty.

Various uncles and aunts of mine also hunt moose, which tastes like beef, only gamier. It carries none of the stigmas of beef, since the moose lead normal, moosey lives—munching wild foods—until my relatives encircle them. Arne Brimi, Norway's famous chef, prepares his game using ingredients the animal itself would eat. Following his lead, we pair moose sirloin with a sauce of lingonberries, sautéed mushrooms, crushed juniper, and spruce shoots. It tastes of Norway's body.

We've had some mishaps with our wild-food preparations, of course. The dandelion wine we brewed was good enough for cooking but not for imbibing. The syrup we boiled from cherries tasted like tree bark. But when we fly home to the States, our fingernails blueberry purple, our suitcases heavy with honey, raspberry jam, dried porcini, pesto, and black-currant *saft,* we bring with us not only the flavors of a Norwegian summer to carry us through a long American winter but the memory of what it means to have truly eaten.

⸎

Baby Greens with Roasted Beets and Potatoes

ACTIVE TIME: 40 Min   START TO FINISH: 1³/₄ HR

FOR VINAIGRETTE

    1 ½ tablespoons tarragon white-wine vinegar
    ¼ teaspoon Dijon mustard
    ½ teaspoon salt
    ⅛ teaspoon black pepper
    ¼ cup olive oil

FOR SALAD

    2 medium beets (1 lb with greens; 14 oz without greens), stems
        trimmed to 2 inches
    1 lb small new potatoes (about 1 inch in diameter) or finger-
        lings (1 to 1 ½ inches long), scrubbed well
    1 teaspoon olive oil

⅛ teaspoon salt

5 oz microgreens such as baby Bibb, red-leaf, and oak-leaf let-
    tuces and baby arugula, or mesclun (about 10 cups)

4 cups baby spinach (3 oz)

⅓ cup lovage leaves, coarsely chopped

⅓ cup fresh chervil and/or dill leaves

⅓ cup fresh tarragon leaves

20 unsprayed organic nasturtium blossoms

Make vinaigrette:

Whisk together vinegar, mustard, salt, and pepper. Add oil
in a slow stream, whisking until emulsified.

Roast beets and potatoes:

Put oven racks in upper and lower thirds of oven and preheat oven to 425°F.

Wrap beets individually in foil and roast on a baking sheet
in upper third of oven until tender, 1 to 1¼ hours. Once
beets have roasted for 30 minutes, toss potatoes with oil and
salt in a small baking pan and roast in lower third of oven, shaking pan occasionally, until potatoes are tender, 25 to 30 minutes. Carefully unwrap beets and cool slightly, then slip off and
discard skins.

Assemble salad:

Cut beets into ⅓-inch dice and put in a large salad bowl. Cut
potatoes into ⅓-inch-thick slices and add to beets along with all
greens and herbs. Add vinaigrette and toss gently to coat.

Sprinkle blossoms on top and serve immediately.

SERVES 6 TO 8

Wok Fragrant

by John Thorne

from *Simple Cooking*

John Thorne's quarterly newsletter is something to look forward to—funny, down-to-earth, and amazingly informative. Enthusiastically parsing the nuts and bolts of cooking, he also somehow gets at the heart and soul of why we cook.

It was my grandfather who introduced me to the world of Chinese restaurants, at least as they were in the 1950s, beguilingly ersatz palaces spun of velvet and gold. As a teenager, I spent my summers with him, working at odd jobs at his apartment house in the daytime and otherwise generally hanging around with him when I wasn't off somewhere by myself.

Grampa was drawn to Chinese restaurants for all the usual reasons: here was food that, while piquantly exotic, hit all the right notes so far as price, quantity, and greasy goodness were concerned. But the selling point that clinched the deal was that in Boston's Chinatown they not only stayed open past midnight but were actually bustling then. If there's just you and a waiter in an otherwise empty place, it's hard to ward off inner tremors of self-pity. But if the joint is jumping, you feel instead like a welcomed initiate to a secret club.

So it was that, whenever the Jack Paar Show started to bore him, Grampa would launch himself from his prone position on the couch and come drag me out of my bedroom and away from my science fiction tale. He would rev up the '52 Cadillac Series Sixty and we would head off to downtown Boston. Once we turned onto

Harrison Avenue, I started eagerly inhaling that ineffable—for a six-teen-year-old, at least—after-midnight aroma of the louche.

Our destination was China Pearl at 9 Tyler Street, and my grand-father always ordered *ho yu gai pu,* a dish of crisp, batter-coated pieces of fried chicken. (I remember this because every visit he had to work out with the waiter which of the many chicken dishes on the menu it was.) For me, the high points of the meal were the appe-tizers—spareribs and egg rolls—and the pork fried rice.

It would only take five more years for me to learn enough about Chinese food to become embarrassed at how touristy my taste was then, especially my fondness for the fried rice. This new awareness certainly affected how I ordered and ate in Chinese restaurants, as well as immediately dispelling any fondness I might have had for ital-icizing whatever was set before me with the cruet of soy sauce.

However, I would also be a liar if I said that I never ordered red-glazed pork ribs or fried rice again. On the contrary. Like many peo-ple who reach this point, my tastes simply bifurcated. The lover of *real* Chinese food—clams with black bean sauce, mu-shu pork, fra-grant crispy duck, *chiao-tzu*—went his own way, not entirely dis-owning but hardly ever mentioning his slightly furtive shadow, the lover of sham Chinese food.

For years in the early eighties, I worked in an office building that sat right at the corner of Boston's Chinatown, and I did a lot of happy culinary exploring there, in places like Henry's, Tai Tung, Moon Villa. Even so, one year when the assistant director of my department offered to treat me to a birthday lunch—anywhere and anything I wanted—I opted for spareribs and pork fried rice . . . and not from any of my Chinatown finds but from a takeout joint in the down-town shopping district. (Although the place itself was blatantly uncool, their sparerib portions blew away the competition's.)

There was an element here, no doubt, of that rarely discussed inclination to just eat bad food—which has more in common with taking a fistful of uppers, drinking moonshine whiskey, or smoking vile cheroots than it does with the pleasures of eating. But in this instance something else was also at work.

Restaurants in Chinatown that were frequented by actual Chinese diners had two menus with corresponding attitudes toward those who ordered from each. I had spent a lot of time getting recognized in such places as that unusual (and, in my own mind, highly estimable) *gwai lo* who wanted to eat the real thing. All it would have taken was three words—"pork fried rice"—to permanently erase everything I had so far managed to accomplish. In fact, by then I'd come to believe that fried rice, like chop suey, had no true roots in China at all, but was a phantasm created to please American eaters.★

The truth, however, turns out to be more complex. Ken Horn, in his affecting and delightful cookbook-as-autobiography, *Easy Family Recipes from a Chinese-American Childhood*, tells how the workers at his uncle's restaurant used to joke about the abandon with which non-Chinese customers added soy sauce to everything in sight. His explanation for this—that Americans "prefer foods on the salty side"—seems an odd accusation, coming from a culture that relishes so many salt-laden sauces, condiments, preserved vegetables, bean pastes . . . the list is endless. Overuse of soy sauce may be ignorant, but it isn't perverse.

I also think he is a bit misleading when he goes on to say that "never would soy sauce be . . . used in fried rice, especially when one wants the clean, mild taste of rice made subtly smoky as it is stir-fried in the wok."

Point of fact: American customers have never had the opportunity to become familiar with real fried rice, because the ersatz stuff is way too profitable. Take yesterday's leftover white rice, thoroughly dampen it with soy sauce, toss in bits of barbecued pork and various vegetables, leave it a vat on the steam table all day, and listen to that mental cash register ring every time another order goes out. The result, if not the method, isn't all that different from the so-called rice pilafs that many restaurants offer as an alternative to baked or fried potatoes. So, lets call the stuff "Chinese pork-flavored rice pilaf" and be done with it.★★ But hold onto that phrase "subtly smoky," because, as we shall now see, those two words encapsulate the heart of true fried rice.

★ Although many Chinese have said this about chop suey, they are wrong—or, rather, didn't come from the right part of China. Li Shu-Fan, in his autobiography, *Hong Kong Surgeon* (1964), remembers eating chop suey in a restaurant in Toishan [China] in 1894 and speculates that the dish was brought to America by the people of that region, who were among the earliest immigrants to the U.S.

★★ This shouldn't be confused with what might better be called "rice-tossed" dishes. In these, cooked rice is stirred into a mélange of wok-cooked ingredients and served directly after the rice is heated and has absorbed the small amount of cooking liquid. These are part of the repertoire of Chinese home cooking and are very good. But while they, too, can be called "fried rice," they aren't our subject here.

> Back in 1979 I was an exchange student at the Chinese University of Hong Kong. My college's cafeteria had a few regular items on the menu, one of which was a plate of fried rice topped with an over-easy fried egg or two, which I would break up and mix into the rice. The rice was very lightly fried with some scallions, a dried chile, and a bit of minced meat, probably pork.—R. W. Lucky, *personal note*

It was a prewar account of a long train journey in China that shook my mind free of Chinese restaurant fried rice—and it is, alas, all too symptomatic of my reading habits that I can't recall the book. I'm rather good at remembering bits and pieces from my reading but terrible at remembering *where* it was that I actually read them. So, although what follows is to a certain extent confirmed in Buwei Yang Chow's *How To Cook and Eat in Chinese* (1945), it is extrapolated from memory and inked in by imagination.

When you wanted something to eat on a long train trip in China in the 1930s, what you got, most likely, was fried rice. The ingredients—cooked rice, eggs, scallion, seasonings—were easy to store, and it required only a few moments to make. Cooking oil was heated to smoking in a large wok. The rice and bits of scallion were tossed in, resulting in a burst of sizzling, as the damp surface of the rice vaporized. The cook tossed this around for a moment until all the rice was lightly seared in this manner. Then he pushed this up the wok's sides and poured a beaten egg onto the freed-up surface. With a few rapid twists of his spatula, this mass was first scrambled and then broken into pieces, which were quickly mixed into the rice. Finally, he dribbled over some soy sauce, rice wine, and toasted sesame oil and, with one quick motion, scooped everything, smoking hot, into an eating bowl . . . and was ready to start on the next order.

What enchanted me—enchants me still—about all this is a near-magical economy—of fuel, of ingredients, of effort, of equipment, of space—that produces—out of nothing! in seconds!—something filling and truly delicious to eat. Once perceived, this image prevented me from ever looking at fried rice the same way again. Afterwards, whenever and wherever I came across that dish, I looked hopefully for some sign of this magic, even though I never found it.

There's a Chinese phrase for this sort of instantaneous, high-heat cooking, where even slivers of food retain their inner moisture and fresh taste beneath a crisply seared exterior—*wok hai* or, roughly, "wok fragrance."† I've never seen this discussed in Chinese cookbooks, perhaps because it is generally considered the province of restaurant cooking, requiring as it does a well-honed deftness and the ability to endure furnace-like working conditions.

However, with the advent of the home-kitchen restaurant stove and, more to the point, the much cheaper wok-friendly outdoor propane burner, now aspiring home cooks also can achieve *wok-hai* creations. I've cast more than one longing glance at the Eastman Outdoors "Big Kahuna" burner, which retails for around fifty dollars, has a rating of 65,000 BTUs (*ten times* the average burner on a gas stove), and can handle a 22-inch wok with éclat.

However, such a unit isn't necessary to make wok-fragrant fried rice. Because cooked rice is light and particulate, it doesn't cool down a hot wok the way heavier, wetter ingredients can. This means it can be sear-fried pretty quickly, even when made on an ordinary home range.

―――∞∞∞―――

Wok-Fragrant Fried Rice

Caveat. Be aware that this is one of those seemingly simple dishes where every word—including "and" and "but"—is the subject of fierce contention. Some cooks heat the wok before adding the oil. Some cook the eggs in the wok before adding the rice; others wait until the very end, then push the finished rice up the sides of the wok and scramble the eggs in the hollow in the center. Still others stir the beaten eggs directly into the rice and stir-fry until set. Seasonings are various and optional—both Barbara Tropp and Ken Hom make a point of using nothing but salt. This is how I make mine, at least right now, in the summer of 2004.

† It is also sometimes called *wok chi*, which means, again loosely, "wok energy" or "wok spirit"—*chi* being a hard word to pin down. Almost always the word "elusive" is appended to the phrase, since *wok chi* is considered to be something nearly mystical—hard to obtain and easily dissipated. Its presence is an indication that the chef is working at the very top of his form.

The Rice. The Qing Dynasty poet and essayist Yuan Mei (1716–1798) wrote of savoring the "juices" of rice, which is only possible, he said, if the rice is properly cooked in just the right amount of water. Ideal fried rice enhances this further by encapsulating the moistness within a crusty coating. (This is why the rice must be boiled in advance; during the resting time it absorbs the moisture clinging to its surface, which makes it less sticky and keeps it from sopping up all the oil.) A super-hot wok can achieve this with tender long-grain rice, but if you're preparing it on a kitchen range, you're much better off selecting a plump short-grain rice (but *not* the super-sticky "sweet" rice). My favorite for wok-fragrant fried rice is Chinese Royal rice, but I get good results using Lundberg organic short-grain "sushi" rice, which is commonly available.

The Wok. To do this properly, you'll need a standard cold-rolled-steel wok. These are the inexpensive, metal-colored woks sold at Asian grocery stores (my 14-inch one cost $9.95). One with a flat bottom is fine—and necessary on an electric burner. If you're buying such a wok new, know that it may have been coated with machine oil to keep it from rusting and needs to be thoroughly cleaned, then seasoned with peanut oil. To do this, heat a tablespoon or so until the oil is almost at the smoking point, swirl it around the inside of the wok, let it cool down, wipe it clean with a paper towel, then repeat that process two or three more times. Once seasoned, the wok should not be washed but wiped out, scouring away any stubborn bits with coarse salt.

The Thing Itself. Wok-fragrant fried rice is as hard to describe as it is good to eat, and the best way to tell when you've achieved it is by taste. Don't bring any expectations to the cooking. The rice won't be visibly crusty, and it shouldn't be burnt or scorched. But if you take a bite now and then as you cook it, you'll find you can't miss the transformation. It really is that noticeable . . . and that delicious.

AT LEAST FOUR HOURS IN ADVANCE

　1 cup uncooked short-grain rice
　1 ⅔ cups water

Put the rice in a large bowl and rinse it in two changes of cold water. Meanwhile, bring the measured water to a boil in a small (1½-quart) saucepan. Stir in the salt, then the strained rice. Reduce the heat to the lowest flame possible. Cover the rice, and cook for 15 minutes. Then uncover the rice until most of the steam has evaporated. Turn off the heat, place a folded napkin over the rice, replace the cover, and let the pot sit off the heat for another 15 minutes. Finally, turn the cooked rice into a large bowl, breaking up any clumps. Cover it with plastic wrap and, depending on how soon you plan to make the fried rice, either put the bowl in the refrigerator or leave it on the counter. Jim Lee, in *Jim Lee's Chinese Cooking*, says that even in summer you can leave it out for a day or two. I certainly do overnight.

COOK'S NOTES

The Chinese prepare boiled rice without adding salt. When making fried rice, this adds to the "sweetness" of the kernels and thus emphasizes the contrast with the savory seasonings. By the way, this is twice the amount called for in the recipe below. Save half for the next batch.

MAKING THE FRIED RICE

about 1 ½ cups day-old cooked rice, at room temperature

2 scallions, trimmed and cut into slivers

1 garlic clove, minced • 1 tablespoon minced fresh ginger

½ Chinese sausage, cut into shreds (see note) *or* 1 tablespoon
    coarsely chopped prosciutto or country ham

1 or 2 eggs, beaten • pinch of salt

Chinese rice wine or dry sherry • toasted sesame oil

2 tablespoons good fresh lard or peanut oil

light (ordinary) soy sauce (see note)

hot red pepper flakes or coarse-ground black pepper

Use a spatula or your fingers to break up any clumps in the rice. Put the scallion slivers, minced garlic, minced ginger, and shredded Chinese sausage or ham in a small bowl.

Season the beaten eggs with a pinch of salt, a drizzle of the toasted sesame oil, and the Chinese rice wine/sherry. Lightly wipe a 9-inch nonstick skillet with about a teaspoon of the lard/peanut oil and put it over medium heat. When it is hot, pour in the eggs. When they have set at the bottom, tilt the pan slightly and use a spatula to lift this layer, allowing the uncooked egg on top to run underneath. Keep doing this until the egg is just set. Remove from the heat and cut into small pieces with a spatula.

Put the remaining lard/peanut oil into the wok. Turn up the flame beneath it as high as it will go. Let it heat until the fat starts to haze—i.e., just before it starts to smoke. Swirl it gently to coat the lower sides of the wok, then turn in the scallions, garlic, ginger, and meat. Notice how, immediately, your kitchen smells like a Chinese restaurant. Stir a few times with a spatula and add the cooked rice. Toss with the spatula to thoroughly coat it with the oil and to mix it and the seasonings together.

Keep turning the mixture over. After a minute, dribble in some soy sauce and more Chinese rice wine/sherry with one hand, while still turning the mixture with the other. If you want to measure this, use no more than ½ tablespoon of each. When this has been absorbed, toss in a pinch of red pepper flakes or coarse-ground black pepper.

Continue tossing the rice over high heat until the surface of the grains becomes slightly translucent and toasted-looking. This will take from 4 to 5 minutes. At this point remove the wok from the heat. Stir in the chopped egg and, if you wish, a little more sesame oil. Serve at once.

COOK'S NOTES

The brand of **soy sauce** I use is Pearl River Bridge Superior Light, **sesame oil** is Kadoya Pure, **Chinese sausage** is Sun Ming Jan (the one with gin in it). I should note that cookbooks tell you to poach Chinese sausage before using it in a stir-fry. My own feeling is that by shredding it and cooking it over this kind of high heat, there's no danger, and I love the densely chewy result.

As to **rice wine,** food writers universally condemn Chinese rice cooking wines as grossly inferior, which they doubtlessly are. However, in the world of bad choices, I think I prefer it over the usual substitute, dry sherry, with which it really has nothing in common except some flavor notes. Rice wine is not, in the true sense, a wine at all, but grain-based brew like sake or barley wine. In any case, when Matt and I were pondering the three or four versions of cooking wine at our Asian market, a Chinese woman, pleased by our interest in her country's cooking, struck up a halting conversation with us. We asked her about rice wine, and without hesitation she plucked Yu Yee Brand Chinese Shao Shing Cooking Wine from the shelf. No lectures, no sad sighs. Instead, she proffered the selected bottle with a smile. "This one is the best, I think," she said.

VARIATIONS: WITH FRIED EGGS—use these instead of the usual scrambled eggs • WITH SHRIMP—substitute 6 to 8 shelled and coarsely chopped raw shrimp for the ham • WITH COOKED GREEN PEAS OR EDAMAME (tender green soybeans)—add ¼ cup with the scallions, garlic, and ginger.

SERVES 1

After I had made this one or two times, I realized that I could never eat pork fried rice in a Chinese restaurant again; I would only burst into tears. I haven't been eating many glossy red spareribs either, having discovered crispy-skin roast pork belly, which blows the ribs out of the water. But the *gwai-lo* factor still comes into play. When I go into a Chinese BBQ store to order some, the cashier confers with the cook, then comes back to ask, "You sure you not want *sparerib?*"

Despite my happiness with my own wok-fragrant fried rice, I still like to imagine that in every Chinatown in America, there's an unmarked four-table joint where Chinese can sneak off to order fried rice—the real stuff, served smoking from the kitchen. But I know I'll never find it. And if I do, they probably won't let me in.

Brisket Brought Us Together

by Karen Stabiner

from *Gourmet*

Time-honored holiday dishes knit a family together—even when they aren't technically a family, as is the case with Stabiner's cluster of guests at a now-annual Passover seder, originally born of a hankering for brisket.

I grew up after the crinoline and before the slip dress, on propriety's waning edge. When I was little, I wore a dotted-swiss and organdy party dress to Passover Seder at my aunt's house, and I dutifully scanned my patent-leather shoes for nicks while I waited for the service to end. But by the time I graduated to a kilt with matching sweater and kneesocks, questioning the status quo had become the politically correct attitude, and so my sister and my cousins and I perfected an array of disaffected expressions to let everyone at the table know that we had far more important things to do.

I fled to college determined never again to endure what I now considered the endless patriarchal ritual of the Seder. I majored in English lit and minored in rejecting the past: All I wanted to know was why it took Grandpa Abe more time to work through the Haggadah than God needed to part the Red Sea and Moses to march our ancestors across it.

Time passed. I wish I could say that the wisdom of years drew me back to belief and observance, but in fact it was brisket. Grandma Ethel's brisket, to be precise, cooked until the tender slices had to be hoisted on a serving spoon lest they break on the tines of a fork, and eaten with molten prunes and chunks of caramelized carrot and sweet potato, all of it coated with a mahogany syrup. Ethel was for the most part a perfunctory cook, known on the other 364 nights of the year for overcooked vegetables and a serviceable roast chicken. Brisket with tzimmes was her one voluptuous dish, and the only part of my childhood meal that I recalled with favor, aside from the bottomless crystal pitcher of Fanta orange soda.

My preoccupation with brisket unnerved my new and nonobservant husband, Larry, since seven pounds of beef required either guests or a commitment to two weeks of cold brisket sandwiches, and I preferred the former. I tried to reassure him that this would not be a *real* Seder, just a dinner party with a Seder menu. Okay, we might sing "Dayenu" and rattle off the four questions, but nothing major. I wrote to Grandma Ethel for the recipe, which came down to this: Cover the brisket with water, bring it to a boil, cover the pot, and simmer for two or three hours. Add prunes, carrots, sweet potatoes, salt, and pepper, and continue to simmer. Slice and serve.

It wasn't much to go by. The first two hours were torture, for there is nothing quite so ugly as a big piece of tan meat burbling around in a pot of thin brown liquid. I threw in way too many prunes and vegetables and fretted some more.

When Larry came home from buying wine, he slumped against the front door in disbelief.

"It smells great," he said.

So it did. Ethel had failed to mention faith and patience, two essential ingredients for both a successful brisket and a successful Seder. Somewhere in the middle of hour three, the liquid had begun to turn dark and glossy, and by dinnertime we had a platter of the kind of meat that made our guests get sloppy and lick their fingers.

The following year, one of the couples called to ask if we were doing Passover dinner again—and so this spring we celebrate our 20th Seder, bound to a growing number of friends who want to spend an evening together thinking about how fortunate we are. We began with a handful of childless adults; now we are two dozen adults and ten children, the eldest of whom leaves for college next fall. Many of the guests aren't Jewish, and we work from a radically abridged prayer book. It is an invented, ecumenical ritual.

The menu is etched in stone, like commandments on a tablet, because the polite if reflexive "Can I bring something?" takes on a profound new meaning when three dozen people are coming to dinner in the middle of the workweek. About eight years ago, I handed out the most general of assignments—please bring a vegetable, a salad, something for dessert—to the known cooks in the crowd. After a few missteps (homemade gefilte fish is not worth the trouble), we settled on our immutable menu:

Chopped liver for the adults and matzo-ball soup for the kids. Lots of Italian haroseth, made with chopped apples, dates, raisins, almonds, matzo meal, and, when I remember, a hard-boiled egg. Lots of horseradish. Grandma Ethel's brisket. Roast chicken for the few people who won't be seduced by even great red meat. Mountains of asparagus, green beans with a raspberry vinaigrette, and roast carrots. Two salads—one spicy with arugula, the other a cooler dish that's heavy on the cucumbers. A table full of desserts, including fresh and dried fruit, chocolate and vanilla macaroons, and a jam-topped spongecake that nobody eats anymore but was a favorite of a guest who moved away. It's a totem, that cake: Someone inevitably asks about the departed family when they see it, and we all stand around and reminisce.

These are not the trendiest preparations on the planet; if they were clothes they would be broken-in jeans and a sweater. But the dishes people bring to the Seder are infused with nostalgia, felt memory, and a passion for family—real or, like our Seder crowd, concocted—that heighten our senses and make a big noisy dinner into a feast.

Nineteen years ago, Lori learned to make those green beans from the nice lady who lived across the hall from Roy, the man Lori was about to marry. A lifetime ago, Laura watched her mother make chopped liver from scratch and listened to her apologize for one of the ingredients ("Miracle Whip!"); now she makes a vat of it and continues to apologize for the source of its incredibly creamy texture. Lucy is a renowned home cook, but on this night she channels her sophistication into a perfect platter of springtime asparagus with lemon, because it makes the meal harmonious. And I answer the inevitable queries about the roast carrots, descendants of the carrots prepared by both of my grandmas, Ethel and Mattie

Ann: "Just olive oil and salt on a jelly-roll pan at four hundred degrees. They get like that all by themselves."

It is the offering, not the intricacy, that counts. The first year that Carolyn joined us, she brought strawberries in a beautiful bowl that she forgot to take home. I returned it a month later, but in subsequent years she forgot to ask and I forgot to remember. Now she brings the fruit in a grocery bag, and the bowl sits out on our kitchen counter all year, waiting. It is our guarantee, our promise of another year, its presence more potent than the pledge we recite ("Next year in Israel") when what we really pray for is next year at the table again, together.

In the kingdom of the heart, where we dine with our friends once each spring, even a strawberry in a particular bowl is a magical dish. The youngest among us reminds us that this night is different from all other nights, and we nod our assent, sure that our collective, cobbled dinner is the best meal on earth. We might as well be right.

Grandma Ethel's Brisket with Tzimmes

ACTIVE TIME: 50 MIN

START TO FINISH: 22½ HR
(INCLUDES MAKING STOCK AND CHILLING BRISKET)

Everything is approximate with brisket and tzimmes, since some people can't stand prunes and others want nothing but. The amounts listed below are estimates; feel free to change them. Though Karen Stabiner calls for first-cut brisket, which is relatively lean, we prefer the more evenly marbled second cut for moister, more succulent meat.

1 (6- to 7-lb) first-cut brisket
1 ¾ teaspoons salt
1 teaspoon black pepper
3 tablespoons olive oil
4 cups brown chicken stock or reconstituted brown chicken demi-glace
¾ cup Sherry vinegar
2 lb carrots, peeled and cut crosswise into 2-inch-long pieces

4 medium sweet potatoes, peeled and cut into 2-inch pieces
2¾ cups dried pitted prunes

•Put oven rack in middle position and preheat oven to 350°F.

•Pat brisket dry and rub all over with 1 teaspoon salt and 1\2 teaspoon pepper. Heat oil in a 17- by 11-inch heavy roasting pan (3 inches deep) over moderately high heat, straddled across 2 burners, until hot but not smoking, then brown brisket, starting with fat side down, on both sides, about 5 minutes per side. Remove from heat, then add stock and vinegar to pan. Cover pan tightly with heavy-duty foil and braise brisket in oven 2 hours. Add carrots and potatoes to pan and braise, covered, 1 hour. Add prunes and braise, covered, until meat is fork-tender, about 30 minutes more. Cool meat, uncovered, to room temperature, about 1 hour, then chill, covered, at least 12 hours.

•Put oven rack in middle position and preheat oven to 350°F.

•Transfer brisket to a cutting board and slice across the grain about ¼-inch thick. Discard as much fat as possible from surface of vegetables and sauce, then return sliced meat to pan and reheat, covered with foil, until heated through, about 40 minutes. Sprinkle with remaining ¾ teaspoon salt and remaining ½ teaspoon pepper, then arrange meat with tzimmes and sauce on a large platter.

COOKS' NOTE
Brisket can be chilled up to 3 days.

SERVES 8 TO 10

Brown Chicken Stock

ACTIVE TIME: 15 MIN START TO FINISH: 6 HR

1 (3 ½- to 4-lb) chicken, cut into 8 pieces
1 onion, quartered and then quarters halved crosswise

2 carrots, peeled and cut into 1-inch pieces
1 celery stalk, cut into 1-inch pieces
2 teaspoons vegetable or olive oil
13 cups cold water
2 teaspoons salt

•Put oven rack in middle position and preheat oven to 425°F.

•Pat chicken dry and put in a large flameproof roasting pan (not glass) along with onion, carrots, and celery. Drizzle chicken and vegetables with oil and toss to coat, then arrange chicken pieces skin sides down. Roast, stirring once halfway through, until chicken and vegetables are golden brown, 1 to 1 1/4 hours.

•Straddle roasting pan (with chicken and vegetables still in it) across 2 burners, then add 1 cup water and deglaze pan by boiling over high heat, stirring and scraping up any browned bits, 1 minute.

•Transfer chicken and vegetables with pan sauce to a 6- to 8-quart stockpot and add salt and remaining 12 cups water, then bring to a boil over high heat. Reduce heat and simmer, uncovered, skimming foam from surface, 3 hours.

•Pour stock through a large sieve lined with cheese-cloth or a triple layer of paper towels, discarding solids. If not using stock right away, cool to room temperature, uncovered, and then chill, covered.

COOKS' NOTE
Stock can be chilled in airtight containers 1 week or frozen 3 months.

MAKES ABOUT 8 CUPS

One-Room Wonder

by Evan Rail

from the *Prague Post*

Rail's simple account in this English-language Prague paper of a quirky ad hoc sort of restaurant says worlds about what people are looking for when they dine out, and what satisfies them most.

You might have trouble finding the new restaurant U Jednoho pokoje (At the One Room), a.k.a. Chez Julien. There's no sign out front marking its location or operating hours. Nor, for that matter, is there an advertisement in any newspaper or magazine or on any Web site. You can't find it in any guidebook or restaurant listings. U Jednoho pokoje is an underground restaurant, and strictly speaking, it's illegal. You'll find out about U Jednoho pokoje only if someone tells you about it.

When you do find out about U Jednoho pokoje, you dial the number or send a text message to make a reservation—drop-ins are not allowed. If you're accepted, you'll be given the address and the name to look for on the buzzer.

When you get there, there's a good chance you'll be let in by Julien himself, a short young Frenchman in a clean white chef's coat. He'll lead you upstairs two flights to the restaurant, hidden on a busy street inside a typical Vinohrady apartment building. In fact, U Jednoho pokoje is an apartment, a high-ceilinged one-bedroom located not too far from the neighborhood's main square. Julien might apologize for the mess, as the only entrance to the dining room is through the tiny kitchen where the meals are prepared. (It is called

At the One Room for a reason, after all.) And then you're seated—by Julien himself, naturally.

Choosing what you're going to eat is easy: Julien offers just one starter, two or three main courses—one vegetarian and chicken, beef or fish—and one dessert. The wine list is just about as limited. Except on especially busy nights when he enlists outside help, Julien himself will take your order. Once he cooks it, Julien will be your server.

The dining room is a dark, atmospheric square, set off from the kitchen by two cockeyed doors and dimly lit with a slew of candles. In one corner, a small boombox plays Nick Cave and other moody tunes. On the walls are artworks donated by friends of Julien, most of which are for sale. The furniture is a mismatched lot of nicely refurbished Czech antiques—on one visit, just two tables and a couch, though more can be brought out as needed. Counting the couch, it looks like the capacity is maybe 10 people, though Julien claims he's served as many as 15.

On the menu one recent night: a simple quiche Lorraine. A lemony millefeuille of chicken and peppery roast vegetables, and a cod fillet with ratatouille. For dessert, a fragrant peach tart.

How is it? To be honest, U Jednoho pokoje is not about the food. At Julien's place, the overall experience is far greater than what's on the plate. The cooking is very good, even excellent, but the effect of being served a dish by the hopeful young man who prepared it is quite powerful, especially in such intimate surroundings. It feels as though you have a private chef, only more personal. When you eat at Julien's place, all of a sudden you find yourself rooting for Julien. You want things to come out right. You want him to succeed. And what's more, you love coming here because it means you know something that most people don't: that this place even exists.

People go to restaurants to satisfy all kinds of hunger. Simple physical hunger can be satisfied with a sandwich or a bowl of noodles, and it doesn't matter where you pick that up. But the deep hunger of wanting to see something unusual is far harder to satisfy. That's what you're offered at U Jednoho pokoje: not mere food, but a kind of spiritual sustenance. A meal for the emotions. You are given the rare opportunity to see a restaurant in its purest form, a distillation of the oft-complicated dining experience down to its bare minimum. And you are let in on a hidden secret that you know only a few people know about. To say the end result is charming would be an understatement. It is magical.

A word of warning: Don't write or call asking for Julien's phone number. Even if I could give it out, I wouldn't. Ask around and maybe you'll find someone who knows someone, and maybe you'll get in.

And maybe not—and it might just be better that way. Not being able to find U Jednoho pokoje would give you cause to think about why you go out to eat at all, why you're never really satisfied with a simple sandwich or a bowl of noodles. It would give you a reason to think about what it means to be hungry beyond physical hunger—what it means to be hungry for something unknown, for something pure and beautiful.

Many Happy Returns

by Monique Truong

from *Food & Wine*

> If we are what we eat, we also may be
> defined by where we eat. Fiction writer
> Truong (*The Book of Salt*) traces thirteen
> years of her New York City life through her
> relationship to a local restaurant.

In New York City trying out new restaurants is like riding in a fleet of unreliable taxis—transporting one night, an ordeal of wrong turns the next. Most places just thankfully disappear into the darkness, never to be seen again: About 70 percent of restaurants close or change hands within five years of opening. When checking out a new spot, I've found it best to keep my expectations low. I've broken this rule only once: From my first visit, I've been devoted to Bar Pitti, a Tuscan place in Greenwich Village.

My first meal there, crostini with chicken liver pâté, was really more of a snack, albeit the kind usually consumed with a glass of Chianti Classico by those lucky enough to be whiling away an afternoon in Florence. The bread, with a chewy, almost malty crust, was grilled and topped with a generous spread of house-made pâté, which was seasoned in a way that didn't mask the mineral flavor of the liver. Before I even took a bite, I was impressed. On my plate were no pedestrian parsley sprigs or crisscrossing lines of sauce from a squeeze bottle. I had ordered crostini with chicken liver pâté, which is exactly what I was served.

That was in 1992. I had moved to New York City the previous fall to live with a boyfriend whom I had been dating for about a year (my prudent rule about restaurants never applied to men). It was late summer, but I remember little or no humidity that day. The weather was what I would call forthright—lots of sunshine and not a cloud in sight. The boyfriend and I were making the rounds of his favorite Village haunts, mostly comic book shops and record stores. We found ourselves hungry in the limbo hours between lunch and dinner, when a good meal is especially hard to find. That's when I saw Bar Pitti—it was new, though I didn't know it at the time—with its glass doors opening onto a block of Sixth Avenue where the sidewalk is unusually wide and there's plenty of space for *all'aperto* dining. Eating outdoors seemed particularly appropriate given the weather and the context of romance. I was 24, and as I sat there looking at this young man, backlit by the sun, I was hoping I'd made the right decision.

When we next returned to Bar Pitti, the weather had turned cool, and we sat inside for dinner. Bar Pitti's two small rooms, painted a lemon yellow, had as their only decorations a band of mirrors and several black-and-white photographs. The largest one was of Florence as glimpsed from one of the surrounding hills, with the Duomo rising like a hot-air balloon from among the city's rooftops. My boyfriend and I looked at that image and imagined traveling there together. We were at Bar Pitti that night to celebrate the start of my first year in law school and his first fall free from classes. We tore pieces of bread and dipped them into a plate of olive oil, a way to begin a meal that now seems almost too banal to mention, but it was at Bar Pitti that we were first introduced to this worthwhile ritual.

That night my boyfriend and I ignored Bar Pitti's list of specials written in Italian on a chalkboard, which was brought to the table and recited at varying speeds and levels of descriptiveness by a member of the waitstaff. The reason was purely financial: The specials cost more than the regular dishes. We were content, though, with our taglierini *all'Empolese,* a fragrant tangle of fresh pasta, artichoke hearts, leeks and just enough tomato to give it a bit of color and a pleasing tang.

During the next three years, Bar Pitti, which took cash only, became my carefully-saved-for reward, my gold star for surviving moot court, a civil procedure exam or an especially demoralizing week of the Socratic method. My boyfriend, who had begun architecture school in 1993, saved his money for new CDs and concert tickets. A pattern of consumption therapy was emerging: I took us out for dinner, and he kept us rocking. Though we were living together, we still kept our money separate. We began, nonetheless, to use the word *partner* when introducing each other to friends and acquaintances. We thought about using the word *lover*, but that just made us laugh. We knew, though, that we should say it because we meant it. We were changing in ways that frightened us, and a meal at Bar Pitti was the reassuring constant that reminded us of our first summer together in the city, of sunlight and no fussy clouds.

Our gradual exploration of Bar Pitti's chalkboard menu of specials began one night when *fegato di salvia,* calves' liver with sage, made an appearance. Bar Pitti's version was a generous but not-too-thick portion of liver pan-fried in olive oil with cloves of garlic and fresh sage leaves. I would eat almost anything prepared with those ingredients, but calves' liver cooked this way was economy in the best sense of the word.

What began as a splurge became a habit, especially once I became a practicing attorney. By 1996, my first full year of practice and our fifth year of living together, we were eating at Bar Pitti so often— an average of three times a week—that one night the waiter came over to our table with the chalkboard, placed it on a nearby chair, said "You two know what these are" and immediately left to attend to another table. His statement was undeniably true. Between the two us, we knew the items on the chalkboard by heart. That wasn't the remarkable thing. What really made me blink was that the waiter had noted our steady patronage and acknowledged it in a manner that was so essentially New York City. I'm not sure what the term for it would be. Convivial indifference? Friendly disregard? In any case, the significant thing was that we had been acknowledged as regulars. Sure it took half a decade, but I figured Bar Pitti, like me, also had the right to take a don't-expect-I'll-see-you-again attitude.

In all honesty, my partner and I truly became regulars at Bar Pitti when we started to have our fights there (me yelling, him silent), which also began, not surprisingly, in 1996. Being an attorney meant I was not only full of cash but also of misery. The cash I still kept in a separate account; the misery I shared completely. Bar Pitti had become our de facto home. It was cleaner than our apartment. It was always filled with the good smells of cooking, an act that, along with writing, I no longer had the time or the heart to do. In addition to the bread and the olive oil, we began our meals with a fight. Then we would glare at the photograph of the Duomo. Then the food, never disappointing, would arrive, and by dessert we were making up with a kiss—a cycle of fighting, eating and making up that took place in full view of the waitstaff, our fellow diners and Sixth Avenue.

In 1998 we came to Bar Pitti late one night with a group of friends—mostly writers, as I had begun joyfully to leave the legal profession behind, a change that also had a positive effect on our relationship. It was a mild fall night, and we sat at one of the outside tables. We were the largest party there and definitely the loudest. A waiter came by with the chalkboard and gave us a look that asked: Is this a table of slightly tipsy, good tippers or a nightmare of indecisiveness and wants? He recognized my face and delivered the now standard "You know what these are." Yes I did, and I proved it by reciting a near-perfect description of the specials that night. I remember a round of light applause. During the course of our meal, the temperature outside dropped, but we didn't want to leave. As a group, we were broke, spending anyway, and intent on enjoying ourselves. I was about to take a 180-degree turn in my life, and I knew, looking at the faces around me, including that of my fiancé, that I was making the right choices.

Those 16 or so dishes on Bar Pitti's chalkboard were always enticing and always a satisfying way to learn Italian. When we finally saw the Duomo in 1999, on our honeymoon, my husband and I knew that pappardelle *al coniglio* was wide strips of pasta with a sauce of rabbit, cooked slowly until the meat fell off the bones. We knew that *puntarelle* was a wild chicory—more white stalks than greens—served with an anchovy-and-garlic vinaigrette. We knew that *polpettine di vitello* was veal meatballs, tender and light.

Bar Pitti is once again a restaurant we save up for. Being cash poor comes with the writing life, and Bar Pitti, after all these years, still takes only cash. The food there has remained terrifically unchanged. What hasn't stayed the same is the reason we go there. These days, more often than not, it's to celebrate some small wonderful thing that life has offered up, like a favorite restaurant that's sticking around for the long haul, more of a friend with a car than a taxi for hire.

Expatriate Games

by John Burnham Schwartz

from the *New York Times Magazine*

In Schwartz's funny yet elegiac essay about a youthful sojourn in Paris, delicious meals shared with a gang of gathered friends become the medium through which to recall a special time in one's life.

When I moved to Paris in 1989 to work on a second novel, I hadn't seen Alex in 20 years. We played together as kids, then fell out of touch. By the time we became reacquainted in Paris, I barely recognized him. He had thick, ink black, curly hair, ringlets almost, that seemed to shine with some secretly applied ointment, and he wore a hat, a cool, slightly insouciant number, part Belmondo and part Boyer, that went nicely with his patterned waistcoats and the long key chain that looped out of his pants pocket and the hand-rolled cigarettes he smoked day and night.

He had come to Paris to study at the Ritz cooking school, then landed an apprenticeship at Taillevent, one of the world's most celebrated restaurants. Yet in no time, fed up with chopping onions 10 hours a day, he quit Taillevent. Quit Taillevent! But that was to be expected. It was the feeding of friends he believed in; in his mind, chopping onions for strangers was an entirely different, somehow smaller-hearted enterprise. He cooked the way he ate, and he ate like Orson Welles or Brando in their later, Roman emperor days—as if he were going to swallow the world, but all in his own good time.

I introduced him to my circle of 20-something American friends: Deb, a photojournalist; Josh, a television executive; Olivia, a philosopher; Phyllida, an editor; Lucy, a playwright. Most of us had gone to college together but had made our way to Paris for our own reasons, which, as with young people everywhere, had to do mostly with longing and possibility, a kind of permanent hunger. We wanted to step outside our normal lives and rebuild a community from scratch. We did this by spending a lot of time together, and by eating and drinking as much as possible. This, of course, was the sort of mission Alex was born to join. No one in my gang had ever met anyone quite like him. He said that he cooked, and we thought, Oh, he cooks, but we didn't know what that meant until the night he invited all of us for dinner.

He was renting a drafty artist's studio off the Rue du Temple. The kitchen was primitive, just two electric burners and an old toaster oven. None of the dining chairs matched. The silverware had been stolen from various cafes, and the glasses were shirt-cleaned.

That night Alex cracked open fat cloves of garlic with the side of a chef's knife and rubbed them, with the best virgin olive oil, over thick slices of peasant bread, then toasted them lightly in the toaster oven. Next he served us a slow-cooked Bolognese sauce of such earthy sweetness and meaty depth that it seemed at once ancient and new. To this day, the memory of its taste is wedded in my mind to the cymbal-like crash of Alex banging pots in the kitchen.

From that night onward, Sunday dinner at Alex's became our weekly ritual. Between feasts—and sometimes during—life-altering decisions were made, hearts broken, songs badly sung. People came and went. For a few uncomfortable months, Josh the TV executive and I shared a girlfriend. Lucy the playwright arrived in the City of Light with an arrogant, pasty-faced, vegan boyfriend none of us liked, but then one Sunday she showed up at dinner on the back of a Frenchman's motorcycle, suffused with an unmistakable glow. Overnight she had become, as it were, a carnivore, and we responded by toasting her liberation and welcoming Yves into the gang. Ditto for Paul, the huge-hearted Russian who stole Deb the photojournalist's heart one night at a party; the following Sunday he became one of us, and is still.

And so it went. Sunday morning would roll around, and each of us would receive a mumbled phone call from a very hungover Alex: You, bring bread! You, haricots verts! You, wine! You, fresh sage! The meal's centerpiece—the lamb shoulder, the Cornish hens, the poulet de Bresse—our chef would trust to no one but himself. Dressed like a dandified gangster, he would roam the narrow streets around the Place du Temple and in his highly eccentric French discuss the freshly killed birds with the butcher.

That evening we would arrive on his doorstep with our packages and find him already on his third glass of Bordeaux and his umpteenth cigarette. An apron, folded in half and tied at his waist, a dish towel draped over his left shoulder: the calm before the storm.

He always started slowly. But as the group arrived and the room grew lively with voices in French and English, Alex's spirits seemed to rise commensurately with the delicious odors. By 10 o'clock we would be salivating like animals and he would just be warming up. He was one of those insane people, a renegade magician, insufferable to live with but impossible to look away from, who could spin culinary gold out of the dross of a few dried herbs and a handful of grain. It was like being in an artist's studio as he painted—face to face with the creative moment, the choices made on the spot, the diving forward. He finished Cornish game hens in the toaster oven, using a sable-hair paintbrush to glaze them. On Thanksgiving, he peeled back the skin of a turkey, stuffed it with truffles, then sewed it back together again. He sautéed brussels sprouts with cubes of pancetta and stood poached pears upright in a frangipani tart dusted with crushed almonds.

Thinking about him now, I'm struck by what seems an obvious thought: that it was not the back-breaking toil that Alex hated in restaurant jobs, or even the submission to the necessities of commerce, but the insulation of the closed kitchen door. Who wants to be a madman locked away in a closet? For our part, we were as much alarmed by him as we were enthralled by the tastes he introduced us to.

Then, all too soon, it was over. Deb and Paul left for Moscow, Josh for Madrid, Lucy and Phyllida and I for America. Alex wrapped up his chef's knives and went home, too. I had dinner with him in New York a couple of times, but somehow, after Paris, any other city was an uneasy fit. I remember him coming to my apartment one night and emptying my vodka supply and dropping burning cigarette ash on my rug and inadvertently breaking a chair—but also, of course, roasting the best capon I have ever eaten in my life.

Sixteen years later, our old Paris group remains in close touch. Everyone except Alex, that is. The rumor is that he's on the West Coast making priceless objets d'art out of bronze. We talk about him the way you talk about a bungee jump once made from a very high, very beautiful cliff: How vivid the colors were! How alive we felt! How pathetically safe not to have him now in our mature, ordered lives! Yet one day without warning—I simply feel it—he will come back to us, his knives sharp as ever, his pots and pans filled with music.

Appendix:
A Taste of Blogworld

O ne of the pleasures of owning a computer with a high-speed connection is that you can waste many an afternoon on the Internet, scrolling through multifarious foodie web logs when you should be working instead. Formats differ from let-it-all-hang-out dining reviews to meticulously annotated recipe files to rambling food diaries (some by eaters, some by home cooks, some by professional chefs, all of them apparently with a lot of spare time to devote to these labors of love). The quality is equally all over the map—sophisticated graphics and layout, alas, are no guarantee that the writing will be any good. Below are excerpts, all plucked from the same randomly chosen mid-April week, from six blogs that I've found consistently fun to read. For the names of others, visit these sites: www.sautewednesday.com, www.chocolateandzucchini.com, or www.thefoodsection.com.

From *www.grubreport.com*
April 11, 2005

Back when I wanted to recreate Osama Bin Lasagne in my kitchen in Boston, Dr. Mathra called around to all the ethnic stores within our reach and asked for Greek Lebné yogurt. It was not to be had. Out here? It flows down the streets like white wine. It grows heavy on trees like white fruit. It falls from the sky like white manna from heaven. Okay, not really, but I'm getting a lot of "Girl, you crazy" looks when I go into raptures over the fact that I finally, FINALLY found Lebné yogurt and that I found it down at our little corner organic store! I guess the crazy looks stem from the fact that this is California and you can find everything good and foodie in California.

Fine, but I'm still going to have my raptures. Lebné yogurt is full-fat Greek yogurt so thick and rich you don't need to drain off excess water before making tzatziki. It's the consistency of mascarpone and I want to swim in it. Following Alton [Brown]'s instructions (I hardly make a move in the kitchen without first checking to see how he does things), I seeded, diced, and salted one large cucumber before wrapping the crisp chunks in a thin towel and leaving it over a bowl to drain a bit. Thirty minutes later, after Dr. Mathra strangled the excess water out of the cucumber, I dumped it in a bowl with 16 oz. of the Lebné yogurt, 4 minced garlic cloves, 6 chiffonaded mint leaves, a pinch of salt, 1 tablespoon Good Olive Oil (Stonehouse, of thee I sing!), and 2 teaspoons red wine vinegar.

Since pretty much any cold mixture of things can stand to be left alone for a few hours before you can hope to judge their true, melded flavors, I covered the bowl and stuck it in the fridge. Oh, god, was it perfect a few hours later or what?

From *deependdining.com*
April 13, 2005

Level One: It took nearly two hours of your life just to nab a table at the Empress Pavilion, are you just having har gow (shrimp dumpling) and siu my (pork dumpling)? Har gow and siu my, arguably the two most popular dim sum dishes, are considered Level One challengers in this "Game of Death" scenario, as are most dumplings and rice rolls. These dishes, however, represent but a few specks of this pointillist dim sum painting. They're significant but there's so much more. It's also like eating "my first dim sum" all the time. What are you a baby?

Level Two: Even at this early level, many diners drop out. Here we have daring fare such as squid, deep fried tentacles or fried shrimp (heads still intact). Snappy, crispy, crunchy. Easy to eat and delicious. Next . . .

Level Three: This is when we really begin to weed out the casually bold from the hard core. Pig's blood cubes, thousand-year-old egg in pork congee, soy sauce duck feet and, of course, chicken feet. Most would argue that the infamous chicken feet should be in the final level of this dim sum challenge hierarchy. Not even close. Chicken feet are fairly popular dishes and common. Most patrons are somewhat familiar with them as well. However, there are some things that are supremely outlandish and we would rather not come face to face with, let alone put in our mouths. Level Four is where you'll find these bad boys.

Level Four, the final floor: Welcome to Dante's dim sum hell. Do you dare partake in one of these nightmarish delights? C'mon, they don't look that grotesque, do they? But before you get your mad dog on, you have to locate these tantalizingly twisted tidbits and that's not easy to do. As you might imagine, these Dali-esque plates are not in high demand even among dim sum loyalists. This makes it more difficult to flag down a dim sum dame who's carting these goodies around. When I say "goodies" I mean selections like marinated beef tripe (omasum tripe) and, in phonetic Mandarin, "nyoh doo" also known as "bowl of guts" (rumen tripe, honeycomb tripe, pancreas and sometimes intestines). You've come a long way. It's on the table. Don't stop here. Have a taste.

From *foodmusings.typepad.com*
April 16, 2005

Oh, happy day! Quite by accident, I have discovered a wonderful new cheese! . . . I was experimenting with goat butter one day and, without my glasses on, mistakenly nabbed this cheese instead from the market shelves. It sat directly next to the goat butter (which Fate later decreed I would eat and find, and I quote, "icky, nasty, like lard in flavor and texture." Don't go running out to try it all at once, folks.)

But this gjetost was a revelation. Though it sat in the fridge for a month or more, in a fit of curiosity (no, no, not desperation, I had a cheddar ripe and ready for the eating if I'd wanted it) I opened the package. Curious color, I thought, and sniffed it like all good foodies do. It smelled like a caramel, a childhood favorite, so I cut off a chunk and ate it. Mildly tangy, like a chevre but infinitely less so, with just enough sweetness to temper, even dominate, the traditional goat flavor.

I went running around the apartment in a fit of glee. And then, in a show of great discipline that is my hallmark, sat down to tell you about it.

In its native land, it is served on brown bread, but if you don't have any (or like me, don't like it) try it with crisp sesame crackers, thick wheat biscuits or on a fruit tray with pears and melon. Or eat it alone. And pretend to others that it's a revolting, acquired taste so you don't even have to share.

from www.movable-feast.com
April 19, 2005

KNIGHT AND SHINING ARMOUR

Just when I thought my trusty little Wusthof Culinar paring knife would be fucked up for a little while - at least until the weekend when I could take it to my sharpening stone - a strange man darkened my doorway. I was working away on my mise en place and I noticed my co-workers here and there approaching this stranger. One by one they handed over to him their knives - their very own knives! He seemed to consult them - console them - and take each knife in like some orphan charge. He wrapped each one in a bit of cloth - like a foundling - and tucked it into a big metal toolbox. And then I realised that the Knife Man was here. Every once in a while in the top kitchens in France, a skilled Knife Man comes around. You hand over your knives - your very own knives! And he heals them. He takes them away for a day or two - does what he needs to do to them - and then returns them to you. . . . I picked up my trusty little paring knife and approached the Knife Man. I showed him the tip. "Can you fix this?" He looked at the knife, then me, then nodded with an understanding and assuring smile. And then it was done. I'd done it. I'd turned over my knife - my very own knife! I have to admit that I worried about it a little all day. The knives were due back right before dinner service. As soon as the Knife Man came back, I swooped over to the pass and claimed mine - where he'd laid them all out - the bigger ones with a bit of cork protecting the tips. I can tell that it's different. It's a shade shorter - really just a hair - but slices effortlessly. I think my knife is still forgiving me - or maybe I haven't forgiven myself yet for letting it out of my sight. She's almost as good as new. But maybe better. Having been damaged - and survived. And now honed to a new gleaming edge.

From *www.domesticgoddess.ca/*
April 19, 2005

The gorgeous stalks of asparagus jumped out at me at the market. Standing there among their friends, waiting to go home with some-one who'd love them, someone who'd take care of them and not simply allow them to rot in a darkened vegetable drawer. They whispered sweet nothings in my ear and promised me thoughts and tastes of spring when I carefully picked them up and placed them in my shopping basket. I didn't know how I was going to cook them at the time but I knew they would be delicious - I mean how could they not be? . . . I got home and opened up all the windows and the balcony door and cooked in my breeze-laden kitchen while S. enjoyed the smells emanating from the kitchen. We ate, enjoying the tastes and textures and the warm almost summer-like evening . . . it was absolute perfection.

The garlic risotto with roasted asparagus was delicious. My aller-gies even calmed down enough so that I could actually see the gor-geous green colour of the asparagus highlighted against the pale cream of the risotto. It looked beautiful but tasted even better. The creaminess of the risotto beautifully complementing the bite of the roasted asparagus. How much better does it get? I guess we'll just have to wait and see. There are many more warm spring evenings in front of us.

From *www.idlewords.com*
April 20, 2005

THE UNBEARABLE THINNESS OF CRUST

The worst pizza in the world is sold at a certain snack counter in Edinburgh. Walk down Princes Street until it turns left onto Leith Walk, and then continue for about a block until you see on your right a diner with pink neon lights in the window. Then turn around and run as fast as your legs can take you, because even the faintest whiff of that shriveled red square of ketchup and shortbread in the display case with its clinging particles of haggis will haunt you all the days of your life.

Back in the heady post-Soviet days, it used to be possible to get really bad pizza in Warsaw. Vendors in the little plastic booths on every corner would sell you a hot dog bun spread with tomato paste and pressed ham for about ten American cents. Then the Vietnamese showed up, with their cut-rate lunch specials and even smaller booths, and the Warsaw pizza market was no more. Finally the Health Department got funding, shut everyone down, deported the Vietnamese, and now the nation's capital is a desolation of McDonald's and hipster cafés.

You can find really bad pizza in New York, but it takes a little work. One promising place is at Penn Station near the A, C, E subway line (not to be confused with the good pizza near the Amtrak lounge). The slices there are thick and sweaty, and the mushroom slice in particular has a vague sliminess to it, as if the mushrooms had been eaten and rejected earlier by an animal whose diet consisted exclusively of garlic.

Ray's Pizza is an entire franchise specializing in bad slices, but the Ray's near Lexington Avenue and 62nd deserves special mention for its combination of bad service and egregious pricing. The flavor is not quite so off (think of a dish sponge boiled in olive oil) but it is the only New York slice I have ever come across that clocks in at over four dollars. As always, for that special extra level of "screw you" lunchtime service, you really have to come to Midtown.

The most overrated pizza in the world requires a little bit of a road trip, to New Haven, Connecticut. Sally's Apizza (not a typo, just an affectation) is only two blocks down from Pepe's, a perfectly wonderful pizza place. . . . Pepe's pizza is stellar while Sally's tastes like something that was accidentally dropped into a mop bucket on its way out of the Pepe's dumpster. The plain tomato-and-cheese pie at Sally's is edible (no more), but their white clam pizza (which at Pepe's is a little hymn to Poseidon, with garlic and olive oil and big salty pieces of clam) is an absolute abomination. It tastes like a matzoh drizzled with Mazola and pencil erasers.

Recipe Index

Acknowledgments

Grateful acknowledgment is made to all those who gave permission for written material to appear in this book. Every effort has been made to trace and contact copyright holders. If an error or omission is brought to our notice, we will be pleased to remedy the situation in future editions of this book. For further information, please contact the publisher.

"Apple Crumble" by Gina Mallet. From *Last Chance to Eat: The Fate of Taste in a Fast Food World.* Copyright © 2004 by Gina Mallet. Used by permission of W.W. Norton & Company, Inc. and McClelland & Stewart Ltd, *The Canadian Publishers.* ✤ "Food without Fear" by Dan Barber. Copyright © 2004 by the *New York Times* Co. Used by permission of the *New York Times* Co. Originally appeared in the *New York Times* November 23, 2004. ✤ "Two Americas, Two Restaurants, One Town" by Rebecca Skloot. Copyright © 2004 by Rebecca Skloot. Used by permission of the author. Originally appeared in the *New York Times Magazine,* October 17, 2004. ✤ "I Married A Restaurant Critic" by Nancy Grimes. Copyright © 2004 by Nancy Grimes. Used by permission of the author. Originally appeared in *Bon Appétit,* September, 2004. ✤ "Big Cheese" by Cynthia Zarin. Copyright © 2004 by Cynthia Zarin. Used by permission of the author. Originally appeared in *The New Yorker,* August 23, 2004. ✤ "Diatribes for Dinner" by Jay Rayner. Copyright © 2005 by Jay Rayner. Used by permission of *Saveur.* Originally appeared in *Saveur,* March, 2005. ✤ "Berry Bonanza" by Rick Nelson, *Star Tribune* Staff Writer. Copyright © 2005 by *Star Tribune.* Republished with permission of *Star Tribune,* Minneapolis-St. Paul. No further republication or redistribution is permitted without the written consent of *Star Tribune.* Originally appeared in the *Star Tribune,* August 19, 2004. ✤ "Extending the Olive Branch" by Dai Huynh. Copyright © 2005 by *The Houston Chronicle* Publishing Company. Reprinted with permission. All rights reserved. ✤ "From *At Mesa's Edge: Cooking and Ranching in Colorado's North Fork Valley* by Euge-

About the Editor

Holly Hughes is a writer, the former executive editor of Fodor's Travel Publications and author of *Frommer's New York City with Kids.*

Submissions for
Best Food Writing 2006

Submissions and nominations for *Best Food Writing 2006* should be forwarded no later than June 1, 2006, to Holly Hughes at *Best Food Writing 2006*, c/o Avalon Publishing Group, 245 W. 17th St., 11th floor, New York, NY 10011, or emailed to bestfoodwriting@avalonpub.com. We regret that, due to volume, we cannot acknowledge receipt of all submissions.

Best Food Writing 2000
Foreword by Alice Waters
1-56924-616-5
$14.95
Contributors include Maya Angelou, Eric Asimov, Anthony
Bourdain, Rick Bragg, Fran Gage, Jeffrey Steingarten, Jhumpa
Lahiri, Nigella Lawson, and Ruth Reichl.

Best Food Writing 2001
1-56924-577-0
$14.95
Contributors include Jeffery Eugenides, Malcom Gladwell,
David Leite, Molly O'Neill, Ruth Reichl, David Sedaris, Jeffrey
Steingarten, and Calvin Trillin.

Best Food Writing 2002
1-56924-524-X
$14.95
Contributors include Anthony Bourdain, Greg Atkinson,
Rand Richards Cooper, John T. Edge, Barbara Haber, Paric Kuh,
John Mariani, Mimi Sheraton, and James Villas.

Best Food Writing 2003
1-56924-440-5
$14.95
Contributors include Susan Choi, Fran Gage, Adam Gopnik,
Amanda Hesser, David Leite, Jacques Pépin, Inga Saffron, Nigel
Slater, and John Thorne.

Best Food Writing 2004
1-56924-416-2
$14.95
Contributors include Steve Almond, Greg Atkinson, John
Kessler, David Leite, Dara Moskowitz, Molly O'Neill,
Mimi Sheraton, James Villas, and Robb Walsh.

Please note that limited quantites are available on some previous
editions in the Best Food Writing series. Your local bookseller
should be able to help you obtain previous editions.